A History of the Church..

Yours Truly,
H. C. Wickersham.

A

History of the Church

FROM THE BIRTH OF CHRIST TO THE
PRESENT TIME.

EMBRACING AN ACCOUNT OF

THE LIVES OF THE APOSTLES, AND MANY EMINENT
CHRISTIANS AND REFORMERS THAT HAVE
LIVED SINCE CHRIST;

ALSO A

BIOGRAPHICAL NOTICE OF THE PRINCIPAL MARTYRS
AND PROMOTERS OF CHRISTIANITY, ILLUSTRAT-
ING THEIR CONSTANCY AND ZEAL, SUF-
FERING AND FORTITUDE

Illustrated by numerous engravings.

Compiled by
HENRY C WICKERSHAM.

MOUNDSVILLE, W. VA., U. S. A.
GOSPEL TRUMPET PUBLISHING COMPANY.
1900.

GENERAL DIVISION.

As considered in this work the history of the Christian church is divided into four periods.

Period I. extends from the establishing of the church by Jesus Christ to A. D. 270. This period embraces (1) The Life of Christ, (2) The Labors of the Apostles, (3) Pagan Persecution.

Period II. extends from A. D. 270 to A. D. 1530. This period embraces (1) The Decay of Vital Godliness, and the Decline of Paganism; (2) The Establishment of the Supremacy of the Roman Pontiff, and the Dark Ages; (3) The Dawn of the Reformation.

Period III. extends from A. D. 1530 to A. D. 1880. This period embraces (1) The Reformation by Martin Luther, and the Decline of the Roman Supremacy; (2) Other Reformers, and Sect-making; (3) Holiness Reformation.

Period IV. extends from A. D. 1880 to the present time. This period embraces a General Reformation and a Gathering of God's People into the One Church.

PREFACE.

IT is the design of this compilation to provide the church in the "evening time" with the means of acquainting itself with the accurate history of the church. This volume covers the periods from the commencement of the Christian era to the present time. Many of the Christian writings of the obscure opening era of the church's history have perished altogether. This, however, increases the value of the fragments which remain, and serves to throw light upon the church's history of that period. With a view to accommodating those who do not have the time or do not wish to read extensive and unabridged ecclesiastical histories, we have condensed the present volume, yet not leaving out anything of importance.

Many have written very extensively, but most of the people that do read, can not read such extensive works. We do not claim to have gathered the materials for this work from the heavy and many-volumed folios of ancient and foreign authors. It will, doubtless, be admitted that a few modern writers in the English language have selected all that is valuable in church history. From these this volume is chiefly gathered. Eusebius, Moshcim, Kitto, Goodrich, Sabine, Buck, Stowe, Clark, and Jackson are among the writers principally consulted for the material which forms this history. All extracts and quotations will not be inclosed in quotation marks, neither will the names of the authors be given unless thought best.

Of the young, and indeed of all, it may be inquired, What more interesting and important field of knowledge can you enter, than that of ecclesiastical history? Where exists more striking instances of virtue, benevolence, and patriotism? Where are to be found more useful lessons on the subject of degraded human nature? I would say to all that want knowledge, Read carefully. It is a true saying, that if a book be worth reading once; it is worth reading twice, and if it stands a second reading, it may stand a third. This, indeed, is the one great test of the excellence of books. Many books require to be read more than once in order to be seen in their proper colors and latent glories.

Henry C. Wickersham.

Moundsville, W. Va., Feb. 22, 1900.

CONTENTS.

LIST OF ILLUSTRATIONS.

A

HISTORY OF THE CHURCH

FROM THE BIRTH OF CHRIST
TO THE PRESENT TIME. . . .

PERIOD I.

CHAPTER I.

THE LIFE OF CHRIST.

JESUS CHRIST, the Lord and Savior of mankind. He is called Christ (anointed) because he is anointed, furnished, and sent by God, to execute his mediatorial office; and Jesus (savior) because he came to save his people from their sins.

His coming had been long foretold by prophetic oracle, and long expected by the house of Israel. At last he was born in the land of Judea, in a small town called Bethlehem, about six miles from Jerusalem. His birth may be dated, according to the best authorities, in the 26th year of the reign of Augustus Cæsar, emperor of Rome, four years before the date commonly assigned for the Christian era. His mother was a virgin espoused to a man whose name was Joseph, of the house of David; and the virgin's name was Mary. His early infancy was spent in Egypt, whither his parents fled to avoid the persecutions of Herod, at that

time king of Judea. After his return from Egypt, he
dwelt at Nazareth, until his entrance upon his public
ministry From this place, at the age of twelve, he
paid his memorable visit to Jerusalem; returning from
which, he lived with his parents and followed the
humble occupation of a carpenter.

At the age of thirty, Jesus came forth from obscurity, and made his first appearance to John on the
banks of the Jordan, where his forerunner had been
baptizing and bearing testimony to his coming. The
baptism instituted by the son of Zacharias was under
the inspiration of God; to which the Savior applies,
and thus fulfills an act of righteousness. This was
witnessed by the outpouring of the Holy Spirit, and a
voice, saying, "Thou art my beloved Son, in whom I
am well pleased." His temptation in the wilderness
follows "And Jesus returned in the power of the
Spirit into Galilee; and there went out a fame of him
through all the region round about. The ministry of
Christ continued about the space of three years and a
half, during which time the events of his life, and holy
diligence were so numerous, and so full of expression,
that if all had been written, the world itself could not
have contained the books.

The doctrines which Christ taught related to the
nature and perfection of God; to the sinfulness and
miserable condition of man; to his own character as the
Son of God and promised Messiah; to the atonement
which he should accomplish by his death; to repentance and justification and sanctification by faith; to
love and obedience; to a resurrection from the dead;
and to a state of future rewards and punishments

These were the great doctrines of the Christian system —doctrines which he commissioned his disciples to preach through the world; and which the Christian church was required to maintain to the end of time. In Christ all the types, prophecies, and promises center

The reader is now referred to the character of Jesus, which, while it affords the most pleasing subject of meditation, exhibits an example of the most perfect and delightful kind. Every grace that can recommend salvation, and every virtue that can adorn humanity, are so blended as to excite our admiration and engage our love He was always ready to do good, by doing his Father's will, in comforting and helping those around him that were distressed or in need. Though possessed of the most unbounded power, we behold him living continually in a state of humiliation and poverty We see him daily exposed to almost every species of want and distress; afflicted without a comforter; persecuted without a protector, and wandering about according to his own pathetic complaint; because he had not where to lay his head. In every period and circumstance of his life, we behold dignity and elevation blended with love and pity. We see power; but it is power which is rather our security than our dread—a power softened with tenderness, and soothing while it awes With all the gentleness of a meek and lowly mind we behold a heroic firmness, which no terrors could restrain. Never was a character so commanding and natural, so resplendent and pleasing, so amiable and venerable

His labors were confined chiefly to the land of the

Jews. The grand object of Jesus was, by his obedience, to bring in everlasting righteousness; and by his death, to make atonement for sin. We see that everything during the course of his ministry combined to accomplish so great an end. Such was the authority with which he was clothed, and such was the evidence of his divine commission, who came to set aside the Jewish rites and ceremonies, and, in the place of the Jewish church, to found a church which should embrace Jew and Gentile, bond and free; and against the ultimate increase and glory of which not even the gates of hell should be suffered to prevail. He sealed his work by his blood. The Jewish rulers plotted his death; as a prophet, they declared him an impostor; as a priest, a blasphemer; as a king, a usurper. These things considered, no death was too cruel, too degrading; so they condemned him to death, and he suffered the crucifixion of the cross upon Calvary, between two thieves. This event occurred in the eighteenth year of Tiberius, the successor of Augustus Cæsar.

The death of Christ was apparently a signal triumph to his enemies, and as signal a defeat to all his followers. Christ had indeed repeatedly foretold his resurrection to his followers; and this intelligence had been communicated to the Jews at large. The former anticipated, though faintly perhaps, this glorious event; but the latter believed it not. They only feared that his disciples might steal his body, and pretend that he had risen from the dead. They therefore sealed his sepulcher, and round it stationed a guard, until the day should pass on which it was said he would arise from the dead. But neither the precau-

CHRIST BEARING HIS CROSS.

tion, nor the power of his enemies, could prevent an event which was connected with the salvation of millions of the sons of men. The third day at length arrived, the appointed hour and moment came; and he arose from the dead. "This Jesus hath God raised up, whereof we all are witnesses."—Acts 2:32. The resurrection of Jesus has ever been regarded by the church as a doctrine of vast importance. We will now give some

SCRIPTURAL, HISTORICAL, AND CIRCUMSTANTIAL EVI-
DENCE OF THE DEATH AND RESUR-
RECTION OF CHRIST.

The account of his death is mentioned by both Tacitus and Lucian. The facts of his trial and execution were communicated by Pilate to the Roman senate; for both Justin Martyr and Tertullian appeal to the "Acts of Pilate," then extant, to corroborate their testimony concerning Christ. Nor do they refer to them in an indefinite and obscure manner, or among those who had not the means of refutation. The former, who lived only about a century after our Savior's death, and who suffered martyrdom at Rome, boldly asserts the fact in a letter to the Emperor Antoninus Pius, and refers him to the "Acts" themselves for confirmation. The latter in his Apology, written about fifty years after Justin Martyr, affirms that Tiberius, the emperor, was so struck with the accounts received from Palestine concerning Christ, that he would have defied him, had the senate assented, and even challenges the senate to consult their records for confirmation of the fact This certainly was very rash on the part of those men, were they not borne out by the

CHRIST SCOURGED BY THE SOLDIERS.

facts in the case. But again, Julian the apostate, Celsus, and Porphyry—all violent enemies to Christianity—not only admit the existence of Christ, but, to account for his "wonderful works," are compelled to ascribe them to his wonderful skill as a magician. How kindred in spirit to the unbelieving Jews who were personal witnesses of the mighty works performed by Christ, and, unable to deny the fact of their performance, ascribed them to Beelzebub! We find recorded the fact that modern research has brought to light the following curious relic

Sentence rendered by Pontius Pilate, acting Governor of Lower Galilee, stating that Jesus of Nazareth shall suffer death on the cross.

In the year seventeen of the Emperor Tiberius Cæsar, and the 24th day of March, in the city of the holy Jerusalem, Annas and Caiaphas being high priests, sacrificators of the people of God, Pontius Pilate, Governor of Lower Galilee, sitting in the presidential chair of the Prætory, condemns Jesus of Nazareth to die on the cross between two thieves—the great and notorious evidence of the people saying: 1 Jesus is a seducer 2 He is seditious 3. He is an enemy to the law 4 He calls himself falsely the Son of God. 5 He calls himself falsely the King of Israel 6 He entered the Tem·le followed by a multitude bearing palm branches in their hands Orders the first Centurion, Quilius Cornelius, to lead him to the place of execution Forbids any person whomsoever, either poor or rich, to oppose the death of Jesus The witnesses who signed the condemnation of Jesus are· (1) Daniel, Rabboni, a Pharisee, (2) Joannes Rorobable, (3) Raphael, Rabboni, (4) Capet, a citizen Jesus shall go out of the city of Jerusalem by the gate Struennus

The foregoing sentence is engraved on a copper plate. It was found in an antique vase of white marble while excavating in the ancient city of Aquilla, in the kingdom of Naples, in the year 1850.

The prophets not only foretold his appearance and character, but also his death and resurrection.

It was the joyful exclamation of Philip, when he had become conversant with Christ, "We have found him, of whom Moses in the law, and the prophets did write, Jesus of Nazareth, the son of Joseph."—Jno. 1:45. The Messiah was symbolized in the types of the Jewish dispensation. The offering of Isaac upon Mount Moriah, the lifting up of the brazen serpent in the wilderness, the entombing of Jonah in the belly of a whale, and indeed every sacrifice offered upon Jewish altars—all were typical of the sufferings, the sacrificial death, the entombing, and the resurrection of the Lord Jesus Christ.

But what was dimly shadowed forth in the types is exhibited with greater distinctness and with more significant particularity in the prophets. A messenger was to prepare the way before him. He was to come, the desire of nations; to come before the scepter departed from Judah, four hundred and ninety years from the building of the second temple, and before it was destroyed; and also to be born of a virgin. The very tribe, and family, and place of his nativity are foretold. He was to preach, to work miracles, to purge the temple, to ride in triumph into Jerusalem. But he was also to suffer, to be despised and rejected of men, to be hated and persecuted, to be betrayed by his professed friend, and sold for a specified sum; he was to be forsaken by his friends, mocked and smitten by his enemies; his hands and feet were to be pierced, and he was to be "lifted up," to be "cut off," to be "numbered with transgressors." The parting of his garments, the casting of lots upon his vesture, the gall and vinegar with which he should be insulted upon the cross, and the very language he should utter in his dying agony—all are foretold. Thus was he to die;

but when dead, his bones were not to be broken, although it was customary to break the bones of those crucified. Though executed as a malefactor, he was to be buried with the rich; and yet not to be left in the grave, nor his body permitted to see corruption. Having risen from the dead, he was to ascend up on high, to be seated at the right hand of God, there to make intercession for his people, and to carry forward the grand designs of his mediatorial office till he shall come to execute final judgment upon all the nations of the earth. Such was the prophetic delineation of the sufferings, death, and resurrection of our Lord Jesus Christ.

To show the reader how comprehensive the prophecies were, and yet how minute in their statement of particulars, a condensed summary of them will be given.

1 *A messenger, or forerunner, was to announce his coming* "I will send my messenger, and he shall prepare the way before me."—Mal. 3:1. "The voice of him that crieth in the wilderness, Prepare ye the way of the Lord "—Isa. 40:3. "I will send you Elijah the prophet."—Mal. 4:5. These predictions were fulfilled in John the Baptist: "In those days came John the Baptist preaching in the wilderness of Judea, saying, Repent ye; for the kingdom of heaven is at hand."—Matt. 3:1, 2; Luke 1:17. This is Elias, which was for to come."—Matt. 11:14. "Elias is come already."—Matt. 17:12; Mark 9:13.

2. *He was to come the desire of nations.* "The desire of all nations shall come."—Hag. 2:7. Ancient writers give evidence of the awakened expectation of eastern nations about the time of the birth of Christ.

THE CRUCIFIXION.

3. Before the scepter departed from Judah. "The scepter shall not depart from Judah, nor a lawgiver from between his feet, until Shiloh come."—Gen. 49:10. Judea was required to pay taxes, indicative that the scepter had departed to the Roman emperor; and "this taxing was first made" at the birth of Christ. Luke 2:1-7.

4. He was to come while the second temple was yet standing. "I will fill this house"—that is the second temple—"with glory." "The glory of this latter house shall be greater than of the former house."—Hag. 2:7, 9. Christ suffered crucifixion only forty years before the destruction of this second temple.

5. The time of his birth is distinctly specified. "Seventy weeks are determined upon thy people and upon thy holy city, to finish the transgression, and to make an end of sins, and to make reconciliation for iniquity, and to bring in everlasting righteousness, and to seal up the vision and prophecy, and to anoint the Most Holy. Know therefore and understand, that from the going forth of the commandment to restore and to build Jerusalem unto the Messiah the Prince, shall be seven weeks, and threescore and two weeks: the street shall be built again, and the wall, even in troublous times. And after threescore and two weeks shall Messiah be cut off, but not for himself: and the people of the prince that shall come shall destroy the city and the sanctuary; and the end thereof shall be with a flood, and unto the end of the war desolations are determined. And he shall confirm the covenant with many for one week: and in the midst of the week he shall cause the sacrifice and the oblation to cease, and

for the overspreading of abominations he shall make it
desolate, even until the consummation, and that determined shall be poured upon the desolate."—Dan.
9:24-2^ The most reliable ʼchronology shows that
from the decree of Artaxerxes to Ezra to rebuild
Jerusalem to the death of Christ, was a period of 490
years, corresponding precisely to the prophetic period
of "seventy weeks," each "week" comprising seven
years. On this supposition, let us apply the subdivi-
sions mentioned in verses 25, 26, and 27:

1. From the decree till inspiration left Judah
   —"seven weeks," each of seven years, -   49 yrs.
2. From that date till the public appearance
   of Christ—"sixty-two weeks," each of seven
   years, -   -   -   -   -   -   -   434 "
3. The period of Christ's ministry, in the
   midst of which he was to be "cut off"—
   "one week," -   -   -   -   -   -   7 "
                                   ———
                                   490 yrs.

6. *He was to be born of a virgin.* "Behold, a virgin
shall conceive, and bear a son, and shall call his name
Immanuel."—Isa 7:14. Christ was born of the
Virgin Mary Matt. 1·18-25; Luke 1 28-35.

7 *His tribe is declared.* "ʼThe scepter shall not
depart from Judah," etc.—Gen 49.10 "It is evident
that our Lord sprang from Judah "—Heb. 7:14.

8 *His family is specified* "And there shall come forth
a rod out of the stem of Jesse, and a branch shall grow
out of his roots."—Isa. 11:1. "Of this man's seed
hath God according to his promise raised unto Israel
a Savior."—Acts 13:23.

9. *The place of his nativity is not forgotten.* "Thou Bethlehem Ephratah, though thou be little among the thousands of Judah, yet out of thee shall he come forth unto me, that is to be ruler in Israel "—Micah 5.2. "Jesus was born in Bethlehem of Judea."—Matt. 2:1. "Christ cometh of the seed of David, and out of the town of Bethlehem, where David was."—Jno. 7:42.

EVIDENCE DIRECT OF THE RESURRECTION OF CHRIST.

It has already been shown that, beyond all question, Christ was crucified, dead, and buried. Now, if it shall be shown that he was subsequently seen, conversed with, handled, gave and received communications, walked, ate, reproved, and instructed, declared himself to be alive, and performed the functions of a living man, and if it shall be shown that the personal witnesses of these facts were competent witnesses, that the number of them was large, that they had opportunity to investigate and know the things whereof they affirmed, that their testimony was given at the time and in the place where the things occurred, and finally, that it was given under such circumstances as attested, on the part of the witnesses, a full conviction and certainty of the fact, if all these facts shall be shown, then, we say, that according to all the rules of evidence and the established laws of human belief, we must credit the actual resurrection of the Lord Jesus Christ from the dead. Let us now mention some of the circumstances connected with the crucifixion, death, and burial of our Lord.

When he was led away to be crucified, a great company of his disciples, relatives, and friends followed, bewailing and lamenting him. Some of them stood so near the cross that he could speak to them, others stood afar off. Many of them remained till the mysterious darkness that overwhelmed the land had passed away, and the Lord had given up the ghost. Among those who not only witnessed his crucifixion, but tarried till he was laid in the sepulcher, were "Mary Magdalene and the other Mary"; that is, Mary the mother of James. Several women appear to have agreed to embalm the body of our Lord, and, after leaving the tomb, they "prepared spices and ointments" for that purpose. This being done, they rested on the sabbath, and came as the day was dawning, on the first day of the week, to execute the design. They appear to have been ignorant that the Jews had scaled the tomb, and placed a guard over it; and the two Marys and Salome, who were in advance of the other women, were perplexed how they might roll away the stone from the door of the sepulcher. About this time—before the women had reached the tomb— an angel descended from heaven, rolled the stone from the sepulcher, and sat upon it. The guard were struck with astonishment, and for a moment were like dead men; but recovering themselves, and finding that the body of Christ was gone, they fled into the city and reported the fact to the Jews

As the women approached the tomb, they beheld that the stone was rolled away. This filled them with alarm; and Mary Magdalene, concluding that the body had been taken away, ran back to tell Peter and John. The other Mary and Salome approached the tomb, determined to ascertain whether the body was

there; but as they entered the tomb, and saw the
angel, but not the body, they were affrighted. The
angel sought to calm their fears, told them the Lord
had risen, and bade them behold the place where they
had laid him, and then go and tell his disciples. But
the women went out quickly from the sepulcher, and.
fled trembling with affright, saying not a word, but
hasting to report what they had seen to the eleven
apostles. They had hardly gone, when Peter and John
came running in advance of Mary Magdalene, and
went into the sepulcher. They found that the body
was not there, but saw the grave-clothes lying folded
up; and after that they returned to their own home,
wondering at what had occurred.

1. *First appearance of Christ after his resurrection.*
Mary Magdalene was left alone at the tomb. She had
lingered behind to weep, being in much doubt and
perplexity as to what had become of the body of Jesus.
While weeping she stooped down and looked again into
the sepulcher, if perchance there might have been some
mistake about the body having been removed. There
she saw two angels, robed in white, one at the
head and one at the foot, where the body of Jesus had
lain. How touchingly beautiful her reply when they
asked her why she wept. "Because they have taken
away my Lord, and I know not where they have laid
him " Turning back she saw Jesus standing by her;
but blinded by her tears, and bewildered by her appre-
hensions, she did not recognize either his personal
appearance or yet his voice when he tenderly inquired
the cause of her grief; but supposing him to be the
gardener, who might have removed the body, she said,

"Sir, if thou hast borne him hence, tell me where thou hast laid him, and I will take him away." Jesus said unto her, "Mary!" She could doubt no more—the voice and the bodily appearance are both recognized, and she, uttering an exclamation of surprise and joy, prostrating herself before him, held him by the feet and worshiped him. But he bade her make no delay; the time was short; he was about to ascend to his Father and his God; therefore, to haste and tell his disciples. Then she went and told the disciples, as they were mourning and weeping, that she had seen the Lord, and that he had said these things to her; but they believed it not.

2. Second appearance of Christ. The other Mary and Salome appear to have fled away to some retired place, and perhaps were so astounded at what they had witnessed that they could not for some time sufficiently recover their self-possession to carry the tidings to the disciples. While in this state their Lord himself met them, calmed their fears, and bade them go boldly and carry the tidings of his resurrection to the apostles, and tell them to meet him, as he had appointed, in Galilee. Still the apostles were incredulous.

3. Third appearance of Christ. After the two Marys, Salome, Peter, and John had departed from the grave, Joanna, and a company of women with her, not knowing the events that had taken place, came bringing spices and ointments to assist in the embalming of the body. Finding the tomb open, they went into it, and discovered that the body had been removed. While they were full of amazement and per-

plexity, two angels appeared to them, and said, "Why
seek ye the living among the dead? He is not here,
but is risen." When Joanna returned and reported
this to the disciples, Peter appears to have gone again
in haste to the sepulcher; and it is probably at this
time that the risen Savior "was seen of Cephas,"
according to the declaration of St. Paul   1 Cor. 15:5.

4 Fourth appearance of Christ. That same morning, after the women had returned from the sepulcher, two of the disciples—one of them Cleopas, or
Alpheus, the father of James, and the other probably
St. Luke—had left Jerusalem, and were journeying
on foot to Emmaus, a village seven or eight miles west
of the city. They had probably been up to Jerusalem
to attend the Passover, and were now returning home;
they were returning with grieved and aching hearts;
their Lord, in whom they had trusted and through
whom they had hoped for the redemption of Israel, had
been crucified and slain. As they talk over the sad
events of the feast a third traveler falls in with them,
and joins in their conversation. He expounds to them
the prophecies relating to the Messiah, and shows that
the very events they lamented were necessary, and also
that Christ must rise again, that the prophecies might
be fulfilled. All this time they did not recognize him;
they saw him, heard his voice, and walked with him,
as they would with any other man   But when they
reached the village, and were about to sup together,
near the close of 'the day, he took bread, and blessed
it, and brake, and gave it to them. This opened their
eyes, and they were filled with astonishment and wonder to recognize their Lord in the person of their

fellow traveler. But he vanished from their sight
So joyful were they at what they had seen, that they
immediately arose and returned to Jerusalem; and when
they reached the city, they found the disciples assembled, and were assured by them that the report received from the women concerning the resurrection of
Christ, before they left in the morning, had been confirmed; for, they said, he "hath appeared to Simon."
Then the two disciples rehearsed what they had wit
nessed in the way, and also at the village whither they
went.   Thus the evidences of his resurrection were so
multiplying that the disciples, who had at first
doubted, were constrained to say, "The Lord is risen,
indeed."

5. *Fifth appearance of Christ* It was now the evening of the day of our Lord's resurrection, and he had
already appeared to six witnesses   Ten of the apostles
and many disciples were now assembled to talk over
the events that had occurred, and especially to consider to what the reports of that day concerning the
resurrection of the Lord might grow.   For fear of the
Jews, they had closed the door   Just then the Savior
appeared in their midst, and said to them, "Peace
be unto you."   But the suddenness and the unexpect-
edness of his appearance filled them with terror and
affright.   He, however, calmed their fears, bade them
look upon him and feel of him, behold his hands
and his feet, and assure themselves that he was flesh
and bones; then also he ate before them; and afterward, still further to confirm their faith, he opened to
their understanding the scriptures, and showed them
that "thus it is written, and thus it behooved Christ

to suffer, and to rise from the dead the third day."

6 Sixth appearance of Christ.   Soon after our
Savior had appeared on the previous occasion, Thomas
came in, and the disciples told him that they had seen
the Lord. He, however, disbelieved, and said, "Except
I shall see in his hands the print of the nails, and put
my finger into the print of the nails, and thrust my
hand into his side, I will not believe." On the eighth
day after the resurrection, the eleven apostles, and
probably others of the disciples, were again assembled
together, Thomas being present with the rest; and
Jesus stood in their midst, and addressed them with
his salutation of peace. Then turning to Thomas,
he upbraided his unbelief, and said to him, "Reach
hither thy finger, and behold my hands; and reach
hither thy hand, and thrust it into my side; and be
not faithless, but believing." It was enough. The
skepticism of Thomas could withstand no longer, and
he cried out, "My Lord and my God!" The special
object of this appearance of Jesus seems to have been
to convince Thomas of the reality of the resurrection,
and thus to extinguish the last doubt of the fact from
the minds of his apostles

7. *Seventh appearance of Christ.* The feast of the
passover being now ended, the eleven returned into
Galilee as the Savior had directed them. This was their
native place, and here they would be less exposed to
the malice of the Jews, and could, therefore, with
more calmness receive the instructions of Christ, and
prepare themselves for that public ministry so soon to
begin at Jerusalem. While here they probably resorted
to their several callings as a means of livelihood.

Simon Peter, with Nathanael, James, and John, and
two others, engaged in fishing, but toiled all night and
caught nothing.   In the morning Jesus stood upon
the shore; and when his disciples did not recognize
him, having first asked them if they had anything to
eat, he bade them cast the net on the right side of the
boat, which being done, they inclosed no less than a
hundred fifty-three great fishes, which were drawn
to the shore and secured.   Then they knew it was the
Lord; and coming to him, they saw a fish that had
been prepared on a fire of coals, and bread.   Jesus
said to them, "Come and dine," and gave them bread
and fish, and they did eat.

8. *Eighth appearance of Christ*   The grand assem-
blage of the disciples where our Savior was to give a
still more public demonstration that he was alive, was
upon a mountain in Galilee.   This meeting he had
appointed before his crucifixion; the angel that announced his resurrection to the women bade them
remind the disciples of the Savior's appointment; the
Lord himself, also, when he appeared to Mary and
Salome, renewed the same message; and it is probable
that on the preceding appearance he gave the disciples
more explicit information where he would meet as
many as might assemble.   The number assembled on
this occasion exceeded five hundred.   Twenty years
after this St. Paul publicly declares that the greater
part of this five hundred were then living witnesses of
the resurrection of our Lord.   Here he gave infallible
proofs of his resurrection, and spoke of things pertaining to the kingdom of God   Here also he renewed the
promise of the Holy Ghost, and bade them go back to
Jerusalem and tarry till it came.

3

9. Ninth appearance of Christ. Jesus after this seems to have made his appearance to James. This appearance the apostle refers to as an evidence of the resurrection, though he gives no particulars of the case. They were omitted probably because they were well known. The James spoken of was James the Lord's brother, bishop at Jerusalem, the only apostle, except Peter, with whom St. Paul was favored with an interview when he came up from Damascus after his conversion. It is to be presumed that he then had the fact from the lips of James himself.

10. Tenth appearance of Christ. The apostles having returned to Jerusalem according to the command of their Master, about forty days after the resurrection Jesus again appeared to them. Here, after renewing their commission, he gave them the promise of the speedy descent of the Holy Spirit, and commanded them not to depart from Jerusalem till they should "be baptized with the Holy Ghost." Having completed his instructions, he led them out toward Bethany, upon the mount of Olives. Here probably upon the sacred spot where he had often instructed his disciples and prayed for them—the spot that had witnessed his awful agony that forced his sweat from every pore as great as drops of blood; the spot where he had been betrayed by the traitorous kiss of one disciple, and forsaken by all the rest—upon this spot he lifted up his hands and blessed his disciples; and as he blessed them he was parted from them, "he was taken up; and a cloud received him out of their sight. And while they looked steadfastly toward heaven as he went up, behold, two men stood by them in white apparel; which also said, Ye men of Galilee, why stand ye gazing up into heaven? this same Jesus, which is taken up from you into heaven, shall so come in like manner as ye have seen him go into heaven."—Acts 1:9-11.

The resurrection and ascension proved his divine authority and mission; his disciples believed in him, his enemies were confounded.

TRADITION

has added somewhat to the *letter* of Christ's history. Eusebius has preserved in his writings a story of letters passing between Jesus and Agbarus, king of Edessa. For their genuineness, he appeals to the public registries and records of the city of Edessa, in Mesopotamia, where Agbarus reigned, and where he affirms that he found them written in the Syriac language. He published a Greek translation of them in his Ecclesiastical History. The learned world has been much divided on this subject; but, notwithstanding the learned Grabe, and Archbishop Cave, Dr. Parker, and other divines, have strenuously contended for their admission into the canon of scripture, they are deemed apocryphal. Jeremiah Jones observes that the common people in England have this epistle in their houses, in many places, fixed in a frame, with the picture of Christ before it; and that they generally, with much honesty and devotion, regard it as the word of God, and the genuine epistle of Christ. But as the whole is unnoticed, and most likely was unknown in the apostolic age, it probably is fabulous.

CHAPTER II.

THE CHURCH.

The church was founded upon Christ the rock of our salvation. "Upon this rock I will build my church, and the gates of hell shall not prevail against it." In this text the building of the church is spoken of as in the future. Now read 1 Cor. 3.9—"Ye are God's husbandry, ye are God's building." "And are built upon the foundation of the apostles and prophets, Jesus Christ himself being the chief corner-stone, in whom all the building fitly framed together groweth unto an holy temple in the Lord: in whom ye also are builded together for a habitation of God through the Spirit." "Ye also, as lively stones, are built up a spiritual house, an holy priesthood, to offer up spiritual sacrifices, acceptable to God by Jesus Christ."

In A. D. 32 Christ said, "I will build my church." In A. D. 59, and after that, the apostles said, "Ye are God's building," "are built up a spiritual house." According to these scriptures the church must have been built between A. D 32 and A D. 59. It is true that the church was begun under the labors of John the Baptist, Jesus, and his apostles before the day of Pentecost. Many believed and entered the kingdom then, and constituted material for the church. But the coming of the Holy Spirit was the point of time when the church was fully organized, and set in operation.

The church is called in the New Testament *the body of Christ,* and those that compose it *members in par-*

ticular. Believers are denominated *disciples, brethren, Christians, saints.* These in their collective character acknowledge *one Lord* and *one faith,* and by *one Spirit* are all baptized into one body; and all constituting the church of God, however separated by time or place, or condition, do hold the same head, and exhibit the same character.

In the Morning, or Apostolic, Period the church had wonderful power; they met together "with one accord," and the power of God was wonderfully manifested in and through them, and many were added unto the church. God places the members in the church. 1 Cor. 12:18. Christ is the door of the church, and salvation the mode of induction, and that is a door that stands open continually, and no man can shut. Christ is not the door of any sect, therefore no sect is the church of God. The experience of salvation does not constitute a person a member of any sect on earth; therefore they are not the church of God. All sects have a door, a manner of admitting members, that is open and shut by men; hence, are unlike the church of God, which no man can open and shut. They are therefore not his church.

Jesus founded his church in unity. The night of his apprehension he prayed for the sanctification of his people, that they might be made perfect in one. The apostolic church retained perfect unity for a time. In the Acts of the Apostles it is recorded that "all that believed were together." "They lifted up their voice to God with one accord." "The multitude of them that believed were of one heart and of one soul."

CHAPTER III.

THE LIVES AND LABORS OF THE APOSTLES.

On the death of Jesus the disciples were scattered; every one went to his own home, and to his occupation; but the event of the resurrection again brought them to one rallying point, and by the directions of their divine and risen Master, they abode waiting at Jerusalem till the day of Pentecost.

Ten days after the ascension of Christ, and fifty from his crucifixion, the promise of the Holy Spirit was fulfilled. By the descent of the Holy Spirit, the apostles were suddenly endued with great power and boldness; also with the gift of tongues, which enabled them to speak in other languages, of which before they had no knowledge. The effects produced on the minds of the apostles on this occasion, were of an extraordinary kind. A flood of light seems to have broken in upon them at once. Their remaining doubts and prejudices were removed; their misapprehensions were rectified; and their views conformed to the scope of the doctrines which had been taught by Christ.

A rumor of this stupendous miracle spreading abroad in the streets of Jerusalem, a multitude of Jews, residents and strangers, were soon collected to the spot. To these, Peter explained the mystery, by declaring it to be effected by the power of that Jesus whom they had wickedly slain. The explanation and the charge, being accompanied to their consciences by the Spirit of God, led to the very sudden conversion of about three thousand souls. Jerusalem was at this time the resort of Jews and Jewish proselytes dispersed throughout the various parts of the Roman empire, who had come to celebrate the feast. The promiscuous throng who were collected by so strange a report, and had been accustomed to different languages, were therefore greatly astonished to hear the apostles declare, each one in his own tongue, the wonderful works of God. While some expressed their surprise at this, others ascribed it to the effects of wine. This weak and perverse slander was, however, immediately refuted by the apostle Peter, who, standing up with the other apostles, lifted up his voice, and said unto them: "Ye men of Judea, and all ye that dwell at Jerusalem, be this known unto you, and harken to my words; for these men are not drunken, as ye suppose, seeing it is but the third hour of the day. But this is that which was spoken by the prophet Joel." He then quotes the words of Jehovah, in which he promised to pour out his Spirit upon all flesh, attended with the most awful denunciations against those who should despise it, but ;with a gracious promise of salvation to all that should call upon the name of the Lord. The illustration of this remarkable prophecy, and its application to what was now obvious to all their senses, paved the way for the apostles, drawing their attention to the great subject of his ministry, the death, and resurrection of Jesus of Nazareth, whom they had taken, and by wicked hands had crucified and slain.

Shortly after the day of Pentecost the healing of a poor cripple, accompanied by a second discourse from Peter, led to the conversion of about five thousand more. This rapid increase of the followers of Christ, greatly alarming the priests and Sadducees, they seized the two apostles Peter and John, and committed them to prison. The next day, being brought before the Sanhedrin, the language and conduct of Peter were so bold, that it was deemed unpolitic to do anything further than to dismiss the apostles, with a strict injunction not to teach any more in the name of Jesus. As soon as the two apostles were dismissed, they returned wih great joy to their brethren, who with great satisfaction heard them tell the things that had happened unto them. They then all glorified God, who by his holy prophet David had foretold what was now come to pass: that the Jews should oppose Christ, say false things of him, deny and crucify him first, and, when God had raised him from the dead, oppose the preaching of him; that the princes and governors should combine against him, and the rulers should in council endeavor to suppress the propagation of his doctrine. "And now, Lord," said they, "behold their threatenings: and grant unto thy servants, that with all boldness they may speak the word, by stretching forth thine hand to heal; and that signs and wonders may be done by the name of thy holy child Jesus. And when they had prayed, the place was shaken where they were assembled together; and they were all filled with the Holy Ghost, and they spake the word of God with boldness. And the multitude of them that believed were of one heart, and of one soul; neither said any of them that aught of the things which he possessed was his own; but they had all things common. And with great power gave the apostles witness of the resurrection of the Lord Jesus: and great grace was upon them all.''

After the punishing of Ananias and Sapphira with death for their hypocrisy and lying, the Lord did many signs and wonders among the people by the hands of the apostles. The fame of these cures, and the great success which Christianity gained by the miracles and preaching of the apostles reaching the ears of the high priest, and some others of the Sanhedrin, they were highly incensed against the apostles, and therefore caused them to be apprehended, and thrown into the common prison. But that very night they were released from their confinement. The prison doors, though fastened with the utmost caution, opened of themselves at the approach of a messenger from the courts of heaven, who commanded the apostles to leave the dungeon, repair to the temple, and preach the glad tidings of the gospel to the people. Early the next morning the council again assembled, and, thinking the apostles were safe in the prison, sent their officers to the prison with orders to bring them immediately before them. The officers went as they were commanded, but, behold, they could not find the apostles. They returned and reported the fact to the council. This greatly surprised the council, but while they were in this state of perplexity a messenger arrived with news that the men whom they had put in prison were in the temple preaching to the people. They then were brought again before the council, and questioned why they still persisted in teaching the people in the name of Jesus, to which Peter answered to this effect: We certainly ought to obey God rather than man. Jesus

whom ye slew on the cross, God has raised up again,
as a Savior, to give the Jews new and patient hearts,
and forgive their sins.   This answer greatly enraged
the council, and they first consulted to put them to
death, but this was overruled by one Gamaliel.   His
speech so diverted their intention that they sentenced
them to a lighter corporal punishment, which was
carried into execution by scourging.   But this punishment did not prevail.   They returned home with triumph.   All the opposition of man, blinded with the
malice of the powers of darkness, could neither discourage them from performing their duty to God, nor
lessen their zeal for preaching, both in public and
private, the doctrine of the gospel.

The next thing of much importance was the ordain-
ing of seven; namely, Stephen, Philip, Prochorus,
Nicanor, Timon, Parmenas, and Nicolas.   These
were ordained by prayer and the laying on of the
hands of the apostles.   The names of these seven are
all of Greek extract, whence we may infer that very
probably they were all natives of Greece, and that,
consequently by their designation, the church was desirous to give full satisfaction to the complaint of those
whose widows had been neglected.   Of the first two of
these, viz., Stephen and Philip, the sacred history has
given us a sufficient account; but of the rest we have
nothing certain, except we will admit what the Latins
tell us of Prochorus, viz., that on the 9th of August he
suffered martyrdom at Antioch, after having made
himself famous for his miracles; of Nicanor, that on
the 10th of January he suffered in the isle of Cyprus,
after having given demonstrations of his faith and

virtue; of Timon, that on the 19th of April, he was first-thrown into the fire, and when he had miraculously escaped thence, he was fixed upon a cross at Corinth; of Parmenas, that on the 23d of January he suffered at Philippi, in Macedonia; and of Nicolas, that either by design or by indiscretion he gave rise to the infamous sect of Nicolaitanes.

Notwithstanding the persecuting spirit of the Jewish rulers, none of the followers of Christ had been called to suffer death for his name until near the end of the year 35 when Stephen, one of the seven, full of the Holy Ghost, was called to lead in the noble army of martyrs. He was not less distinguished by his eloquence than by his piety. His defense delivered before the Sanhedrin, recorded in the seventh chapter of the Acts of the Apostles, is a practical illustration of the zeal and boldness of the primitive disciples of Christ. But what avail signs and wonders, the most splendid appeals of eloquence, or the most forcible convictions of truth, among the obdurate and incorrigible? For, notwithstanding the goodness of his cause, the miracles which he had wrought to support it, the luster with which he now appeared, and the eloquence which flowed in torrents from his lips, "they cried out with a loud voice, and stopped their ears, and ran upon him with one accord, and cast him out of the city, and stoned him."—Acts 7:57-60. His dying deportment evinced how eminently he was filled with the spirit of his Master, and is a pattern to all who are called to suffer in the same righteous cause.

From this point, A. D. 35, a persecution against the church arose, which lasted about six years. In the

beginning of this persecution (A. D. 36) the miraculous conversion of Saul, or Paul, took place—the latter
being his Grecian name, the former his Hebrew. The
first mention made of Saul is at the trial of Stephen,
on which occasion, though a young man, he was active
in putting him to death. He was a native of Tarsus,
the chief city of the province of Celicia, and had come
to Jerusalem to pursue his studies under Gamaliel, a
celebrated doctor of the Jewish law. Saul having
enlisted himself against Jesus and his cause, and being of an ardent temperament, sought opportunity to
distinguish himself in putting down the advancing
interests of the despised Galilean. Having intimation
that not a few of the disciples had taken refuge in
Damascus, a noted city of Syria, Saul petitioned for a
commission from the high priest against them. This
being readily granted, he, with several companions,
was soon on his journey, breathing out threatenings
and slaughter against the Christians. When he came
near Damascus, a refulgent light, far exceeding the
brightness of the sun, darted upon him, and a great
light from heaven shone around him, and he fell to
the earth as one dead. He was then addressed by a
voice saying, "Saul, Saul, why persecutest thou me?"
To this Saul replied, "Who art thou, Lord?" He was
immediately answered, "I am Jesus whom thou persecutest. It is hard for thee to kick against the
pricks." As if he had said, "All thy attempts to extirpate the faith in me will prove abortive, and like
kicking against the spikes, wound and torment thyself."
Jesus said unto him, "Arise, and go into the city, and
it shall be told thee what thou must do." And Saul

MARTYRDOM OF ST. STEPHEN.

arose from the earth, but the splendor of the vision had overpowered his bodily eyes, so that he was led by the hand into Damascus, where he remained three days without sight or food. It is necessary only to add, that in a few days Saul was numbered with the disciples, and began "to preach Christ in the synagogues, that he is the Son of God."

That such a person should become a convert to the faith in the then infant state of the church, was eminently important, for this particular reason: "that all the other apostles were men without education, and absolutely ignorant of letters and philosophy; and yet there were those in the opposition, Jewish doctors and pagan philosophers, men of deep learning, whom it was essential to combat. Hence the importance of such an auxiliary as Saul, who, to great boldness of character, united an amazing force of genius, and the most thorough knowledge of the times." He was called to be an apostle, last in order, but first in eminence, standing forward as the *Apostle of the Gentiles.* His manner of life, his decision of character, his zeal, his labors in detail, his writings, need not be recorded here, as they would be too extensive for a work of this kind: they form a conspicuous feature of the New Testament.

Paul's testimony. "But by the grace of God I am what I am: and his grace which was bestowed upon me was not in vain; but I labored more abundantly than they all: yet not I , but the grace of God which was with me." "In labors more abundant, in stripes above measure, in prisons more frequent, in deaths oft. Of the Jews five times received I forty stripes save one. Thrice was I beaten with rods, once was I stoned, thrice I suffered shipwreck, a night and a day I have been in the deep; in journeyings often, in perils of waters, in perils of robbers, in perils by mine own countrymen, in perils by the heathen, in perils in the city, in perils in the wilderness, in perils in the sea, in perils among false brethren; in weariness and painfulness, in watchings often, in hunger and thirst, in fastings often, in cold and nakedness. Beside those things that are without, that which cometh upon me daily, the care of all the churches." "In Damascus the governor under Aretas the king kept the city of the Damascenes with a garrison, desirous to apprehend me: and through a window in a basket was I let down by the wall, and escaped his hands." That such a man should at the end of his career receive the crown of martyrdom, is congenial with his history, though it is not in the sacred writings asserted in so many words; but from his own words, together with a train of events attending his latter days, it is a circumstance more than probable. In his second letter to Timothy he speaks of his death as *near at hand*, and from his phraseology, it is not a natural death he expects, as the result of old age, or a worn out constitution, but a violent death—"*I am ready to be offered.*"

CHAPTER IV.

BIOGRAPHICAL SKETCHES OF THE APOSTLES.

WITH the exception of Peter and Paul, the notices of the lives and labors of the apostles, as contained in the sacred narrative, are very meager. They were alike commissioned to go into all the world and preach the gospel to every creature; and they were all endued with power from on high, when they received the baptism of the Holy Ghost on the day of Pentecost. The center of their first field of missionary labor was Jerusalem, when Peter was the prominent character in the apostolic circle. Thence their mission extended to Samaria, and the center of their second field of activity was Antioch, in which Paul was the principal actor to the time of his martyrdom at Rome. From this time the third period of apostolic missionary agency begins. From this period, during which the apostles and fellow laborers were actively employed in various and distinct fields in the Gentile world, very little is found recorded in the sacred narrative concerning their lives and labors, and other historic sources are incomplete and not in all respects reliable.

The historic sketches following in this chapter are derived, with the exception of a few scripture notices, from the early ecclesiastical writers, and the best encyclopedias of the present time. Though the verity of some of their statements lacks authentic confirmation, yet the current traditions, generally received at the time, doubtless had a basis of historic facts, and may, therefore, be accepted in the main as credible. Such was the zeal and 'success of the apostles that at the close of the first century Christianity had been preached and embraced in most or all the provinces of the Roman empire. We will now begin our biographical sketches with the apostle

SIMON PETER.

Simon Peter was a native of Bethsaida, on the lake of Gennesaret. His father was called Jonas, and the name by which Peter is known in Christian history was given to him by our Lord, who changed his name of origin (Bar-Jona) into Cephas, a Syro-Chaldaic word, which means rock or stone, and for which *Petra*, or, in the masculine form *Petros*, is the Greek equivalent. He was a fisherman by occupation, and together with his brother Andrew, was actually engaged in this occupation on the sea of Galilee when our Lord called both of them to be his disciples, promising to make them fishers of men. For this invitation they had been prepared by the preaching of John the Baptist, and they accepted it without hesitation. For the incidents recorded of Peter's life as a disciple, we must refer to the gospel narrative.

He was one of the three apostles who were present at the transfiguration, and it was to him particularly that the Savior commended the care of his sheep. When Jesus was betrayed Peter displayed great courage; but when he saw that his Lord was detained as a malefactor, his courage failed him, and he denied him. But after the ascension of Christ Peter evinced great boldness in the cause of the gospel. By his preaching, about three thousand souls were converted on a single occasion; and a little after, five thousand. He was the spokesman on the day of Pentecost. He it was who answered to the charges when they were brought before the council. He is the chief actor in the tragic scene of the death of Ananias and Sapphira. He was the first to break down the wall of prejudice of race by receiving a Gentile convert; he was the first to propound to the church at Jerusalem the question to be discussed as to the obligation of the Mosaic observances. The last incident of Peter's life supplied by the scripture narrative is his presence before the church at Jerusalem in A. D. 49. Of his subsequent career, our only knowledge is derived from tradition. His special mission was to the Hebrew race, as Paul's was to the Gentile; and he is supposed to have preached through Pontus, Galatia, Cappadocia, Asia, and Bithynia, chiefly to those of his own nation dispersed in these countries, all of which are named in the address of the first of the two epistles which he has left. He is supposed to have gone to Rome about the year 63 or at all events a short time before his martyrdom, which is fixed with much probability in the year 66, and is supposed to have been at the same time and place with that of St. Paul. Peter was sentenced to be crucified, and according to the tradition preserved by Eusebius from Origen, prayed that he might be crucified with his head downward, in order that his death might exceed in ignominy that of his divine Master.

ANDREW.

Andrew, the first disciple of Christ and brother of Peter, also a fisherman of Galilee, was a disciple of John the Baptist previous to his recognition of Christ

CRUCIFIXION OF ST. ANDREW.

as the Messiah.   The career of Andrew as an apostle
after the death of Christ is unknown.   Tradition tells
us that after the day of Pentecost he departed to
preach the gospel to the Scythians; and on his journey to their country, preached in Cappadocia, Galatia,
Bithynia, and along the Euxine sea, winning many
souls.   At Sinope, where he met Peter, the inhabitants of the city did what they could to oppose the
apostle's doctrine.   Afterward he traveled through
many provinces, till he came to Byzantium (now Constantinople), where he ordained Stachys (whom Paul
calls his beloved Stachys) bishop of that city.   He
then took his journey through Thrace, Macedonia,
Thessaly, Achaia, and, as some affirm, Ephesus; and
having planted the gospel in many places, came to
Patræ, a city of Achaia, where he sealed his testimony
with his blood.   He was fastened upon the cross with
ropes, that he might be longer dying, the cross being
two beams like the letter X.   From this cross, after
he was fastened to it, he preached to the people for the
space of two days; and by his admirable patience converted many to the faith.   His death was thought to
be A. D. 62 or 70.

JAMES, THE SON OF ZEBEDEE.

James, the son of Zebedee, and brother of John, is
distinguished rather by his death, than by his life and
labors.   He was by birth a Galilean, and by occupation a fisherman.   With Peter and John, he was a
spectator of our Savior's transfiguration upon the
mount, and was with him in the garden, at the time
of his agony.   This apostle preached to his countrymen the Jews.   Herod Agrippa, grandson of Herod

the Great, caused a great number of Christians to be imprisoned, and among the rest this apostle. A short time after sentence of death was passed upon him, and he was slain with the sword. As for the tyrant, divine justice overtook him; he was eaten of worms until he died. James was slain in the year 44 A. D. There is an incredible legend of his having planted the gospel in Spain, and he is the patron saint of that country.

JAMES, THE SON OF ALPHÆUS.

Of the life and labors of this apostle very little is known. He probably spent his time largely preaching the gospel in Judea. Hippolytus tells us that he met his death at the hands of a mob of Jews who came upon him while he was preaching in Jerusalem, and stoned him to death. He is said to have been buried by the temple.

JAMES, THE LORD'S BROTHER.

James, the Lord's brother, was the author of that epistle bearing his name. In church history he is distinguished by the title of *the Just.* His communications, his writings, and even his enemies, contribute to prove him worthy of such marked approbation. The enmity of the more bigoted Jews, however, procured his condemnation, and the high priest Ananus gave order that he should be stoned to death. According to Josephus, the execution of the sentence excited great dissatisfaction among the people of Jerusalem. The date of his death can not be precisely fixed, but it was probably about 62 or 63 A. D.

JOHN.

John was the brother of James the son of Zebedee,

and pursued the same profession. From his respect and attention to Jesus he seems to have been his favorite disciple, "the disciple whom Jesus loved"; and tradition makes his last words to have been, "Little children, love one another." He was born at Bethsaida. The events of his life from the time he became a disciple, to the ascension of Christ, are to be learned from the Gospels. After the outpouring of the Spirit on the day of Pentecost he appears to have labored for the spread of the gospel first in Jerusalem and Samaria, and afterwards to have had his residence chiefly in Ephesus. During the reign of the emperor Domitian, he was driven by persecution to the isle of Patmos, but returned to Ephesus under Nerva, and died there at a great age, about A. D. 100. It is believed that he was the only one of our Lord's apostles who died a natural death. Tradition accounts for this by representing his life as miraculously preserved.

PHILIP.

Philip was born at Bethsaida. Our Savior, while in Galilee, called Philip to follow him. Happy in having found the Messiah, Philip sought for Nathanael, to whom he imparted the glad tidings. It is supposed he preached in Upper Asia. It is affirmed also that he preached in Scythia. After many years, he came to Hierapolis, a city in Phrygia, where the people worshiped a serpent by the name of Jupiter Ammon. There it is related that he preached the gospel, and many of the idolaters became ashamed of the god they had worshiped, and were converted to the Christian faith. Satan, perceiving his kingdom falling, raised a persecution, and the apostle was carried to prison, scourged, and there hanged by the neck to a pillar. The martyrdom of Philip happened about the year 52 A. D.

BARTHOLOMEW.

Bartholomew is supposed by the ancients to be the same person as Nathanael, that "Israelite indeed." He was a native of Galilee, but nothing authentic is known regarding his life and labors. According to the traditionary record of Eusebius, he carried Christianity into India; Chrysostom speaks of him as a missionary in Armenia and Asia Minor. It has been said that at Hierapolis, a city in Phrygia, he would probably have suffered with Philip, had not an earthquake overawed his executioners. From thence he traveled to Lycaonia, and thence departed to Albanopolis, in Armenia the Great, a place much given to idolatrous worship. The governor of the city caused him to be apprehended. His sentence was crucifixion; and when the day of execution came, he went cheerfully to death, sealing the truth of the doctrine he had preached, with his blood.

THOMAS.

Thomas and Didymus are names of the same apostle. Origen informs us that he preached at Parthia, and Sophronius says that he preached the gospel to the Persians, Medes, Caramenians, Hyrcanians, Bactrians, and other people. He probably went to Asiatic Ethiopia, and at last to the East Indies, and preached the gospel so far as Pabroban. When the Portuguese first visited these countries after their discovery of a passage by the Cape of Good Hope, they received the following particulars, partly from constant and uncon-

troverted traditions preserved by the Christians in
those parts; namely, that Thomas came first to
Socotra, an island in the Arabian sea, and then to
Cranganore, where, having converted many from the
error of their ways, he traveled further into the East. ·
Having great success in winning souls to the faith, the
hand of persecution arose against him, and he was slain
by the Brahmans. Thomas, who at first was the weak-
est and most incredulous of all the apostles, is said to
have become the most active and invincible of them
all; traveling over most parts of the world, and living
without fear in the midst of barbarous nations.

MATTHEW

Matthew, called Levi, was born at Nazareth. He
was a publican, or tax-gatherer. He preached in Judea
for several years, and at his departure wrote his Gospel.
The ancients assign two dates to the composition of
his Gospel, one from A D 40 to 45, the other from
the year 60 to 65. It is quite evident that he wrote
his Gospel twice; first in Hebrew then in Greek, and
the reason for this is very plain. After the overthrow
of Jerusalem the Jews were dispersed and ceased to
speak their own language, and the Greek became their
usual tongue, as the Hebrew had been before. Matthew seeing this, prepared for them his Greek Gospel,
and there being no further use for the Hebrew one, it
gradually disappeared; though Jerome affirms that he
had not only seen it in the famous library of Pamphilus at Cesarea, but actually himself translated it
into Greek and Latin. Our present Greek is no translation, but an original from Matthew's own hand; and
we have the evidence entirely satisfactory of a Hebrew

ST. THOMAS'S INCREDULITY.

Gospel of his written some twenty years earlier. The
Hebrew Gospel, as we are informed by Eusebius, was
found among the Christians in India in the latter part
of the second century. According to the testimony of
antiquity, which there is no ground for contradict-
ing, the Hebrew Matthew was the first of the four
Gospels that was written. Eusebius says that after
our Lord's ascension Matthew preached in Judea,
and then went to foreign nations. He is said to
have visited Ethiopia, Persia, and Parthia, and to
have died a martyr's death at Naddabar, a city of
Ethiopia.

THADDEUS.

Thaddeus, Lebbeus, or Jude, was the author of an
epistle, one of the smallest books in the canon of the
New Testament. It was placed among the doubtful
writings of the primitive church, while some even considered it spurious. Even as late as the Reformation
it was held in suspicion. The epistle must have been
written at a late period, for he mentions as historical
facts already occurring what Peter in his second epistle
had predicted as still future at the time when he was
writing. 2 Pet. 2. The late date of the epistle, and
the fact that not much was known in the church
respecting its author, were probably the reasons why
it was slow in coming into universal use. But little
is known of the life and labors of Jude. He was the
brother of James, and consequently he was a younger
son of Mary, the mother of Jesus. He is said to have
preached the gospel in Lydia, Mesopotamia, Syria,
Idumea, and Arabia, and suffered martyrdom at Berytus about A. D. 80.

SIMON THE CANAANITE.

Simon, in the catalogue of our Lord's chosen apostles, is styled Simon the Canaanite, also known as Simon Zelotes. It occurs in Matt. 10:4; Mark 3:18. The word does not signify a descendant of Canaan, nor a native of Cana, but it comes from a Chaldean or Syriac word *Kannean,* by which the Jewish sect or faction of "the Zealots" was designated. Simon continued in communion with the rest of the apostles and disciples at Jerusalem, and at the feast of Pentecost received the gift of the Holy Ghost and was qualified with the rest of his brethren for the great work of an apostle. Some say he went into Egypt, Cyrene, and other parts of Africa preaching the gospel to the inhabitants of those countries; and others add that he also preached the gospel to the inhabitants of the western parts, and even in Britain, where, having converted great multitudes, and sustained the greatest hardships and persecutions, he was at last crucified, and buried in some part of the island, but the exact place is unknown.

JUDAS ISCARIOT.

Judas, by transgression, fell from the honors of the sacred college, that he might go to his own place. His bag and his halter he has left behind, with which to enshrine his awful memory. Let every one that reads notice these relics of a wicked heart, and beware of covetousness.

MATTHIAS.

Matthias was one of the seventy whom Jesus made choice of as one of his disciples. After the crucifixion he was chosen by the apostles to supply the place of

Judas. After the ascension he spent the first year of his ministry in Judea, where he was successful in bringing over a great number of people to the Christian faith. From Judea he traveled into other countries, and came at length to Ethiopia. Here many were converted; but the inhabitants in general being of a fierce and untractable temper resolved to take away his life, which they effected by first stoning him, and then severing his head from his body.

This closes the biography of the twelve apostles; but we will sketch a few others that were apostles and noted characters in the apostolic age.

CHAPTER V.

BIOGRAPHICAL SKETCHES CONTINUED.

IN chapter three we have given a sketch of the great apostle Paul. We shall in this chapter relate the particulars concerning some of his fellow laborers in the cause of Christ.

MARK.

Mark was the son of a pious woman in Jerusalem, and the intimate friend of the apostle Peter. He was also the friend and companion of Paul till some neglect of his, which occasioned a misunderstanding between Paul and Barnabas respecting him, produced a separation. Paul afterwards became reconciled to him, perhaps when he met him at Rome in company with Peter, and spoke of him in several of his epistles with great confidence and affection. According to the almost unanimous testimony of antiquity, his gospel was written at Rome, under the superintendence of the apostle Peter, a little after that of Matthew, and it was intended for the instruction of the Roman converts from paganism. He carefully explains allusions to Jewish customs, as if writing for those who were unacquainted with them. He is much more brief than the other evangelists, and has but twenty-four verses the substance of which is not found in Matthew and Luke. Unlike Matthew he is very particular in narrative, and very much condenses the conversations and discourses of Jesus. Ecclesiastical tradition speaks of a missionary expedition of his to Egypt and the west of Africa, of his suffering martyrdom about the year 62 or 66, and of the transmission of his corpse to Venice, which city has chosen him for its patron saint.

LUKE.

Luke was a Gentile by birth, and a physician, and according to the prevailing testimony of the ancients, a citizen of Antioch, where the followers of Christ were first called Christians. He was familiar with Greek literature (says Stowe), as is evident from the style and structure of his two works, the Gospel and the book of Acts, and his method of addressing them to Theophilus. He became a zealous Christian and by personal investigation familiarly acquainted himself with all the circumstances attending the origin of Christianity, diligently studied the Hebrew scriptures, and was the constant companion of the apostle Paul. Of Theophilus, the friend to whom he ascribes his two works, nothing is known with certainty. He was probably a Greek who lived out of Palestine, and perhaps at Antioch. Of all the evangelists Luke is the only one who gives a detailed account of the circumstances which preceded and attended the births of John the Baptist and Jesus. Luke was the companion of Paul in many of his missionary journeys, and it is said that after Paul's martyrdom he preached in Italy, Dalmatia, Macedonia, Bithynia, and finally suffered martyrdom at a very advanced age.

BARNABAS.

Barnabas, properly Joses, is mentioned in the Acts of the Apostles as a fellow laborer of Paul, and even honored with the title of apostle. Eusebius says, "Barnabas, indeed, is said to have been one of the apostles, of whom there is distinguished notice in the Acts of the Apostles; and also in St. Paul's epistle to the Galatians." According to tradition, he became the first bishop of Milan. He is supposed to have suffered martyrdom at the hands of the Cypriot Jews, A. D. 61. The epistle ascribed to him is held as apocryphal. This epistle contains twenty-one chapters. Its aim is obviously to strengthen the faith of believers in a purely spiritual Christianity. It commences by declaring that legal sacrifices are abolished, and then proceeds to show, though not in a very coherent or logical manner, how variously Christ was foretold in the Old Testament. In the tenth chapter, it spiritually allegorizes the commands of Moses concerning clean and unclean beasts; in the fifteenth it explains the true meaning of the sabbath; and in the sixteenth, what the temple really prefigured. This concludes what may be termed the doctrinal portion of the epistle; the remainder, which is of a practical charac-

ter, describes the two ways of life—the way of light
and the way of darkness, and closes with an exhortation that those who read it may so live that they may
be blessed to all eternity. It is a simple, pious, and
earnest work. This epistle lays a greater claim to
canonical authority than most others. It has been
cited by Clemens Alexandrinus, Origen, Eusebius, and
Jerome, and many ancient Fathers. Cotelerius affirms
that Origen and Jerome esteemed it genuine and
canonical; Cotelerius himself did not believe it to be
either one or the other; on the contrary, he supposes
it was written for the benefit of the Ebionites (the
Christianized Jews), who were tenacious of rites and
ceremonies. Bishop Fell feared to own expressly what
he seemed to be persuaded of, that it ought to be
treated with the same respect as some of the books of
the present canon. Dr. Bernard, Savilian professor
at Oxford, not only believed it to be genuine, but that
it was read throughout in the churches in Alexandria,
as the canonical scriptures were. Dodwell supposed it
to have been published before the epistle of Jude, and
the writings of both the Johns, Vossius, Dupuis, Dr.
Cave, Mill, Dr. S. Clarke, Whiston, and Archbishop
Wake, also esteemed it genuine: Menardus, Archbishop
Lud, Spanheim, and others, deemed it apocryphal.

TIMOTHY.

Timothy was a native of the city of Lystra in
Lycaonia in Asia Minor, the son of a Greek father and
a Jewish mother. He was converted to the faith of the
gospel by the preaching of Paul, and became his companion and fellow laborer in Macedonia and Achaia, and
was his fellow prisoner at Rome. When Paul returned

from Rome, in 64, he left Timothy at Ephesus to take
care of that church, of which he was the first bishop,
as he is recognized by the council of Chalcedon. Paul
wrote to him from Macedonia the first of the two letters which are addressed to him. It is quite probable
that it was written from this place, about A. D. 63 or
64, and it is not impossible that it might have been
written from Laodicea according to the old superscrip-
tion. After the apostle came to Rome in the year 65,
being then very near his death, he wrote to him his
second letter, which is full of marks of kindness and
tenderness. He calls to mind various interesting personal incidents, exhorts to purity of life and fortitude
under affliction, warns of corruptions and false teachers, and expresses his own calmness and happiness in
view of his approaching martyrdom. He no doubt
was an eye-witness of the martyrdom of Paul, which
happened at Rome in the year 68. After Timothy had
visited Paul at Rome he returned to Ephesus, where
he acted as bishop in that place for a while without
interruption, till at length he fell a victim to the
malice of the pagans, and by their hands suffered
martyrdom.

TITUS.

Titus, a Greek by birth, was an assistant of the
apostle Paul, was with him on his journey to Jerusalem; fulfilled commissions for him in Corinth, and
was left in Crete to attend to ecclesiastical duties in
that island. This was about A. D. 63. The following year Paul wrote to him to desire that as soon as he
should have sent Tychicus to him for supplying his
place in Crete, he would come to him at Nicopolis, in

Epirus, where the apostle intended to spend the winter. The epistle was probably written between the first and 'second epistles to Timothy. The object of this epistle is to represent to Titus what are the qualities that a bishop should be endued with. Titus was deputed to preach the gospel in Dalmatia, where he was situated when the apostle wrote his second epistle to Timothy. He afterwards returned into Crete, from which it is said he propagated the gospel into the neighboring islands. He died at the age of ninety-four, and was buried in Crete.

PHILEMON.

Philemon was a wealthy citizen of Colosse, a relative of Apphia and Archippus, who had been converted to Christianity by the apostle Paul. He was a generous believer, full of faith and good works, and the apostle had entire confidence in him.

CLEMENT.

Clement of Rome, the same spoken of by Paul in his epistle to the Philippians 4:3, was a Roman by birth, a disciple of the apostle Peter, and bishop of Rome at the close of the first century. Clemens Alexandrinus calls him an apostle; Jerome says he was an apostolic man; and Rufinus, that he was almost an apostle. Under his name we have two epistles to the church at Corinth; the first genuine and entire, but the second a mere fragment and of doubtful authority. Eusebius calls his epistle the wonderful epistle of St. Clement, and says that it was publicly read in the assemblies of the primitive church. It is included in one of the ancient collections of the canons of scripture. Its genuineness has been much questioned. But the

5

points of objection are comparatively groundless.

In what manner Clement conducted himself, and how he escaped the general persecution under the emperor Domitian, we have no certain accounts; but we are very well assured that he lived to the third year of the emperor Trajan, which is the hundredth of the Christian era. Rufinus and Pope Zosimus give him the title of Martyr; and the Roman church, in its canon, places him among the saints who have sacrificed their lives in the cause of Christ.

IGNATIUS.

Ignatius, surnamed Theophorus, was a pupil of the apostle John, and by him ordained second bishop of Antioch, which office he held forty years. He lived through the persecution of Domitian, but in the reign of Trajan, he was condemned to death. In the year 107, Trajan, being on his way to the Parthian war, came to Antioch. Ignatius, fearing for the Christians, and hoping to avert any storm which might be arising against them there, presented himself to the emperor, offering to suffer in their stead. Trajan received the apostolic man with great haughtiness; and being exasperated by the frankness and independence which he manifested, ordered him to be sent to Rome, there to be thrown to the wild beasts for the entertainment of the people.

From Antioch, Ignatius was hurried by his guards to Seleucia. Sailing thence, he arrived after great fatigue at Smyrna, where, while the ship was detained, he was allowed the pleasure of visiting Polycarp, who was the bishop of the church of that city. They had been fellow disciples of the apostle John. The mingled emotions of joy and grief experienced by these holy men, at this interview, can scarcely be conceived. Intelligence of his condemnation spread through the church, and deputies were sent from many places to console him and to receive some benefit by his spiritual communications. To various churches he addressed seven epistles; four of which were written at this time from Smyrna and Troas. The seven epistles have been known and read in the Christian churches from the very earliest period. There is an edition of them about the sixth century, which undoubtedly contains many interpolations; but the earlier and briefer recensions, of which Archbishop Usher had a Latin translation and I. Voss, the Greek original, may safely be received as genuine throughout. Besides these seven there are others ascribed to Ignatius, which may be rejected as spurious.

At length the hour of final separation came, and Ignatius was hurried from the sight and consolations of his friends. Having arrived at Rome, he was not long after led to the amphitheater and thrown to the wild beasts. Here he had his wish. The beasts were his grave. A few bones only were left; which his attendants gathered, carefully preserved, and afterwards buried at Antioch.

POLYCARP.

Polycarp was a disciple of St. John, and by him ordained bishop of Smyrna, which office he held over sixty years. Of his family and native country nothing is known. He was the companion of Ignatius. The eminence of his character and station marked out Polycarp as the victim of persecution. Perceiving his danger, his friends persuaded him to retire for a season to a neighboring village to elude the fury of his enemies. The most diligent search was made for him; but being unable to discover the place of his concealment, the persecutors proceeded to torture some of his brethren, with a design to compelling them to disclose the place of his retreat. This was too much for the tender spirit of Polycarp to bear. Accordingly he made a voluntary surrender of himself to his enemies, inviting them to refresh themselves at his table, and requesting only the privilege of an hour to pray without molestation. This being granted, he continued his devotions to double the period, appearing to forget himself in the contemplation of the glory of God. Having finished his devotions, he was placed upon an ass, and conducted to the city. When brought before the proconsul, efforts were made to induce him to abjure his faith, and to swear by the fortune of Cæsar. This he refused; upon which he was threatened with being made the prey of wild beasts. "Call for them," said Polycarp, "it does not well become us to turn from good to evil." "Seeing you make so light of wild beasts," rejoined the consul, "I will tame you with the punishment of fire." To this the aged disciple replied, "You threaten me with a fire that is quickly extinguished but you are ignorant of the eternal fire of God's judgment reserved for the wicked in the other world."

Polycarp remaining thus inflexible, the populace begged the proconsul to let out a lion against him. But the proconsul declared the spectacle of the wild beasts was finished. Then it was determined that he should be burnt alive. Accordingly preparations were made, during which this holy man was occupied in prayer. As they were going to nail him to the stake the martyr said, "Let me remain as I am; for he who giveth me strength to endure the fire will enable me to remain unmoved.". Putting his hand behind him they bound him. He now prayed aloud, and when he had pronounced *Amen*, they kindled the fire. The flames encircled his body like an arch, without touching him. On seeing this the executioner was ordered to thrust his sword into him, when so great a quantity of blood flowed out of his body that it extinguished the fire. The Christians begged for his body that they might give it decent burial; but at the instigation of Polycarp's enemies, especially the Jews, their request was denied and his body was ordered to be consumed in the pile. The Christians were allowed to collect the charred bones that remained with the ashes and inter them. His death occurred between the years 164 and 168.

He wrote a letter to the Philippians, which is for the most part still extant. Some answers to Biblical questions are ascribed to him, in regard to the genuineness of which serious doubts have been raised.

CHAPTER VI.

THE DESTRUCTION OF JERUSALEM.

"O JERUSALEM, Jerusalem, thou that killest the prophets, and stonest them which are sent unto thee,

how often would I have gathered thy children together,
even as a hen gathereth her chickens under her wings,
and ye would not."—Matt. 23:37. "And when he
was come near, he beheld the city, and wept over it,
saying, If thou hadst known, even thou, at least in
this thy day, the things which are hid from thine eyes.
For the days shall come upon thee, that thine enemies
shall cast a trench about thee, and compass thee round,
and keep thee in on every side, and shall lay thee even
with the ground, and thy children within thee; and
they shall not leave in thee one stone upon another;
because thou knewest not the time of thy visitation."—
Luke 19:41-44. These predictions came to pass in the
year 70. We will proceed to give a short account of
this event, the most awful in all the religious dispensation of God. All history can not furnish us with a
parallel to the calamities and miseries of the Jews;
rapine and murder, famine and pestilence, within; fire
and sword, and all the terrors of war without.

Our Savior wept at the foresight of these calamities;
and it is almost impossible for any person to read the
account without being affected. The predictions concerning them were remarkable, and the calamities that
came upon them were the greatest the world every saw.
Now, what sin was it that could be the cause of such
heavy judgments? Can any other be assigned than
what the scripture assigns? 1 Thess. 2:15, 16. They
both killed the Lord Jesus and their own prophets, and
persecuted the apostles; and so filled up their sins, and
wrath came upon them to the uttermost. It is hardly
possible to consider the nature and extent of their
sufferings, and not conclude the Jews' own impreca-

tion to be singularly fulfilled upon them, "His blood be on us and our children." The Romans under Vespasian invaded the country, and took the cities of Galilee, Chorazin, Bethsaida, Capernaum, etc., where Christ had been especially rejected. At Jerusalem the war was most wretched of all. Before we enter upon the details of the destruction we will notice some prodigies which preceded the war, as related by Josephus.

A comet, which bore the resemblance of a sword. hung over the city of Jerusalem for the space of a whole year.

A short time before the revolt of the Jews, a mos. remarkable and extraordinary light was seen about the altar of the temple. It happened at the ninth hour of the night preceding the celebration of the feast of the passover, and continued about half an hour, giving a light equal to that of day. Ignorant persons considered this unusual and wonderful appearance as a happy omen; but those of superior judgment averred that it was a prediction of approaching war; and their opinion was fully confirmed by the event.

The eastern gate of the interior part of the temple was composed of solid brass, and was of such an immense weight that it took the labor of twenty men to make it fast every night. It was secured with iron bolts and bars, which were let down into a large threshold consisting of an entire stone. About the fifth hour of the night this gate opened without any human assistance; immediate notice of which being given to the officer on duty, he lost no time in endeavoring to restore it to its former situation; but it was with the utmost difficulty that he accomplished it. There were likewise some ignorant people who deemed this to be a second good omen, insinuating that Providence had thereby set open a gate of blessing to the people, but persons of superior discernment were of a contrary opinion, and concluded that the opening of the gate predicted the success of the enemy, and destruction of the city.

A short time after the celebration of the feast of the passover, before the setting of the sun, the appearance of chariots and armed men was seen in the air, in various parts of the country, passing round the city among the clouds

While the priests were going to perform the duties of their function according to the custom, in the inner temple, on the first of Pentecost they at first heard an indistinct murmuring, which was succeeded by a voice, repeating, in the most plain and earnest manner, these words, "Let us be gone, let us depart hence."

But the most extraordinary circumstance of the whole was this. Some time before the commencement of the war, and while the city appeared to be in the most perfect peace, and abounded in plenty, there came to the feast of tabernacles a simple countryman, a son of Ananias, who without any previous intimation, exclaimed as follows: "A voice from the east; a voice from the west; a voice to Jerusalem, and a voice to the temple; a voice to men and women newly married; and a voice to the nation at large." In this manner did he continue his exclamations, in various parts through all the streets of the city; at which some persons of eminence in the city were so offended that they ordered him to be apprehended and severely whipped. This was accordingly done, but he bore his sufferings not only without complaint, but without saying a word in his own defense; and no sooner was his punishment ended than he proceeded in his exclamations as before. By this time the magistrates were suspicious (and indeed not without reason) that what he had said proceeded from the divine impulse of a superior power that influenced his words. In consequence of this they sent him to the governor of Judea, who directed that he should be whipped with the greatest severity. This order was so strictly obeyed that his very bones were seen, notwithstanding he neither wept nor supplicated, but in a voice of mourning, between each stroke exclaimed, "Woe, woe to Jerusalem!" From this very extraordinary behavior, the governor was induced to interrogate him with respect to his character, and the place of his birth and residence, and what could prompt him to act as he had done. He would not, however, make an answer to any of these questions, upon which the governor found himself under the necessity of dismissing him, as a man out of his senses. From this period to the commencement of the war he was never known either to visit or speak to any of the citizens, nor was he heard to say any other words than the melancholy sentence, "Woe, woe to Jerusalem!" Those who daily punished him received no ill language from him, nor did those who fed him receive his thanks; but what he generally said to every one was an ominous prediction. It was remarked that on public festivals he was more vociferous than at other times; and in the manner before mentioned he continued for the space of more than three years; nor did his voice or strength appear to fail him till his predictions were verified by the siege of Jerusalem. As soon as this event took place, he went for the last time on the wall of the city, and exclaimed with a more powerful voice than usual, "Woe, woe to this city, this temple, and this people"; and concluded his lamentation by saying, "Woe, woe be to myself." He had no sooner spoken these words than, in the midst of these predictions, he was destroyed by a stone thrown from an engine.

The time is now come in which God shall begin to reckon with his enemies, and to verify the predictions of his Son. While Vespasian was spreading the victories of the Roman arms and was preparing more effectually to curb the still unbroken spirit of the Jews, intelligence arrived successively of the deaths of Nero, Galba, Otho, and Vitellius, and of his own election to the throne. Departing therefore for Rome, he left the best of his troops with his son Titus, ordering him to besiege Jerusalem, and utterly to destroy it. Titus lost no time in carrying into effect his father's injunctions; and accordingly, putting his army into motion, he advanced upon the city. Jerusalem was strongly fortified, both by nature and art. Three walls surround it, which were considered impregnable; besides which it had numerous towers surmounting these walls, lofty, firm, and strong. Desirous of saving the city, Titus repeatedly sent offers of peace to the inhabitants; but they were indignantly rejected. Titus, one of the most merciful generals that ever breathed, did all in his power to persuade them to an advantageous surrender, but they scorned every proposal. At length, finding all efforts at treaty ineffectual, he entered upon the siege, determined not to leave it till he had razed the city to its foundation.

A matter will now be related, which took place during the prevalence of the famine, which will show the low state to which they were reduced during the siege. It will be given in full as Josephus has it recorded.

"Now of those that perished by famine in the city, the number was prodigious; and the miseries they underwent were unspeakable; for if so much as the shadow of any kind of food did anywhere appear, a war was commenced presently, and the dearest friends fell a fighting one with another about it, snatching from each other the most miserable supports of life. Nor would men believe that those who were dying had no food, but the robbers would search them when they were expiring, lest any one should have concealed food in their bosoms, and counterfeited dying; nay these robbers gaped for want, and ran about stumbling and staggering along like mad dogs, and reeling against the doors of the houses like drunken men; they would also in the great distress they were in, rush into the very same houses two or three times in one and the same day. Moreover, their hunger was so intolerable, that it obliged them to chew everything, while they gathered such things as the most sordid animals would not touch, and endured to eat them; nor did they at length abstain from girdles and shoes, and the very leather that belonged to their shields they pulled off and gnawed: the very wisps of old hay became food to some, and some gathered up fibers, and sold a very small weight of them for four attic. But why do I describe the shameless impudence that the famine brought on men in their eating inanimate things, while I am going to relate a matter of fact, the like to which no history relates, either among the Greeks or Barbarians? It is horrible to speak of it, and incredible when heard. I had indeed willingly omitted this calamity of ours, that I might not seem to deliver what is so portentous to posterity, but that I have innumerable witnesses to it in my own age: and besides, my country would have little reason to thank me for suppressing the miseries that she underwent at this time.

"There was a certain woman that dwelt beyond Jordan; her name was Mary, her father was Eleazar, of the village of Bethezob, which signifies *the House of Hyssop*. She was eminent for her family and her wealth, and had fled away to Jerusalem with the rest of the multitude, and was with them besieged therein at this time. The other effects of this woman had been already seized upon; such I mean as she had brought with her out of Perea, and removed to the city. What she had treasured up besides, as also what food she had contrived to save, had been also carried off by the rapacious guards, who came every day running into her house for that purpose. This put the woman into a very great passion, and by the frequent reproaches and imprecations she cast at these rapacious villains, she had provoked them to anger against her; but none of them, either out of the indignation she had raised against herself, or out of commiseration of her case, would take away her life: and if she found any food, she perceived her labors were for others, and not for herself, and it was now become impossible for her any way to find any more food, while the famine pierced through her very bowels and marrow, when also her passion was fired to a degree beyond the famine itself; nor did she consult with anything but with her passion and the necessity she was in. She then attempted a most unnatural thing, and, snatching up her son, who was a child sucking at her breast, she said, 'O thou miserable infant! for whom shall I preserve thee in this war, this famine, and this sedition? As to the war with the Romans, if they preserve our lives, we must be slaves. This famine also will destroy us even before that slavery comes upon us. Yet are these seditious rogues more terrible than both the other. Come on; be thou my food, and be thou a fury to these seditious varlets, and a byword to the world, which is all that is now wanting to complete the calamities of us Jews.' As soon as she had said this, she slew her son, and then roasted him, and ate the one half of him and kept the other half by her concealed. Upon this the seditious came in presently, and smelling the horrid scent of this food, they threatened her that they would cut her throat immediately if she did not show them what food she had gotten ready. She replied that she had 'saved a very fine portion of it for them'; and withal uncovered what was left of her son. Hereupon they were seized with a horror and amazement of mind, and stood astonished at the sight, when she said to them, 'This is mine own son, and what hath been done was mine own doing. Come, eat of this food; for I have eaten of it myself. Do not you pretend to be either more tender than a woman, or more compassionate than a mother; but if you be so scrupulous, and do abominate this my sacrifice, as I have eaten the one half, let the rest be preserved for me also.' After which those men went out trembling, being never so much affrighted at anything as they were at this, and with some difficulty they left the rest of that meat to the mother. Upon 'which the whole city was full of this horrid action immediately; and while everybody laid this miserable case before their own eyes, they trembled, as if this unheard-of action had been done by themselves. So those that were thus distressed by the famine were very desirous to die, and those already dead were esteemed happy, because they had not lived long enough either to hear or to see such miseries.''

When the report of this spread through the city, the horror and consternation were as universal as they were inexpressible. The people now for the first time began to think themselves forsaken of God. In the mind of Titus this act awakened the deepest horror and indignation. "Soon," said he, "shall the sun never more dart his beams on a city, where mothers feed on the flesh of their children; and where fathers no less guilty than themselves, choose to drive them to such extremities, rather than lay down their arms." Under this determination the Roman general now pushed the siege with still greater vigor, aiming particularly, in the first place, to obtain possession of the temple. The preservation of this noble edifice was strongly desired by him; but one of the Roman soldiers, being exasperated by the Jews, or, as Josephus thinks, *pushed on by the hand of Providence*, seized a blazing firebrand, and getting on his comrades' shoulders, threw it through a window into one of the apartments that surrounded the sanctuary, and instantly set the whole north side in a flame up to the third story. Titus, who was asleep in his pavilion, awaked by the noise, immediately gave orders to extinguish the fire. But they failed to obey his command. The flames continued to do their work of destruction, until this consecrated edifice, the glory of the nation, the admiration of the priest and prophet of God, became one mingled heap of ruins. To this a horrible massacre succeeded, in which thousands perished, some by the flames, others by falling from the battlements; and a greater number still by the enemy's sword, which spared neither age, nor sex, nor rank. Next to the temple, were consumed the treasury house of the palace, though they were full of the richest furniture, vestments, plate, and other vauable articles. At length the city was abandoned to the fury of the soldiers, who spread rapine, and murder, and fire through every street. The number that perished during the siege has been estimated as little short of a million and a half. The conquest of the city being achieved, Titus proceeded to demolish its noble structures, its fortifications, its palaces, its towers, and its walls. So literally and fully were the predictions of the Savior accomplished, respecting its destruction, that scarcely anything remained which could serve as an index that the ground had ever been inhabited. Thus after a siege of six months was swept from the earth a city which God had honored more than any other; a temple, in which his glory had been seen, and his praises sung by

priest and prophet, for a succession of ages; an altar
was gone, which had smoked with the blood of many
a victim; a dispensation was ended, which had existed
for ages; a nation, as a nation, was blotted from being,
which had outlived some of the proudest monuments
of antiquity.

Such were the consequences to the Jewish nation of
rejecting and crucifying the Son of 'God. From the
day in which the Roman general 'led his triumphant
legions from the spot, the Jews have been "without a
king, and without a prince, and without a sacrifice,
and without an image, and without an ephod, and without teraphim."—Hosea 3:4. Dispersed through the
world, despised and hated by all, persecuted and yet
upheld, lost as it were among the nations of the earth,
and yet distinct, they live—they live as the monuments
of the truth of Christianity—and convey to the world
the solemn lesson that no nation can reject the Son of
God with impunity. This is indeed true of nations
that reject the Bible. Look at the history of the nations where the Bible has been trampled under foot.
Only a few years ago France and England were pretty
nearly equal. ' England threw the Bible open to the
world, and France tried to trample it. Now the
English language is spoken around the world, and its
prosperity has increased, while it stands foremost
among nations. But look at France. It has gone
down and down with anarchy and revolution.

CHAPTER VII.

PAGAN PERSECUTIONS.

PERSECUTION is any pain or affliction which a person designedly inflicts upon another; and in a more restricted sense, the sufferings of Christians on account of their religion. Persecution is threefold—1. *Mental*, when the spirit of a man rises up and opposes another. 2. *Verbal*, when men give hard words, and deal in uncharitable censures. 3. *Actual*, or *open*, by the hand, such as the dragging of innocent persons before the tribunal of justice. Matt. 10:17, 18.

Historians usually reckon ten general persecutions. The Christian church was at all times regarded with suspicion and dislike in the Roman empire. The question may be asked, Why was Pagan Rome so disgusted with Christianity, persecuting it with rancor, when it appeared in its greatest beauty? The answer given by Bishop Warburton is this: that *intercommunity* of worship was a fundamental doctrine of paganism. Had, therefore, the Christians consented to *mingle* with the pagans in their worship, they would not have been persecuted. But so far from this, Christianity exalted itself above paganism, and would have no connection with it. It claimed not only to be the true, but the only true religion on the earth. This excited the jealousy and indignation of the advocates of paganism, and was the true cause why the advocates of Christianity were so often and so grievously persecuted. That this was the cause may be confirmed by the fact that the Jews, who disclaimed all

6

connection with paganism, were persecuted much in the same manner. The emperor Julian, who well understood this matter, frankly owned that the Jews and Christians brought the execration of the world upon them, by their aversion to the gods of paganism, and their refusal of all communication with them. Though persecution has its origin from the devil, God permits it to come upon his children to try them. 2 Tim 3:12. The persecutor no doubt generally thinks he is doing God service. John 16·2

The first general persecution took place about the year 64 under the emperor Nero, when that emperor having set fire to the city of Rome for the pleasure of gazing on the desolation occasioned thereby, to exculpate himself laid the charge upon the Christians—a people universally held in contempt, and to whom nothing was too bad to be imputed. Tacitus, the famed historian of that day, speaking of Nero, and of that event, says, To divert suspicion from himself, he substituted fictitious criminals, and with this view he inflicted the most exquisite tortures on those men who were called Christians. Their death and tortures were aggravated by cruel derision and sport, for they were either covered with the skins of wild beasts and torn in pieces by devouring dogs, or fastened to crosses and wrapped up in combustible garments, that when the daylight failed, they might like torches, dispel the darkness. For this tragical spectacle Nero lent his own gardens, and exhibited at the same time the public diversion of the circus; sometimes driving a chariot in person, and sometimes standing as a spectator, while the shrieks of women burning to ashes supplied music for his ears.

A PRIMITIVE CHRISTIAN BURNED BY HEATHEN PERSECUTORS.

This persecution, not confined to the city of Rome, raged, by the edict of the tyrant, through the empire; and most probably continued though with some abatement of its fury, to the end of Nero's reign (A. D. 68), when this unhappy man laid violent hands upon himself, and so delivered the world from the monster, and the Christians from this bloody scourge.

The second general persecution was under Domitian, in the year 95, when 40,000 were supposed to have suffered martyrdom, which ended with his death, who was assassinated in A. D. 96, at the instigation of his wife, whom the tyrant was designing to destroy.

The third persecution began in the third year of the reign of Trajan, in the year A. D. 100, and was carried on with great violence for several years, or until Adrian, which was nineteen years. With this persecution the history of the second century must commence. We have a fair specimen of the spirit of the times, in the correspondence between Pliny, governor of Bythinia, and his master Trajan. The date of these letters is A. D. 107.

"*C. Pliny to the Emperor Trajan.*

Sir: It is customary with me to consult you upon every doubtful occasion; for where my own judgment hesitates, who is more competent to direct me than yourself, or to instruct me where uninformed? I never had occasion to be present at any examination of the Christians before I came into this province; I am therefore ignorant to what extent it is usual to inflict punishment, or urge prosecution. I have also hesitated whether there should not be some distinction made between the young and the old, the tender and

DREADFUL SUFFERINGS OF THE PRIMITIVE MARTYRS.

the robust; whether pardon should not be offered to penitence, or whether the guilt of an avowed profession of Christianity can be expiated by the most unequivocal retraction—whether the profession itself is to be regarded as a crime, however innocent in other respects the professor may be; or whether the crimes attached to the name, must be proved before they are made liable to punishment. In the meantime, the method I have hitherto observed with the Christians, who have been accused as such, has been as follows. I interrogated them—Are you Christians? If they avowed it, I put the same question a second, and a third time, threatening them with the punishment decreed by law. If they still persisted, *I ordered them to be immediately executed, for of this I had no doubt, whatever was the nature of their religion, that such perverseness and inflexible obstinacy certainly deserved punishment.* Some that were affected with this madness, on account of their privileges as Roman citizens, I reserved to be sent to Rome, to be referred to your tribunal. In the discussion of this matter, accusations multiplying, a diversity of cases occurred A schedule of names was sent me by an unknown accuser, but when I cited the persons before me, many denied the fact that they were or ever had been Christians; and they repeated after me an invocation of the gods, and of your image, which for this purpose I had ordered to be brought with the statues of the other deities. They performed sacred rites with wine and frankincense, and execrated Christ, none of which things I am assured, a real Christian can ever be compelled to do. These, therefore, I thought proper to discharge Others named by an informer, at first acknowledged themselves Christians, and then denied it, declaring that though they had been Christians, they had renounced their profession—some three years ago, others still longer, and some even twenty years ago. All these worshiped your image and the statues of the gods, and at the same time execrated Christ. And this was the account which they gave me of the nature of the religion they once had professed, whether it deserves the name of crime or error, namely, that they were accustomed on a stated day to assemble before sunrise, and to join together in singing hymns to Christ, as a deity; binding themselves as with a solemn oath not to commit any kind of wickedness; to be guilty neither of theft, robbery, nor adultery; never to break a promise, or to keep back a deposit when called upon. Their worship being concluded, it was their custom to separate, and meet together again for a repast, promiscuous indeed, and without any distinction of rank or sex, but perfectly harmless; and even from this desisted, since the publication of my edict in which, agreeably to your orders I forbade any societies of that sort. For further information, I thought it necessary in order to come at the truth to put to the torture two females who were called deaconesses. But I could extort from them nothing except the acknowledgement of an excessive and depraved superstition; and therefore, desisting from further investigation, determined to consult you; for the number of culprits is so great as to call for the most serious deliberation. Informations are pouring in against multitudes of every age, of all orders, and of both sexes; and more will be impeached; for the contagion of this superstition hath spread, not only through cities, but villages also, and even reaches the farmhouses. I am of opinion nevertheless that it may be checked, and the success of my endeavors hitherto forbids despondency; for the temples once almost desolate, begin to be again frequented; the sacred solemnities which had for some time been intermitted, are now attended afresh; and the sacrificial victims, which once could scarcely find a purchaser, now obtain a brisk sale. Whence I infer, that many might be reclaimed were the hope of pardon on their repentance, absolutely confirmed."

To this letter Trajan sent the following reply.

"My dear Pliny.

You have done perfectly right in managing as you have the matters which relate to the impeachment of the Christians. No one general rule can be laid down which will apply to all cases. These people are not to be hunted up by informers; but if accused and convicted, let them be executed; yet with this restriction, that if they renounce the profession of Christianity and give proof of it by offering supplication to our gods, however suspicious their past conduct may have been, they shall be pardoned on their repentance. But anonymous accusations shall never be attended to, since it would be establishing a precedent of the worst kind, and altogether inconsistent with the maxims of my government."

Trajan died in the year 117 and was succeeded by Adrian. During the reign of Adrian the church had peace and prosperity. The successor of Adrian was Antoninus Pius, a senator, who ascended the throne

A. D. 138. He was distinguished for his love of peace,
and his justice and clemency.   Without embracing
the gospel, he so far approved of Christianity, as decidedly to discountenance the persecution of its professors.   Accordingly during the three and twenty
years of his reign, it seems reasonable to conclude
that Christians were permitted to worship God in
peace.

The fourth persecution.   Antoninus Pius adopted
for his successor his son-in-law, Marcus Aurelius Antoninus, who ascended the throne in A. D. 161. He was
a prince of a very different character, and severely the
church found it so.   During his time the fourth persecution took place, during which the Christians were
banished from their houses, forbidden to show their
heads, reproached, beaten, hurried from place to
place, plundered, imprisoned, and stoned.   The martyrdoms of Justin, of Polycarp, of which we have
already given an account, and of the confessors of
Lyons and Vienne stand as an indelible stain upon his
character.   Justin and six others, companions in trib-
ulation, were brought before the magistrate, and urged
to renounce their profession, and sacrifice to the gods;
but standing fast in their attachment to the Crucified
One, sentence was given that they should be first
scourged, and then beheaded, according to the laws.

Lyons and Vienne, two cities of Gaul, or France,
afford a proof, not only of the wide spread of the gospel, but also of the opposition it met with, under the
government of Marcus Aurelius.   The persecution
commenced by the furious attack of the populace.
Christians did not dare to appear in any public place,

such as the markets, the baths, nor scarcely in the streets, much less could they assemble for worship without the greatest danger. They were not safe in their own houses. They were plundered, dragged on the ground, stoned, beaten, and accused to the magistrate of the most abominable crimes. All the tender ties of relationship were dissolved; the father delivered up the son to death, and the son the father. In order to compel them to give up their profession, the most cruel tortures were inflicted. The inhuman ruler commanded them to be scourged with whips, to be scorched by applying heated brazen plates to the most tender parts of their body. To prepare them for a renewal of such barbarous treatment, they were remanded to prison, and again brought forth, some to a repetition of similar cruelties, others to die under the hands of their persecutors. Pothinus, one of the pastors, upwards of ninety years of age, worn out with his labors, suffered many things and expired in prison. Various were the ways in which the martyrs were put to death: some were thrown to beasts, others roasted in an iron chair, and many were beheaded.

The sufferings of a female, and a youth of fifteen deserve particular notice. The good woman was suspended by a rope within reach of the beasts; but the beasts failing to attack her she was taken down and cast into prison. On the last day of exposing the Christians, Blandina, which was her name, was brought forth again, attended by the youth, whose name was Ponticus. They were ordered to acknowledge the heathen deities, and refusing to do so the multitude had no compassion for either of them, and they were

HORRIBLE CRUELTIES INFLICTED ON THE PRIMITIVE CHRISTIANS.

put to extreme tortures.   The youth expired first.
Blandina having endured stripes, the teeth of the
beasts, and the iron chair, was inclosed in a net, and
thrown to a wild bull: after having been tossed some
time, to the gratification of the base mob, she breathed
out her soul, and was numbered with the noble army
of martyrs.

Marcus Aurelius Antoninus was called (A. D. 180)
to stand before the divine tribunal   During the reign
of Commodus and Pertinax, which was together thirteen years, the church throughout the world enjoyed a
large degree of external peace, and greatly increased
in numbers.

The fifth persecution.   On the death of Pertinax,
Septimius Severus took the sovereign rule in A D. 193.
In the tenth year of his reign (A. D. 202) the fifth persecution commenced.   In this persecution happened
the martyrdom of Perpetua and Felicitas, and their
companions.   Perpetua had an infant at the breast,
and Felicitas was just delivered, at the time of their
being put to death.   These two beautiful and amiable
young married women, mothers of infant children,
after suffering much in prison, were exposed before
an insulting multitude to a wild cow, who mangled
their bodies in a most horrid manner; after which
they were carried to a conspicuous place, and put to
death by the sword.   The persecution under Severus
was general.   It extended to Africa, Asia, and the
province of Gaul.   Lyons again became the seat of the
most dreadful ravages.   Irenæus, the pastor of the
church at that place, had escaped death during the
former persecutions; but in this he obtained the crown

of martyrdom.   At this trying season, some of the churches purchased a casual and uncertain peace, by paying money to the magistrates and their informers. After a reign of eighteen years Severus died, in A. D. 211.   The chronology of the Roman rulers that held the throne between the periods of persecution will be omitted.

The sixth persecution.   In the year 235 the virtuous Alexander and his amiable mother were put to death, during a conspiracy raised by Maximinus, the son of a herdsman of Thrace; who, by means of the army, was made emperor.   During his reign the sixth persecution occurred; which, however, fortunately for the church, was limited to three years.   The principal persons who perished under his reign were Pontianus, bishop of Rome; Anteros, a Grecian, his successor, who gave offense to the government by collecting the acts of the martyrs, Pammachius and Quiritus (Roman senators) with all their families, and many other Christians. During this persecution raised by Maximinus, numberless Christians were slain without trial, and buried indiscriminately in heaps, sometimes fifty or sixty being cast into a pit together, without the least decency.

From the death of Maximinus (A. D. 238) to the reign of Decius (A. D. 249) the church enjoyed considerable repose; and the gospel made extensive progress.   During this interval, reigned Pupienus, Balbinus, Gordianus, and Philip, the last of whom was the first Roman emperor who professed Christianity. Following Philip came Decius, whose reign is distinguished for the next great persecution.

The seventh persecution raged with great violence

throughout the empire, for the space of thirty months,
when Decius was succeeded by Gallus.   This persecution was the most dreadful ever known.   The Christians in all places were driven from their homes,
stripped of their estates, tormented with racks, stoned,
scorched with lighted torches, burnt with red-hot
irons, torn with sharp hooks, laid naked upon live
coals, intermingled with glass, cast into prison,
scourged, and beheaded.   This persecution was occasioned partly by the hatred he bore to his predecessor
Philip, who was deemed a Christian, and partly to his
jealousy concerning the amazing increase of Christianity; for the heathen temples began to be forsaken,
and Christians thronged to their places of worship.
These reasons stimulated Decius to attempt the very
extirpation of the name Christian.

Milner, speaking of the state of the church at this
time, says, "It deserves to be remarked, that the first
grand and general declension, after the primary effu-
sion of the Divine Spirit, should be fixed about the
middle of this century." Ambition, pride, and luxury
are the usual result of a season of worldly ease and
prosperity.   The pastors neglected their charges for
worldly preferment, and even embarked in schemes of
mercantile speculation.   From the foregoing account
it might be inferred, as was the melancholy fact, that
the persecution under Decius was distinguished beyond
all that preceded it, for the number of apostates from
the faith.   Until this time, few instances are on
record of the apostatizing of any from the faith, even
in the severest persecutions by which the church had
been afflicted; but now vast numbers, in many parts

of the empire, lapsed into idolatry. At Rome, even
before any were accused as Christians, many ran to
the forum and sacrificed to the gods, as they were
ordered; and the crowds of apostates were so great
that the magistrates wished to delay numbers of them
till the next day; but they were importuned by the
wretched suppliants to be allowed to prove themselves
heathen that very night.

Notwithstanding the numberless apostates of these
times, whose course was deeply wounding to the cause
of Christianity; there were those who rendered themselves illustrious by their steady adherence to the faith,
even amid the pains of martyrdom. During this persecution was laid the foundation of *monkery*, by one
Paul, of Egypt; who to avoid the persecution, retired
to the deserts of Thebais, where, acquiring a love for
solitude, he continued from the age of twenty-three
the remainder of his life, which was protracted to the
unusual length of one hundred thirteen years. From
this example of seclusion sprang, in the course of a
few years, swarms of monks and hermits, a class of
men not only useless but burdensome, offensive, and
disgraceful to Christianity.

In the year 251, Decius being slain, Gallus succeeded him. After allowing the church a short calm,
he began to disturb its peace, though not to the extent of his predecessor. The persecution, however, was
severe; and was borne by the Christians with more fortitude than it had been in the time of Decius. After
a miserable reign of eighteen months, Gallus was slain,
and was succeeded by Valerian.

The eighth persecution. On the ascension of Vale-

rian (A. D. 253) the church enjoyed a state of peace
and refreshment for nearly four years; the emperor
appearing, in respect to Christians, as a friend and
protector; but at the expiration of this period, his conduct was suddenly changed, by means of the influence
of his favorite, the hostile Macrianus, and a deadly
persecution was commenced, which continued for the
space of three years. This was called the eighth persecution. It began in the month of April, A. D. 257.
Both men and women suffered death, some by scourging, some by the sword, and some by fire. The first
person of official distinction who suffered martyrdom
under his orders was Sextus, the bishop of Rome. On
his way to execution he was followed by Laurentius,
his chief deacon; who, weeping, said, "Whither goest
thou, father, without thy son?" To which Sextus
replied, "You shall follow me in three days." This
prophecy was fulfilled. After the death of the bishop,
this noble deacon was brought before the magistrate,
and condemned to death, which was carried out by
broiling him on a bed of iron. At Utica a most terrible tragedy was exhibited: 300 Christians were, by the
orders of the proconsul, placed round a burning lime-
kiln. A pan of coals and incense being prepared, they
were commanded either to sacrifice to Jupiter, or to be
thrown into the kiln. Unanimously refusing, they
bravely jumped into the pit, and were immediately
suffocated.

The ninth persecution, under Aurelian, in 274, was
inconsiderable compared with the others before mentioned.

The tenth persecution began in the nineteenth year

PRIMITIVE MARTYRDOMS.

of Diocletian, A. D. 303. In this dreadful persecution, which lasted ten years, houses filled with Christians were set on fire, and whole droves were tied together with ropes and thrown into the sea. It is related that 17,000 were slain in one month's time; and that during the continuance of this persecution, in the province of Egypt alone, no less than 144,000 Christians died by the violence of their persecutors; besides 700,000 that died through the fatigues of banishment, or the public works to which they were condemned.

Soon after this persecution abated in the middle parts of the empire, as well as in the west, and Providence at length began to manifest vengeance on the persecutors. Maximian endeavored to corrupt his daughter Fausta to murder Constantine her husband, which she discovered; and Constantine forced him to choose his own death, when he preferred the ignominious death of hanging, after being an emperor nearly twenty years. Maximus was governor of Cilicia. He and Galerius were friends to Diocletian, and were his prompters in this great persecution. Galerius was also visited by an incurable and intolerable disease, which baffled all the skill of physicians and surgeons. He was eaten of worms while living. He suffered untold agony. He was in this languishing state a full year, and his conscience was awakened, at last, so that he was compelled to acknowledge the God of the Christians, and to promise that he would rebuild the church houses, and repair the mischief done to them. An edict in his last agonies, was published in his name, and the joint names of Constantine and Licinius, to permit the Christians to have the free use of religion, and to supplicate their God for his health and the good of the empire; on which many prisoners in Nicomedia were liberated.

CHAPTER VIII.

MIRACLES.

THE power of working miracles is supposed by some to have been continued no longer than the apostles' days. Others think that it was continued long after. It seems pretty clear, however, that miracles universally ceased before Chrysostom's time, A. D. 347. Eusebius gives no account of the manifestation of any of the gifts of the Spirit later than A. D. 265. As for what Augustine says (A. D. 596) of those wrought at the tombs of the martyrs, and some other places, in his time, the evidence is not always so convincing as might be desired in facts of importance. As to the miracles of the Roman Catholics, it is evident, as Doddridge observes, that many of them were ridiculous tales, according to their own historians; others were performed without any credible witnesses, or in circumstances where the performer had the greatest opportunity for juggling. There is no doubt that they were all frauds. Yet according to ancient historians, miracles certainly were performed by the true saints of God during the extent of the First Period, or Morning Age, of the church. I will give a few proofs from Eusebius's Ecclesiastical History.

"These accounts are given by Irenæus (A. D. 180) in those five books of his, to which he gives the title of 'Refutation and Overthrow of False Doctrine.' In the second book of the same work, he also shows that even down to his times, instances of divine and miraculous power were remaining in some churches. 'So far are they,' says he, 'from raising the dead, as the Lord raised, and as the apostles by means of prayer, for even among the brethern frequently in a case of necessity, when a whole church united in much fasting and prayer, the spirit returned to the ex-animated body, and the man was granted to the prayers of the saints.' And again he says, after other observations: 'But if they say that our Lord also did these things only in appearance, we shall refer them back to the prophetic declaration, and shall show that all those things were strictly foretold, and were done by him, and that he alone is the Son of God.   Wherefore, also, those that were truly his disciples, receiving grace from him, in his name performed these things for the benefit of the rest of men, as every one received the free gift from him.   Some, indeed, most certainly and truly cast out demons, so that frequently those persons themselves that were cleansed from wicked spirits, believed and were received into the church. Others have the knowledge of things to come, as also visions and prophetic communications; others heal the sick by the imposition of hands, and restore them to health. And, moreover, as we said above, even the dead have been raised and continued with us many years.   And why should we say more?   It is impossible to tell the number of the gifts which the church throughout the world received

from God, and the deeds performed in the name of
Jesus Christ, that was crucified under Pontius Pilate,
and this too every day for the benefit of the heathen,
without deceiving any, or exacting their money. For
as she has received freely from God, she also freely
ministers.' In another place the same author writes:
'As we hear many of the brethren in the church who
have prophetic gifts, and who speak in all tongues
through the Spirit, and who also bring to light the
secret things of men for their benefit, and who ex-
pound the mysteries of God.' These gifts of different
kinds also continued with those that were worthy until
the times mentioned.''

"Many miracles are attributed to Narcissus by his
countrymen, as they received the tradition handed
down from the brethren. Among these they relate a
wonderful event like the following. About the great
watch of the passover, they say, that whilst the deacons were keeping the vigils the oil failed them; upon
which all the people being very much dejected, Narcissus commanded the men that managed the lights to
draw water from a neighboring well, and to bring it to
him. They having done it as soon as said, Narcissus
prayed over the water, and then commanded them in a
firm faith in Christ, to pour it into the lamps. When
they had also done this, contrary to all natural expectation, by an extraordinary and divine influence, the
nature of the water was changed into the quality of
oil, and by most of the brethren a small quantity was
preserved from that time until our own, as a specimen
of the wonder then performed. They relate also many
other matters worthy of note respecting the life of this

man." Eusebius gives another account of miracles
about the year A. D. 265, which is the last we have
any account of during the Morning Age of the church.

REASONS FOR DIVISION INTO PERIODS.

This chapter will be concluded by giving some scriptural and historical reasons why in this work church history has been divided into *four periods; i. e.*, (1) from
Christ to A. D. 270, (2) from 270 to 1530, (3) from
1530 to 1880, (4) from 1880 to the present time.

Period I., or Morning Light Age of the church, was a
period of light and purity. "Who is she that looketh
forth as the morning, fair as the moon, clear as the
sun, and terrible as an army with banners?"—Cant.
6:10. During this period the church was equipped
and endued with great power, and in all its glory manifested its great head Jesus Christ. It was in this
period that the Holy Ghost was given to the church.
"But ye shall receive power, after that the Holy Ghost
is come upon you." "And when the day of Pentecost
was fully come, they were all with one accord in one
place. And suddenly there came a sound from heaven
as of a rushing mighty wind, and it filled all the house
where they were sitting. And there appeared unto
them cloven tongues like as of fire, and it sat upon
each of them. And they were all filled with the Holy
Ghost, and began to speak with other tongues, as the
Spirit gave them utterance." "And when they had
prayed the place was shaken where they were assembled
together; and they were all filled with the Holy Ghost,
and they spake the word of God with boldness. And
the multitude of them that believed were of one heart
and of one soul: neither said any of them that aught

of the things which he possessed was his own; but they had all things common. And with great power gave the apostles witness of the resurrection of the Lord Jesus: and great grace was upon them all.'' During this time miracles of many kinds were performed, and all the gifts of the Spirit were manifest.

Now in order to show the duration of this period, we must find out when the church retrograded from this power and glory, which took place, according to many authors, from the middle to the close of the third century. During the whole of the third century, the work of God in purity and power had been declining. From the accession of Gallienus, in A. D. 260, to 302 (excepting the reign of Aurelian) the church was in a state of peace, as far as outward persecutions were concerned. But at no period since the days of the apostles, had there been so general a decay of vital godliness, as in this. During the pacific part of Diocletian's reign, the great first outpouring of the Spirit of God, which began on the day of Pentecost, appears to have nearly ceased.

A principal cause of this sad declension may be found in the connection which was formed by the professors of religion with the philosophy of the times. Outward peace and secular advantage completed the corruption. Ministers and laity became jealous of one another, and ambition and covetousness became ascendant in the church. The worship of God was indeed generally observed; nominal Christians continually increased; but the spirit which had but a few years before so nobly and zealously influenced a Cyprian, a Dionysius, a Gregory, and which so strongly resembled the spirit of apostolic times, was gone.

Another great event which marks the close of this period is the division and decline of the Roman empire We read that at this time almost half the inhabitants of the Roman empire, and of several neighboring countries, professed the faith of Christ. And when endeavors were made to preserve the unity of belief, and of church discipline, it occasioned numberless disputes among those of different opinions, and led to the establishment of an ecclesiastical tyranny. The phase of things had taken a change in the church; for instead of letting Christ be the head, and the bishops be ensamples to the flock, the bishops aspired to higher degrees of power and authority than they had formerly possessed. The bishops assumed in many places a princely authority, particularly those who had the greatest number of churches under their inspection, and who presided over the most opulent assemblies. They assumed the authority of a temporal magistrate. Sumptuous garments dazzled the eyes and minds of the multitude into-an ignorant veneration for their assumed authority. The example of the bishops was imitated by the presbyters, who, neglecting the sacred duties of their station, abandoned themselves to the indolence and delicacy of an effeminate and luxurious life. The deacons beholding the presbyters deserting thus their functions, boldly usurped their rights and privileges; and the effects of a corrupt official body spread through every rank of the church.

Heresies sprung up in different localities. About A. D. 270, Nepos, a bishop in Egypt, attempted to revive the heresy of Cerinthus, the most noted heretic

of the first century, who taught the church that there
would be a certain millennium of sensual luxury on
the earth.   Nepos endeavored to establish this theory
by the Revelation of John.   He caused a division in
the church, and a great many who opposed his theory
attempted to refute the whole book of Revelation, and
to set it aside.   ·About this time another awful heresy
was brought about by one Paul of Samosata, who then
was acting as bishop at Antioch.   He prepared himself
a tribunal and throne, not as a disciple of Christ, but
having, like the rulers of this world an exclusive seat
or place where he decided cases as a magistrate.   He
attained to excessive wealth, by his iniquities and sac-
rilege, and by those various means which he employed
to extort from the brethren, depressing the injured,
and promising to aid them for a reward.   Eusebius
relates many things concerning this man, which there
is not space here to bring out in detail, but surely he
began to fulfill the saying of Paul in 2 Thess. 2:4.
The Encyclopædia Britannica says that the council at
which this Paul of Samosata was excommunicated was
held probably in the year 268, and that he continued in
his office until the year 272, when the city was taken
by the Emperor Aurelian, making it necessary for Paul[1]
to withdraw, and in church history he is not heard of
afterwards.   Milner, also, shows that the great faith
and love of the gospel ceased about A. D. 270, and the
great Apostasy began.   From the foregoing facts and
citations from ecclesiastical history, it will be seen that
it is not presumption to locate the close of the first
great period of the church's history at A. D. 270.

Measuring from A. D. 270, the twelve hundred sixty

years ascribed in Daniel's vision to the reign of popery, reaches to A. D. 1530, the precise date of the first Protestant league, which marks the close of Period II. Tracing the church from this date for three hundred fifty years the end of the third period (A. D. 1880), is reached, which corresponds with the three and a half days, or centuries, of Rev 11:7-9, and reaches to the exact time when the children of God began to declare themseves free from sect denominations, and really to enjoy and possess salvation outside all Protestant and Roman denominations Further mention of this and the following period will be made in t^he proper places in the course of this history.

PERIOD II.

CHAPTER IX.

THE DECAY OF VITAL GODLINESS, AND THE DECLINE OF PAGANISM.

THE church has waded through several general persecutions, during which she never lost so much of her glory and spiritual power as in times of peace and prosperity.   Though she increased in numbers, wealth, and popularity, she decreased in piety, purity, meekness, and humility.   As external opposition ceased, internal disorders ensued.   During the past history of the church, she has been making her way through seas and fires, through clouds and storms.   And so long as a profession of religion was attended with danger, so long as the dungeon, the rack, or the faggot were in prospect to the disciples of Jesus, their lives and conversation were pure and heavenly.   The gospel was their only source of consolation, and they found it in every respect sufficient for all their wants.   From this time a spirit of pride, of avarice, of ostentation, and of domination will be seen invading both the ministry and the laity; and there will be schisms generated, heretical doctrines promulgated, and a foundation laid for an awful debasement and declension of true religion, and for the exercise of that monstrous power which was afterwards assumed by the popes of Rome.   Such was the spread and establishment of Christianity, that paganism saw its achievements with great jealousy and fear. The whole Roman empire was filled with professors of Christianity, and some of their ministers were men of family and renown. A great crisis seemed evidently to be at hand; Christianity or Paganism must triumph. It might be well here to define paganism.

Paganism, the religious worship and discipline of pagans, or the adoration of idols and false gods; that is, ascribing to things and persons, properties which are peculiar to God alone   The principal source of idolatry seemed to be the extravagant veneration for creatures and beings from which benefits accrue to men. Idolatry had four privileges to boast of. 1. It was a venerable antiquity, more ancient than the Jewish religion; and idolaters might have said to the Israelites, Where was your religion before Moses and Abraham? Go, and inquire in Chaldea, and there you will find that your fathers served other gods   2. It was wider spread than the Jewish religion. It was the religion of the greatest, the wisest, and the politest nations of the Chaldeans, Egyptians, and Phenicians — the parents of civil government, and of arts and sciences. 3. It was more adapted to the bent which men have towards visible and sensible objects. Men want gods who shall go before them, and be among them. God, who is everywhere in power and nowhere in appearance, is hard to be conceived. 4. It favored human passion; it required no morality; its religious ritual consisted of splendid ceremonies, reveling, dancing, nocturnal assemblies, impure and scandalous mysteries, debauched priests and gods who were both slaves and patrons to all sorts of vices. Pagans are

not acquainted with either the doctrines of the Old
Testament or of the Christian dispensation. For
many ages before Christ, the nations at large were destitute of the true religion, and gave themselves up to
the grossest ignorance, the most absurd idolatry, and
the greatest 'crimes. Even the most learned men
among the heathen were in general inconsistent, and
complied with or promoted the vain customs they
found among their countrymen.

During the time of Christ and the apostles and the
Morning Light Age of the church, the chief religion of
the Roman empire was pagan. Most of the emperors
until Constantine favored pagan worship. The death
of Licinius occurred in 323, at which time Constantine
succeeded to the whole Roman empire, which till now,
had not been in subjection to one individual for many
years. Constantine honored and helped to establish
the cause of Christianity. But his fury was turned
against paganism. By his order the pagan temples
were demolished, or converted into places for Christian
worship; the exercise of the old priesthood was forbidden, and the idols destroyed; large and costly structures for Christian worship were raised; and those
already erected were enlarged and beautified. The
episcopacy was increased, and honored with great
favors, and enriched with vast endowments. The
ritual received many additions; the habiliments of the
clergy were pompous; and the whole of the Christian
service at once exhibited a scene of worldly grandeur
and external parade.

The conduct of Constantine towards the pagans also
merits censure, notwithstanding that his power was

exercised in favor of Christianity. Instead of leaving
every one to obey the dictates of his conscience, he
prohibited by law the worship of idols throughout the
bounds of his empire.   In this he obviously trans-
cended the authority invested in him as a civil ruler—
for if a civil magistrate may prohibit religious opinions,
or punish the propagators of them, merely because in
his view they are unscriptural, he has the same right
to punish a professing Christian, whose sentiments, or
practices, differ from his own, as he would have to
punish a pagan, or a Mohammedan.   If the magistrate
may lawfully exercise a control over the human mind,
in one instance, may he not in any other; since, upon
the supposition, his own judgment is the authorized
standard of what is right and wrong, in matters of religion? The truth is, the magistrate derives no authority, either from reason or from the word of God, to
control the human mind in relation to its religious
faith. Upon this principle Constantine and his bishops
were no more justified in abolishing heathenism by the
force of civil power, than Diocletian or Galerius with
the priests were justified in their attempt to break
down and destroy Christianity.   Well has it been
observed: "Let the law of the land restrain vice and
injustice of every kind, as ruinous to the peace and
order of society; for this is its proper province. but
let it not tamper with religion by attempting to
enforce its exercise and duties."

CHAPTER X.

DIVISIONS AND CONTROVERSIES.

As it was stated regarding the commencement of the Period, that "from this time . . . there will be schisms gendered, heretical doctrines promulgated, and a foundation laid for an awful debasement and declension of true religion, and for the exercise of that monstrous power which was afterwards assumed by the popes of Rome," a few of the leading controversies will now be given in their order.

DONATISTS.

A schism denominated Donatists from the leader Donatus, had their origin in the year 311, when in the room of Mensurius, who died in that year on his return to Rome, Caecilian was elected bishop of Carthage, and consecrated, without the concurrence of the Numidian bishops, by those of Africa alone, whom the people refused to acknowledge, and to whom they opposed Majorinus, who accordingly was ordained by Donatus bishop of Casae Nigrae. The Donatists maintained that the sanctity of their bishops gave to their community alone a full right to be considered as the true church. Thus began a schism which continued three hundred years, and overspread the province of Africa. This controversy Constantine took fruitless pains to settle, both by councils and hearings; but finding the Donatists refractory, he was provoked to banish some, and to put others to death. The banished, however, were some time after recalled, and permitted to hold such opinions as they pleased. Under the successors of Constantine they experienced a verity of fortune for many years, until at length they dwindled away.

ARIANS.

Soon after the commencement of the Donatist controversy a controversy originated in the church at Alexandria, well known by the name of the "*Arian Controversy*," which was managed with so much violence, as to involve the whole Christian world. Arius was a presbyter of the church at Alexandria, about 315. He maintained that the Son of God was totally and essentially distinct from the Father; that he was the first and noblest of those beings whom God had created—the instrument by whose subordinate separation he formed the universe; and therefore, inferior to the Father both in nature and dignity; also that the Holy Ghost was not God, but created by the power of the Son. The Arians owned that the Son was the Word; but denied that Word to have been eternal. They held that Christ had nothing of man in him but flesh, to which the Word was joined, which was the same as the soul in us. These sentiments of Arius spreading abroad were adopted by not a few, among whom were some who were distinguished not only for their learning and genius, but for their rank and station.

Alexander, bishop at Alexandria in 320, being alarmed at the propagation of sentiments so unscriptural, remonstrated with Arius; and by conciliatory measures attempted to restore him to a more scriptural system. Finding his efforts vain, and that Arius was still spreading his doctrines abroad, he summoned a council consisting of near a hundred bishops, by which Arius and several of his partisans were deposed and

MARTYRS DEVOURED BY WILD BEASTS.

excommunicated These things threw the Christian
world into a state of great confusion Both parties
were by far too much influenced by the spirit of pride,
and many things, to the disgrace of both, were shamefully practiced.

These disputes awakened the most serious attention
of Constantine. He wrote conciliatory letters both to
Alexander and to Arius, in which he gave no opinion
on the subject of debate, but urged mutual forbear-
ance and forgiveness. In this interference he employed
Hosius, bishop of Cordova, a man renowned for his
faith and piety; but things were too obstinate to be
thus settled. He finding all efforts to reconcile Alexander and Arius fruitless, issued letters to the bishops
of the several provinces of the empire to assemble at
Nice, in Bithynia. This was in A. D. 325, and became
known in history as the

Council of Nice.

This council consisted of three hundred eighteen
bishops and a vast body of presbyters. It is supposed that the number of ecclesiastics present was not
less than six hundred. The council assembled in a
large room, and having taken their places, they continued standing until the emperor, who was clad in
an exceedingly splendid dress, made his appearance.
When at length all were seated, says Eusebius, the
patriarch of Antioch rose, and addressing the emperor,
gave thanks to God on his account—congratulated the
church on its prosperous condition, brought about by
his means, and particularly in the destruction of the
idolatrous worship of paganism. To these congratula-
tions of the patriarch, the emperor replied that he was

happy at seeing them assembled on an occasion so glorious as that of amicably settling their difficulties,
which, he said, had given him more concern than all
his wars. He concluded by expressing an earnest wish
that they would as soon as possible remove every cause
of dissension, and lay the foundation of a lasting
peace. On concluding his address, a scene occurred
which presented to the emperor a most unpromising
prospect. Instead of entering upon the discussion of
the business for which they had been convened, the
bishops began to complain to the emperor of each
other, and to vindicate themselves. Constantine listened to their mutual recriminations with great
patience; and when, at his instance, their respective
complaints were reduced to writing, he threw all the
billets unopened into the fire; saying, that it did not
belong to him to decide the differences of Christian
bishops, and that the hearing of them must be deferred
till the day of judgment. After this the council proceeded in earnest to the business of their meeting.
Their discussions lasted for several weeks, and finally
their decisions were published.

Before this council broke up, some few other matters
were determined; such as would deserve no place here,
were it not to show the sad defection of Christianity in
the increase of superstition and human tradition. It
was decreed that Easter should be kept at the same
season, through all the church; that celibacy was a
virtue; that new converts should not be introduced to
orders; that a certain course of penitence should be
enjoined on the lapsed; with other directions of a
similar nature.

The controversy was far from being settled by the decision of the Council of Nice. The doctrines of Arius had indeed been condemned, he himself banished to Illyricum, his followers compelled to assent to the Nicene creed, and his writings proscribed; yet his doctrines found adherents, and both he and his friends made vigorous efforts to regain their former rank and privileges. It seems proper to give an account of the creed alluded to above, as it is the first account of anything of the kind   Hosius of Cordova drew it up by order of the council.   The following is the creed:

"We believe in one God, the Father Almighty, maker of all things, visible and invisible, and the Lord, Jesus Christ, the Son of God, the only begotten, begotten of the Father, that is of the substance of the Father, God of God, Light of Light, true God of true God; begotton, not made, consubstantial with the Father, by whom all things were made, things in heaven, and things on earth, who for us men, and for our salvation, came down and was incarnate, and became man, suffered and rose again the third day, and ascended into the heavens, and comes to judge the quick and the dead, and in the Holy Ghost   And the catholic and apostolic church doth anathematize those persons who say that there was a time when the Son of God was not, that he was not before he was born; that he was made of nothing, or of another substance of being, or that he is created or changeable, or convertible "

Arius was recalled from banishment by Constantine in two or three years after the Council of Nice, and the laws that had been enacted against him were repealed. Notwithstanding this, Athanasius, then bishop of Alexandria, refused to admit him and his followers to communion.   This so enraged them, that, by their interest at court, they succeeded in having that prelate deposed and banished; but the church of Alexandria still refused to admit Arius into their communion. The emperor sent for him to Constantinople, where, upon a fresh confession of his faith in terms less offensive, the emperor commanded him to be received into their communion; but that very evening, it is said, Arius dropped dead as his friends were conducting him in triumph to the great church of Constantinople. The Arian party, however, found a protector in Constantius, who succeeded his father in the East. They underwent various revolutions and persecutions under succeeding emperors; till, at length, Theodosius the Great exerted every effort to suppress them. Their doctrine was carried in the fifth century into Africa under the Vandals; and into Asia under the Goths. Italy, Gaul, and Spain were also deeply infected with it; and towards the commencement of the sixth century it was triumphant in many parts of Asia, Africa, and Europe; but it sunk almost at once, when the Vandals were driven out of Africa, and the Goths out of Italy by the arms of Justinian. However, it revived again in Italy, under the protection of the Lombards, in the seventh century, and was not extinguished until about the end of the eighth. Arianism was again revived in the West by Servetus, in 1531, for which he suffered death. After this the doctrine got footing in Geneva, and in Poland; but at length degenerated in a great measure into Socinianism. Erasmus, it is thought, aimed at reviving it, in his commentaries on the New Testament; and the learned Grotius seems to lean that way. Mr. Whiston was one of the first divines who revived this controversy in the eighteenth century. Dr. Clarke also advocated it, while Dr. Waterland was one who strongly opposed Arianism.

Those who hold the doctrine usually called *Low Arianism*, say that Christ pre-existed; but not as the eternal Logos of the Father, or as the being by whom

he made the worlds, and had intercourse with the
patriarchs, or as having any certain rank or employment whatever in the divine dispensation. In modern
times the term *Arian* is indiscriminately applied to
those who consider Jesus simply subordinate to the
Father. Some of them believe Christ to have been the
creator of the world; but they all maintain that he
existed previously to his incarnation, though in his
pre-existent state they assign him different degrees of
dignity. Hence the terms *High* and *Low* Arian.

In the year 337 Constantine died, having received
baptism, during his sickness, at the hands of his favorite bishop, Eusebius of Nicomedia. The state of the
church at the death of Constantine was exceedingly
low. It was distracted with baneful divisions; and a
general struggle for power and wealth seemed to pre-
dominate. Constantine, though a much better man
than his predecessors, was yet but a man of the world;
and from all that we can gather, Eusebius did not
possess enough of the genuine spirit of Christianity to
correct him, and teach him the real meekness of Jesus.
Prelatical pride had been rising very high for a century
before this. The pastors had forgotten their Master's
instruction: "Be ye not called Rabbi; for . . . all ye
are brethren." Lord, Bishop, and *Archbishop*, and all
the spirit of such distinctions, had been long enough
upon the advance to congratulate such an emperor as
Constantine. The materials for an hierarchy having
been prepared, it was no difficult thing for a set of
worldly-minded bishops, countenanced by a prince, to
put them together. Under all these circumstances,
really true religion was not likely to be bettered by such

a reverse in external affairs, and so the event proved. The ancient contest which was for the faith once delivered to the saints, declined apace, and a strife for worldly honor, fleshly gratification, and spiritual dominion, was substituted in its stead.

Eusebius of Nicomedia, patriarch of Constantinople, was born toward the end of the third century. He was first tutor to the emperor Julian; then bishop of Berytus, in Syria; and afterwards of Nicomedia. He was at the head of the Arian party. Under the emperor Constantine, he became Patriarch of Constantinople. He died in the year 342, after having in the previous year held an assembly of the church for the establishment of Arianism at Antioch.

Eusebius of Cæsarea, the "Father of Ecclesiastical History," was born in Palestine about 264. He took the surname of Pamphili from his friend Pamphilus, Bishop of Caesarea. He went to Tyre, and afterwards to Egypt, where he himself was thrown into prison on account of his religion. In 315 he succeeded Agapius as Bishop of Cæsarea, took a prominent part at the Council of Nice, and died about 340. He was the head of the semi-Arian, or moderate, party in the Council of Nice. That party was averse to discussing the nature of the Trinity, and would have preferred the simplicity of scripture language in speaking about the Godhead to the metaphysical distinctions of either side.

Eusebius of Emisa was born at Edessa, studied at Alexandria, and was a pupil of Eusebius Pamphili, and the friend of Eusebius of Nicomedia. Averse to all theological controversies, he declined the bishopric of Alexandria. He was afterwards, however, appointed bishop of Emisa. He died at Antioch in 360.

CHAPTER XI.

HERMITISM THE ROOT OF MONKERY.

HERMIT, a person who retires into solitude for the purpose of devotion. Who were the first hermits can not easily be known. The origin of hermits seems to have been this. The persecutions that attended the first ages of the gospel forced some Christians to retire from the world, and live in deserts and places most private and unfrequented, in hopes of finding peace and comfort, which was denied them in public life; and this being the case of some very extraordinary persons, their example gave such reputation to retirement that the practice continued when the reason of its commencement ceased.

Antony, who died in the year 356, may be considered the father of monastic life. He was an illiterate youth of Alexandria. Happening one day to enter a meeting of the church, he heard the words of Jesus to the young ruler· "Sell all that thou hast and give to the poor." Considering this as a special call to him, he distributed his property, deserted his family and friends, and took up his residence among the tombs, and in a ruined tower. Here, having practiced self-denial for some time, he advanced three days' journey into the desert, eastward of the Nile, where, discovering a most lonely spot, he fixed his abode His example and his lessons infected others, whose curiosity pursued him to the desert, and before he closed his life, which was prolonged to the term of one hundred five years, he beheld vast numbers imitating the example which he had set them. Influenced by the example of Antony, a Syrian youth whose name was Hilarion, fixed his dreary abode on a sandy beach about seven miles from Gaza. The austere penance in which he persisted for forty-eight years diffused a similar enthusiasm; and innumerable monasteries were soon distributed over all Palestine. From this time monkery increased very rapidly, and was no less universal than Christianity. Nor was this kind of life confined to males. Females began about the same time to retire from the world, and to dedicate themselves to solitude and devotion. Nunneries were erected, and such as entered them were henceforth secluded from all worldly intercourse. They were neither allowed to go abroad, nor was any one permitted to see them. Here, they served themselves, and made their own clothes, which were white and plain woolen.

One of the most renowned examples of monkish penance upon record is that of St. Simeon, a Syrian monk, who lived about the middle of the fifth century, and who is thought to have outstripped all who preceded him. He is said to have lived thirty-six years on a pillar erected on the top of a mountain in Syria, whence he got the name of "Simeon the Stylite." From this pillar, it is said, he never descended, unless to take possession of another, which he did four times, having in all occupied five of them. He spent the day till three in the afternoon, in meditation and prayer; from that time till sunset he harangued the people, who flocked to him from all countries. Females were not permitted to approach him—not even his own mother, who is said, through grief and mortification in being refused admittance, to have died the third day after her arrival. Many other similar instances of extravagance and superstition in those times abounded.

It is a sad fact that eminent men in the church at that time, and on down for several hundred years extolled these superstitions. Even Athanasius encouraged the institution of monkery. Basil terms monkery "an angelical institution; a blessed and evangelical life, leading to the mansions of the Lord " Jerome declares "the societies of monks and nuns to be the very flower and most precious stone, among all the ornaments of the church." Others were equally eloquent in extolling the perfection of monkery, and commending the practice. The consequence of these praises on the part of men so prominent was, as might be expected, a most rapid increase of both monasteries and monks. Even nobles, and dukes, and princes not only devoted immense treasures in founding and increasing these establishments, but descended from their elevated stations and immured themselves in these convents for the purpose of communion with God. Thousands who still continued to live in the world, consecrated their wealth to purchase the prayers of these devoted saints; and even tyrants and worn-out debauchees considered themselves secure of eternal glory, by devoting their fortunes to some monastic institution. The real history of these establishments, however, would disclose little in favor of religion. There were doubtless many who ripened within their walls for heavenly glory; but there is reason to fear that the majority under the mask of superior piety led lives of luxury, licentiousness, and debauchery.

Almost from its origin monastic life has existed under different classes, or orders. It was first divided into two distinct orders, of which one received the name of Cenobites; the other, that of Eremites. The former lived together in a fixed habitation, and made up one large community under a chief, whom they called *father* or *abbot*, which signifies the same thing in the Egyptian language. The latter drew out a wretched life in perfect solitude, and were scattered here and there in caves, in deserts, in the cavities of rocks, sheltered from the wild beasts only by the cover of a miserable cottage, in which each lived separated from the rest of mankind. The Anchorites were yet more excessive in the austerity of their manner of living than the Eremites. They frequented the wildest deserts without either tents or cottages; nourished themselves with the roots and herbs which grew spontaneously out of the uncultivated ground; wandered about without having any fixed abode, reposing wherever the approach of night happened to find them; and all this that they might avoid the view and the society of mortals. Another order of monks were those wandering fanatics, or rather impostors, whom the Egyptians called Sarabaites, who instead of procuring a living by honest industry traveled through various cities and provinces and gained a maintenance by fictitious miracles, selling relics to the multitude, and other frauds of a like nature. Many of the Cenobites were chargeable with vicious and scandalous practices. This order was not, however, so generally corrupt as that of the Sarabaites, who were for the most part profligates of the most abandoned kind. As

to the Eremites, they seemed to have deserved no other
reproach than that of a delirious and extravagant
fanaticism.   All these different orders were at first
composed of the laity, and were subject to the jurisdiction and the inspection of the bishops   But in
course of time many of them were adopted among the
clergy, even by the command of the emperors; and
the fame of monastic piety and sanctity became so
general that bishops were frequently chosen out of
that fanatical order.

During this time two monstrous errors were almost
universally adopted, and became a source of innumerable calamities and mischiefs in the succeeding ages.
Of these maxims one was, That it was an act of virtue
to deceive and lie, when by such means the interests of
the church might be promoted; and the second,
equally horrible, though in another point of view, was,
That errors in religion, when maintained and adhered
to after proper admonition, were punishable with civil
penalties and corporal tortures.   Of these erroneous
maxims the former was now of a long standing; it had
been adopted for some ages past, and had produced an
incredible number of ridiculous fables, fictitious prodigies, and pious frauds, to the unspeakable detriment of
that glorious cause in which they were employed. And,
it must be frankly confessed that the greatest men, and
most eminent saints of that time were more or less
tainted with the infection of this corrupt principle, as
will appear evidently to such as look with an attentive
eye into their writings and their actions.   The other
maxim, relating to the justice and expediency of punishing error, was introduced in those serene and peace-

ful times which the accession of Constantine to the imperial throne procured to the church. It was from that period approved by many, enforced by several examples during the contests that arose with the Priscillianists and Donatists, confirmed and established by the authority of Augustine, and thus transmitted to the following ages, as will be seen further on in this history. Step by step things grew darker and darker, and religion in its established form was at this time but little removed from the superstitions and idolatry of the ancient heathen. There were indeed some good persons—some who maintained the true principles of faith—but the mass of professors, and even of the ministry, had shamefully drifted from the true spirit of the gospel.

FALL OF THE ROMAN EMPIRE.

About the year 395 important changes began to take place in the Roman Empire, which was one cause of the decline and change brought upon the church at that time. These changes were caused by numerous barbarous tribes inhabiting the north of Europe, who, attacking the Roman Empire, in a course of years reduced it to a state of complete subjection, and divided its various provinces into several distinct governments and kingdoms. These tribes consisted of the Goths, Huns, Franks, Alans, Suevi, Vandals, and various others. They were extremely barbarous and illiterate, at the same time powerful and warlike. The incursions of these tribes into the empire was at a time when it was least able to make effectual resistance. Both Honorius and Arcadius were weak princes. The Roman character was greatly sunk. Their lofty and daring spirit was gone. Their empire had for years groaned under its unwieldy bulk; and only by the most vigorous efforts had it been kept from crumbling to ruins. With Theodosius expired the last of the successors of Augustus and Constantine, who appeared in the field of battle at the head of their armies, and whose authority was acknowledged throughout the empire. Such being the case and state of things, it is not strange that the northern tribes should have seized the opportunity to invade the empire, nor that their efforts at subjugation should have been crowned with success. Still less singular is it that the church of God should have suffered in a corresponding degree.

In the year 410 the imperial city of Rome was besieged and taken by Alaric, king of the Goths, who delivered it over to the licentious fury of his army. A scene of horror ensued which is scarcely paralleled in the history of war. The plunder of the city was accomplished in six days; the streets were deluged with the blood of murdered citizens, and some of the noblest edifices were razed to their foundation. Thus this proud city, which had subdued a great part of the world—which, during a period of 619 years, had never been molested by the presence of a foreign enemy—was itself called to surrender to the arms of a rude and revengeful Goth; who was well entitled the *Destroyer of Nations*, and the *Scourge of God* From this period the barbarians continued their ravages until 476, which is commonly assigned as making the total extinction of the western part of the Roman empire. Of the tribes that had been accessory to this result, the Visigoths took possession of Spain; the Franks, of Gaul; the Saxons, of England; the Huns, of Pannonia; the Ostrogoths, of Italy and adjacent provinces. These conquests effected an almost entire change in the state of Europe. New governments, laws, and languages; new manners, customs, and dresses; new names and countries prevailed. Although the new conquerors were barbarous, they generally, though at different times, conformed themselves to the religious belief of the nations among whom they settled. Many of them were converted to Christianity. It is said of one Clovis, king of the Franks in Gaul, that he and three thousand of his soldiers were converted to Christianity, and were baptized at Rheims. He himself was no honor to the church, but there was something remarkable about his conversion which deserves note, and which no doubt resulted in much good. The Franks (afterwards French) were a German nation, who dwelt about the lower Rhine. Having passed this river, they entered into Gaul, under the conduct of Pharamond, their first king, about the year 420. Clodio, Merovæus, Childeric, and Clovis reigned in succession after him. Like the rest of the barbarous nations who desolated the lower empire, they still advanced slowly in conquest, and Clovis entirely ruined the Roman empire in Gaul. But he had to contend with other barbarous invaders, all of whom, however, he subdued at length, and by much carnage and violence he became the founder of the French monarchy. Wicked as he was, he became a useful instrument in the hand of God in causing many others to accept the gospel of Christ. He married a woman, a niece of Gondeband, king of the Burgundians; she was zealous for the doctrine of Christ. Could her private history be known, it would probably be instructive and edifying; for what but zeal for God could have induced a royal lady brought up among heretics, and given in marriage to a powerful pagan, to persevere alone so firmly in the apostolic faith. She faithfully exhorted and entreated her husband to embrace the doctrine of Christ. Clovis heard her with patience, but remained inflexible. It pleased God at length to give him a striking lesson from which he ought to have learned the true art of happiness. Fighting with the Alemanni he was upon the point of being defeated. While in this great time of need he lifted up his eyes to heaven with tears, and said, "O Jesus Christ, whom Clotilda [his wife] affirms to be the Son of the living God, I implore thy aid. If thou givest me victory, I will believe on thee; for I have called upon my own gods in vain." While he was yet praying his enemies turned their backs and submitted to him. He was as good as his word.

The year 432 was distinguished by the introduction of Christianity into Ireland by Patrick, who on account of his labors in that country has been deservedly entitled the apostle of the Irish.

Under the auspices of Gregory the Great, the Roman pontiff, Christianity was introduced into England, in the year 597, at which time Augustine, with forty monks was sent into that country and began the conversion of the people.

CHAPTER XII.

ESTABLISHMENT OF THE SUPREMACY OF THE ROMAN PONTIFF.

To trace the nominal church through the sixth century would be hard to do. But as some few monuments of the pure religion of Jesus are found even at this time, a brief outline of the corrupt system must for the sake of connection be continued. This work having been designed to be only an abridged history, only those persons and subjects of most importance will be discussed in detail.

Fulgentius adorned the beginning, and Gregory the close of this century, which produced no other authors of equal merit. It seems that the greatest work accomplished during this century was the establishment of the religion of Jesus in England, which was accomplished through the supervision of Gregory. This great prelate, worn out at length with labors and diseases, died in the year 604, after he had enjoyed, or rather endured, his bishopric thirteen years and six months. The labors of Columba, an Irish monk, were attended with success among the Picts and Scots, many of whom embraced the gospel. In Germany the Bohemians, Thuringians, and Boii are said to have abandoned in this century their ancient superstitions, and to have received the light of divine truth: but this assertion appears extremely doubtful to many; for when the accounts of their conversion, and their lives and writings are carefully examined, it is evident that in this and succeeding ages they retained a great part

9

of their former impiety, superstition, and licentiousness, and that they were attached to Christ only by a
mere outward and nominal profession. A vast multitude of Jews, converted to Christianity in several
places, were added to the church during the course of
this century. Many of that race, particularly the inhabitants of Borium in Libya, were brought over to
the truth by the persuasion and influence of the emperor Justinian. In the West the zeal and authority
of the Gallic and Spanish monarchs, the efforts of
Gregory the Great, and the labors of Avitus, bishop of
Vienne, engaged numbers to receive the gospel.

It must, however, be acknowledged that of these
conversions the greater part arose from the liberalities
of Christian princes, or the fear of punishment, rather
than from the force of argument or the love of the
truth. Compulsion seems to have been the method
mostly adopted to bring the people to Christ during
this century, which was only the ripening of the fruit
of the spirit of that man of sin that was to be more
fully manifested in the coming centuries. Tyranny
and superstition had grown gradually in this and the
former centuries. From the very beginning of the
Christian church, even in the days of Christ and his
apostles, the reader can not but have marked the
prevailing disposition of man to corrupt and carnalize
that which the Savior revealed pure and spiritual.
James and John were struggling for the right hand,
and for the left in their Master's kingdom. Paul
clearly points out the coming in of Antichrists, "with
all power, and signs, and lying wonders." He says the
"mystery of iniquity" was working in his day, but two

things then conspired to hinder its progress: *the apostolic power and inspiration within, and the Roman power without.* The first of these impediments doubtless expired about the middle of the third century, but the force of imperial pagan persecution continued to maintain a restraint till the reign of Constantine, upon the accession of whom the church was raised above her enemies, and encouraged to assume those marks of worldly pride and power hereafter denominated, and that justly, "the beast"—"that man of sin."

Constantine instituted the order of patriarchs, and set them up in the chief cities; but these had not long possessed this mark of distinction before they began to quarrel among themselves who should be the greatest, or universal and chief. A variety of circumstances had conspired to throw the weight of power into the scale of the Roman see. This was seen with jealousy by the bishop of Constantinople, who thought himself entitled to the same dignity, his city being the seat of imperial authority. As early as 588 John of Constantinople, called the Faster, assumed the title of Universal Bishop; and the title was confirmed by a council, at that time in session in that city. The successor of John assumed the same proud title. Gregory the Great, contemporaneous with the successor of John, took great umbrage at the boldness of the Bishop of Constantinople in assuming a title which, in point of precedence, belonged to the bishop of Rome, but which his conscience would not permit him to take. Gregory died in the year 604, as we have already stated, and was succeeded by Boniface III.

This latter prelate had no scruple in accepting the title. But he sought it of the emperor Phocas, with the privilege of transmitting it to his successors. The profligate emperor, to gratify the inordinate ambition of this court sycophant deprived the bishop of Constantinople of the title and conferred it upon Boniface; at the same time declaring *the church of Rome to be the head of all other churches.*

CHAPTER XIII.

UNIVERSAL SUPREMACY ACKNOWLEDGED.

THE supremacy of the Roman pontiff was acknowledged by Phocas, emperor of the East, in the year 602. From this time the papal power continued to acquire strength, and to extend its influence until as a sovereign pontiff, the pope of Rome held an enviable rank among the potentates of the earth; and as a spiritual leader received the homage of nearly the whole world. From this time the popes exerted their power to promote the idolatrous worship of images, saints' relics, and angels. In this barbarous age the religion of Christ lay expiring under a motley and enormous heap of superstitious inventions, and had neither the courage nor the force to raise her head or to display her primitive power and beauty. In the earlier periods of the church the Christian worship was confined to one Supreme God, and his Son Jesus Christ: but the professed Christians of this century multiplied the objects

of their devotion, and paid homage to the remains of
the true cross, to the images of the saints, and to
bones concerning whose real owners the information
was extremely dubious.   The primitive Christians in
order to bring people to Christ set before them the
Bible and its promises, Jesus and his love, heaven and
its beauties, God and his mercies; while the professors
of this century talked of nothing else than a certain
fire which effaced the stains of vice, and purified souls
from their corruption.   The former taught that Christ,
by his sufferings and death, had made atonement for
the sins of men; the latter seemed by their superstitious doctrine to exclude from the kingdom of heaven
such as had not contributed by their offerings to aug-
ment the riches of the clergy or the church.   The
former were only studious to attain a virtuous simplicity of life and manners, and employed their principal
zeal and diligence in the culture of true and genuine
piety, while the latter placed the whole of religion in
external rites and bodily exercises.   And in everything
there was a wide difference between the apostolic worship and the worship of this century.

For the purpose of bringing the real state of affairs
plainly before the reader, the author will here give in
full as stated by C A. Goodrich the circumstances and
means that were employed during the supremacy of
the Roman pontiff to advance and strengthen the papal
power.   Three circumstances existed at this time, and
continuing for several centuries contributed to the
increase and establishing of the papal power.   These
were the *ignorance*, the *superstition*, and the *corruption* of the world.

1. Ignorance. The incursion of the northern barbarians spread an intellectual famine throughout all
Europe. The only men of learning were the monks,
and they seldom left their cloisters; and the only
books were manuscripts. Not only were the common
people ignorant of the art of reading, but this ignorance pertained extensively to the clergy. Many of the
latter could scarcely spell out the Apostles' Creed;
and even some of the bishops were unable to produce
a sermon.

2. Superstition. The universal reign of superstition
contributed to the same results. The spiritual views
of religion of primitive times, and the simplicity which
had marked the order of ancient worship, were no
more In their room an unmeaning round of rites,
ceremonies, and festivals was introduced; and in the
observance of these the distinguishing doctrines of the
gospel and the true religion of the heart, were effectually lost sight of The common people were taught to
revere the clergy with idolatrous veneration. More
reverence was paid to the image of the Virgin Mary
than to the Son of God; and greater virtue was attributed to a finger or a bone of an apostle than to the
sincerest prayer of faith. Upon this superstition the
popes fastened; they increased it by every means in
their power, and made it instrumental in extending
their lordly power.

3. Corruption. The universal corruption of the
world accelerated the triumphs of the papal throne
more than all other means. If purity of heart existed,
it was confined to few, and in nations far from Rome.
The influence of the Spirit was unheard of. Even a

POPE ALEXANDER TREADING ON THE NECK OF
FREDERICK, EMPEROR OF GERMANY.

cold morality was scarcely inculcated. Holiness of heart, and the practice of the Christian virtues were seldom named. Vice and falsehood characterized the times. The worship of images, the possession of relics, the contribution of money to the treasuries of the Roman pontiff, were urged, as insuring a passport to heavenly felicity.

Next to the favorable circumstances just mentioned, the means employed by the papal power itself to extend its influence are worthy of note.

1. Preference given to human composition over the Bible. The art of printing was yet for a long time unknown. Copies of the scriptures were few, and so valuable that a single copy was worth the price of a house. The ignorance of the common people was, therefore, in a measure unavoidable. The popes and clergy were willing that it should be so. Taking advantage of this ignorance, they imposed upon the people such opinions of the Fathers, and such decrees of councils, as suited their purpose, and stamped them with the authority of God. In this way the Bible was neglected; its voice was unheard; and upon the strength of human opinions and human decrees the papal power extended its ghostly authority.

2. Efforts under the patronage of the Roman pontiff to convert the heathen. Aware of the importance of first raising the standard of the cross under the auspices of papal authority, the pope was ready to embrace every opportunity to send forth missionaries attached to their cause. Hence many heathen nations were visited, and efforts made to spread the knowledge of Christianity; at the same time care was taken to

send only such as were deeply imbued with the spirit
of the Roman hierarchy. Never were men more faithful in any cause. They taught the heathen to look
upon the Roman pontiff as their spiritual father, and
to bow to his authority as the vicegerent of God on
earth. Where reason failed to accomplish their purpose resort was had to force. Many were the instances,
—among which may be mentioned the Pomeranians,
the Slavonians, and the Finlanders—in which baptism
was administered at the point of the sword.

  3. Introduction of the worship of images. The introduction of images into places of Christian worship
dates its origin soon after the time of Constantine the
Great, but like many other superstitious practices, it
made its way by slow and imperceptible degrees.
There were those who strongly opposed its practice;
but their opposition was ineffectual. The passion
increased, and being fostered by the Roman pontiffs
and their servants it strongly tended to divert the
minds of the people from the great objects of faith
and worship presented in the scriptures, and gave to
the papal throne increasing power over the wandering
and darkened minds of the multitudes.

  NOTE.—Image, in a religious sense, is an artificial
representation of some person or thing used as an
object of adoration, in which sense it is used synony-
mously with idol. The popish divines maintain that
the use and worship of images are as ancient as the
Christian religion itself. To prove this, they allege a
decree, said to have been made in a council held by
the apostles at Antioch, commanding the faithful that
they may not err about the object of their worship, to

make images of Christ and to worship them. ·But no notice was taken of this decree till six or seven hundred years after the apostles.

4. Influence of monkery, which was enlisted in the cause. With scarcely an exception the institutions of monkery were on the side of the papal power, and with sedulous care did the Roman pontiffs foster these institutions, that they might further the object of their ambition. The monks were faithful to their master's cause. Every project started by the popes received their sanction; and the severest denunciations were poured forth from the convents against those who should call in question the wisdom of the papal throne.

5. Sanction given by the popes to the passion for the relics of saints, which about the ninth century reached an extraordinary height. Such was the crazed passion on this subject that many, even in eminent stations, made long pilgrimages to obtain some relic of the primitive saints. Judea was ransacked. The bodies of the apostles and martyrs are said to have been dug up, and great quantities of bones were brought into Italy, and sold at enormous prices. Even clothes were exhibited which were declared to be those in which Christ was wrapped in infancy; pieces of his manger were carried about; parts of his cross, the spear which pierced his side, the bread which he broke at the last supper; and to wind up the whole, vials were preserved which it was said contained the milk of the mother of Christ, and even the Savior's blood. From adoring the relic the senseless multitude passed to adore the spirits of the saints. Seizing upon this love of idolatry, the Roman pontiffs issued the command that no saint should be worshiped except such as had been canonized by them. This at once invested them with an enormous power. They made saints of whom they pleased, and the people were taught to regard these saints as their protectors—as having power to avert dangers, to heal maladies, to prepare the soul for heaven. By these means the Son of God was kept from view, and the deluded multitude made to feel that the power of health, of life, and of salvation emanated from Rome.

6. *The sale of absolution and indulgences.* The Roman pontiff, as the vicegerent of God on earth, claimed to have power not only to pardon sins, but also to grant permission to commit sin. A doctrine so accordant with the corrupt state of manners and morals, which for centuries prevailed, was received with implicit faith. The murderer, the assassin, the adulterer, needed now only to pay the prescribed fee, and his sins would be blotted out; those who wished to commit these crimes, in like manner, needed but to open their purses, to receive a plenary indulgence. The consequence of this sale of pardon was a vast increase of the revenue of the Roman pontiffs, and nearly an absolute control over the minds of the millions who adhered to the Roman faith. Indulgences in papacy signify a remission of the punishment due for sin, granted by the church, and are supposed to save the sinner from purgatory. The power of granting indulgences has been greatly abused. Pope Leo X., in order to carry on the magnificent structure of St. Peter's at Rome, published indulgences and a plenary

remission to all such as should contribute money
towards it.   The form of these indulgences read as
follows: "May our Lord Jesus Christ have mercy upon
thee, and absolve thee by the merits of his most holy
passion.   And I, by his authority, that of his blessed
apostles, Peter and Paul, and of the most holy pope,
granted and committed to me in these parts, do absolve
thee, first from all ecclesiastical censures, in whatever
manner they have been incurred; then from all thy sins,
transgressions, and excesses, how enormous soever they
may be· even from such as are reserved for the cogn-
izance of the holy see.   I remit to you all punishment
which you deserve in purgatory on their account;
and I restore you to the holy sacraments of the church,
to the unity of the faithful, and to that innocence and
purity which you possessed at baptism: so that when
you die the gates of punishment shall be shut, and the
gates of the paradise of delight shall be opened; and
if you shall not die at present, this grace shall remain
in full force when you are at the gate of death.   In the
name of the Father, and of the Son, and of the Holy
Ghost."

7. *The doctrine of purgatory, or a state of temporary
punishment after death*   "Purgatory is a place in
which the just who depart out of this life are supposed
to expiate certain offenses which do not deserve eternal
damnation."   This was a powerful engine, and most
effectually was it used for the purpose of enriching
and enlarging the Roman hierarchy.   From this purgatory and the miseries pertaining to it, the people
were taught that souls might be released if prayers
and masses in sufficient number, and from the proper

sources were offered up. Hence the richest gifts were
bestowed upon the church, by the surviving friends of
those for whom the benefit was sought; and the dying
transgressor readily parted with his possessions to
secure it.

The arguments advanced by the papists for purgatory are these. (1) "Every sin, how slight soever,
though no more than an idle word, as it is an offense
to God, deserves punishment from him hereafter, if
not canceled by repentance here. (2) Such small sins
do not deserve eternal punishment. (3) Few depart
this life so pure as to be exempt from spots of this
nature, and from every kind of debt due to God's
justice. (4) Therefore few will escape without suffering something from his justice for such debts as they
have carried with them out of this world, according to
that rule of divine justice by which he treats every
soul hereafter according to his works, and according to
the state in which he finds it in death." From these
propositions, which the papists consider as so many
self-evident truths, they infer that there must be some
third place of punishment; for since the infinite goodness of God can admit nothing into heaven that is not
clean and pure from all sin, both great and small, and
his infinite justice can permit none to receive the
reward of bliss who as yet are not out of debt, but
have something in justice to suffer, there must of necessity be some place or state where souls departing this
life, pardoned as to the external guilt or pain, yet
obnoxious to some temporal penalty, or with the guilt
of some venial faults, are purged and purified before
their admittance into heaven. And this is what they

teach concerning purgatory, which, though they know
not where it is, of what nature the pains are, or how
long each soul is detained there, yet they believe that
those who are in this place are relieved by the prayers
of their fellow members here on earth, as also by alms
and masses offered up to God for their souls. And as
for such as have no relations or friends to pray for
them, or give alms to procure masses for their relief,
they are not neglected by the church, which makes a
general commemoration of all the faithful departed in
every mass, and in every one of the canonical hours of
the divine office.

Besides the foregoing arguments, the following
passages are alleged as proofs: 2 Maccabees 12:43-45;
Matt. 12:31, 32; 1 Cor. 3:15; 1 Pet. 3:19. The text
cited from Maccabees seems to prove that there is no
such place as purgatory, since Judas did not expect the
souls departed to reap any benefit from his sin-offering
till the resurrection. The texts cited from the canonical books have no reference to this doctrine, as may
be seen by consulting the contexts, which give us no
idea of purgatory. It is contrary to the teachings of
the Bible. If Christ died for us, and redeemed us
from sin and hell, as the scriptures teach, then the
idea of further meritorious sufferings detracts from the
perfection of Christ's work, and places merit still in
the creature; a doctrine exactly opposite to the
scriptures.

Gibbons, Archbishop of Baltimore (of the nineteenth
century), still propagates this doctrine. In comment-
ing on 1 Cor. 3.13-15, he says, " 'The fire shall try
every man's work of what sort it is. If any man's

work abide'; that is, if his works are holy, he shall receive a reward. 'If any man's work shall be burned;' that is, if his works are faulty and imperfect, 'he shall suffer loss; but he himself shall be saved; yet so as by fire.' His soul will be ultimately saved, but he shall suffer for a temporary duration in the purifying flames of purgatory." He still further says, "This interpretation is not mine. It is the unanimous voice of the Fathers of Christendom " The foregoing interpretation and statement are utterly unfounded. All the Fathers that have written and propagated the doctrine of purgatory and hell redemption have been classed among the spurious; and are of that class that Peter speaks of, that are unlearned and unstable, who wrest the scriptures unto their own destruction. Here are a few examples, as recorded by Chiniquy of the nineteenth century, how the priests of Rome use the doctrine of purgatory to extort money from the poor and ignorant.

(The priest, Mr. Courtois, to Mr. Chiniquy's widowed mother.) "Madam, there is something due for the prayers which have been sung, and the services which you requested to be offered for the repose of your husband's soul. I will be very much obliged to you if you pay me that little debt."

"Mr. Courtois," answered my mother, "my husband left me nothing but debts. I have only the work of my own hands to procure a living for my three children, the eldest of whom is before you. For these little orphans' sake, if not for mine, do not take from us the little that is left."

"But, madam, you do not reflect. Your husband

died suddenly and without any preparation; he is therefore in the flames of purgatory. If you want him to be delivered, you must necessarily unite your personal sacrifices to the prayers of the church and the masses which we offer."

"As I said, my husband has left me absolutely without means, and it is impossible for me to give you any money," replied my mother.

"But, madam, your husband was for a long time the only notary of Mal Bay. He surely must have made much money. I can scarcely think that he has left you without any means to help him now that his desolation and sufferings are far greater than yours "

"My husband did, indeed, coin much money, but he spent still more. Thanks be to God, we have not been in want while he lived. But lately he got this house built, and what is still due on it makes me fear that I will lose it. He also bought a piece of land not long ago, only half of which is paid, and I will, therefore, probably not be able to keep it Hence I may soon, with my poor orphans, be deprived of everything that is left us. In the meantime I hope, sir, that you are not a man to take away from us our last piece of bread."

"But, Madam, the masses offered for the rest of your husband's soul must be paid," answered the priest.

"Sir, you see that cow in the meadow, not far from our house? Her milk and the butter made from it form the principal part of my children's food. I hope you will not take her away from us. If, however, such a sacrifice must be made to deliver my poor husband's soul from purgatory, take her as payment of the masses to be offered to extinguish those devouring flames.''

The priest instantly arose, saying, "Very well, Madam," and went out. . . . He directed his steps towards the meadow, and drove the cow before him in the direction of his house, regardless of the screams and cries of the family.

Chiniquy gives an account on another occasion, of a poor man, raising his voice in a most touching way, saying, "I can not leave my poor wife in the flames of purgatory; if you can not sing a high mass, will you please say five low masses to rescue her soul from those burning flames?"

The priest turned towards him and said: "Yes, I can say five masses to take the soul of your wife out of purgatory, but give me five shillings, for you know the price of a low mass is one shilling.''

The poor man answered: "I can no more give you one dollar than I can five. I have not a cent, and my three poor little children are as naked and starving as myself.''

"Well! well!'' answered the curate, "when I passed this morning before your house, I saw two beautiful sucking pigs. Give me one of them and I will say you five low masses.'' The poor man said: "The small pigs were given me by a charitable neighbor that I might raise them to feed my poor children next winter.   They will surely starve to death, if I give my pigs away.''

"But," says Chiniquy, "I could not listen any longer to that strange dialogue, every word of which fell upon my soul as a shower of burning coals. I was

beside myself with shame and disgust.   I abruptly left
the merchant of souls finishing his bargains, went to
my sleeping-room, locked the door, and fell upon my
knees to weep to my heart's content.   It would require
a more eloquent pen than mine to give the correct history of that sleepless night   The hours were dark and
long.''

Mr. Chiniquy was a priest in the Church of Rome at
that time, and as he spent this sleepless night in
prayer to God, he cried, "My God! My God! Is it
possible that, in my so dear Church of Rome, there
can be such abominations as I have seen and heard to-
day? . . . Is it possible that there is such a fiery
prison for the sinners after death, and that neither
thyself nor any of thy apostles has said a word
about it?''

Several of the Fathers consider purgatory as of
pagan origin   Tertullian spoke of it only after he had
joined the sect of the Montanists, and he confesses
that it is not through the Holy Scriptures, but through
the inspiration of the Paraclete of Montanus that he
knows anything about purgatory.   Augustine, the
most learned and pious of the Holy Fathers, does not
find purgatory in the Bible, and positively says that its
existence is dubious, that every one may believe what
he thinks proper about it.

8   The establishing of the Inquisition, which was by
far the most efficient means   The Inquisition dates
its origin in the thirteenth century.   It originated in
an attempt to crush some persons in Gaul (now
France), who had ventured to question the authority
of the Roman pontiffs   In the year 1204 Pope Inno-

CRUELTIES OF THE INQUISITION.

cent III. sent Inquisitors, as they were called, headed
by one Dominic, into Gaul, to execute his wrath upon
persons who had dared to speak in opposition to the
papal throne. These Inquisitors so effectually performed their embassy, that officers with similar power
were appointed in every city. Hence rose the Inquisition, which in time became a most horrible tribunal—
an engine of death; which kept nations in awe, and in
subjection to the papal dominion.

These courts had ordinarily three *Inquisitors*, or
lords of the Inquisition, who were absolute judges,
from whose sentence there was no appeal—no, not to
the pope: of these, two, and often all three, were
priests. The first was a divine, the second a casuist,
and the third a civil judge. They had under them a
great number of *qualifactors*, who, by order of the
lords, examined the crimes alleged against the prisoners, somewhat in the manner of our juries; and
familiars, who by inspecting books, mingling themselves into companies, and other similar methods,
procured information. Of these assistants, chiefly of
the familiars, several hundreds sometimes belonged to
one court. When any person was accused, the accusa-
tion was received in secret. The testimony of two or
sometimes of one was held sufficient for condemnation.
The accused was generally at midnight demanded by
the *coach of the Inquisition*; nor dared even a husband,
a wife, a parent, or a child, in the least retard the
delivery of their dearest relation, without exposing
themselves to Inquisitorial fury. No man was informed who was his accuser; and if he denied the
charge, he, especially if a wealthy layman, was tor-

tured, or at least had the engines of torture presented,
to oblige him to confess himself guilty, whether he was
or not. If nothing could be proved or extorted, and sev-
en persons of credit did upon oath attest his innocence,
he was perhaps released, but so dogged by spies that if
he dropped one word to the dishonor of the Inquisitors,
he was re-apprehended by their order, and might
expect to be ruined. If any one conceived an ill-will
to his neighbor, he had nothing more to do than to
accuse him to the Inquisitors. If the Inquisitors cov-
eted any man's wealth, they had only to demand him
as their prisoner. A young lady's beauty was as dangerous as either heresy or witchcraft; if the Inquisitorial
lord was charmed therewith, the sacred coach was sent
for her at midnight, and conveyed her to their prison,
where, by the terror or torture of their horrible engines of cruelty, the poor creature was forced to submit to the will of those base hypocrites.

CHAPTER XIV.

MOHAMMEDANISM.

BEFORE proceeding further with the subject of the
Roman supremacy, a view will be taken of the principal subject of the seventh century; viz., the *Rise of
the Mohammedan Imposture.* The author of this false
religion was Mohammed, who was born at Mecca, a
city of Arabia, about the year 570. About the year
609 he, having matured his system, began to announce

himself as a prophet of God, and to publish his religion abroad. He was endowed with every talent for lifting himself up in this world. He had followed the business of a merchant in Arabia, and by traveling had gained a thorough knowledge of the country and its inhabitants. Christianity in that country had been debased by superstition, and mixed with heathenism. He therefore conceived the idea of constructing a new religion, of which he himself was to be head and prophet. Adopting the leading feature of Christian and Jewish faith, the unity of the Godhead, and manifesting the highest reverence for the only Jehovah, he marked every species of idolatry with the deepest abhorrence. He pretended a divine commission for reforming the prevalent abuses among the Jews and Christians, and to bring them back to the primitive and pure religion. But knowing those with whom he had to do, and the general practice of polygamy in the East and among the Arabs, he ingrafted this custom into his religious system, and thus conducted the most plausible points of doctrine with the most seductive and indulgent practice. In maturing this plan Mohammed spared no time nor pains From the time of his first asserting his divine authority to the season of his grand experiment, about fourteen years elapsed; during this time he prepared the Koran, in the composition of which he was aided by a renegade Christian and a vagabond Jew, both of whom were fit instruments in the formation of such a confusedly mixed volume.

His preparatory attempts were among his friends and associates, whom he persuaded to renounce their

idolatry, and some of whom he enlisted as his coadju-
tors; these with himself were bound by the most
solemn oaths to abide by certain rules which he gave
them.   He saw the professed Christians divided, disputing, and one party harassing and persecuting the
other.   As Arabia was ignorant, and half pagan, ready
to turn with every wind of doctrine, the people around
him, naturally turbulent and warlike, if united under
one head, were sure to form a tremendous military
force.   His friends and connections were considerable,
but the consciousness of his own native powers afforded
him sure resources.   He began covertly and with
small essays.   Success beyond his most sanguine expec-
tations emboldened his confidence, and he burst forth
as a torrent on every side.   The love of war, and the
love of women, brought thousands to his standard,
and presently we find all Arabia at the feet of this
prophetical sacerdotal prince.   In this exalted character he lived about ten years.   At his death (A. D.632),
as might naturally be expected, a dispute arose about
succession.   Abu-Bekr, father-in-law to the prophet,
and Ali, his son-in-law, were the competitors   A
division in the new empire, a schism in the hierarchy,
was the result.   Had not Divine Providence thrown
the affairs of this vast establishment into confusion,
and turned the swords of the rival caliphs against each
other, it is hard to conjecture where this mighty
usurpation would have stopped   The check this system received at the death of its founder, though great,
did not altogether prevent his successors carrying on
his wonderful plan.   Egypt, Syria, Palestine, and
Persia fell into the hands of these conquerors, and the

whole empire would most probably have fallen a prey but for the circumstance above noticed This great power of darkness in no small degree helped to prevent the spread of Christianity, and added to the awful darkness that was then prevailing in the world.

CHAPTER XV.

THE GREEK CHURCH.

THE Greek church may be considered in regard to its antiquity, as coeval with the Roman, or Latin, church; and for the first eight centuries, the two churches were assimilated, not only in regard to the peculiar doctrines of their faith, but also to their acknowledgment of the supremacy of the Roman pontiff. The schism of these two churches is a most memorable epoch in ecclesiastical history, as it forms the most distinguishing picture of the two religions of the present day. The Greek church is considered as a separation from the Latin. In the middle of the ninth century, the controversy relating to the procession of the Holy Ghost (which had been started in the sixth century) became a point of great importance on account of the jealousy and ambition which at that time were blended with it.

Photius, the patriarch of Constantinople, having been advanced to that see in the room of Ignatius, whom he procured to be deposed, was solemnly excommunicated by Pope Nicholas in a council held at

Rome, and his ordination declared null and void. The Greek emperor resented this conduct of the pope, who defended himself with great spirit and resolution Photius, in his turn, convened a council, in which he pronounced sentence of excommunication and deposition against the pope, and got it subscribed by twenty-one bishops and others, amounting in number to a thousand. This occasioned a wide breach between the sees of Rome and Constantinople. However, the death of the emperor Michael, and the deposition of Photius subsequent thereupon seem to have restored peace; for the emperor Basil held a council at Constantinople in the year 869, in which entire satisfaction was given to Pope Adrian; but the schism was only smothered and suppressed for a while. The Greek church had several complaints against the Latin; particularly it was thought a great hardship for the Greeks to subscribe to the definition of a council according to the Roman form, prescribed by the pope, since it made the church of Constantinople dependent on that of Rome, but, above all, the pride and haughtiness of the Roman court gave the Greeks a great distance, and as their deportment seemed to insult his imperial majesty, it entirely alienated the affections of the emperor Basil.

Towards the middle of the eleventh century Michael Cerularius, patriarch of Constantinople, opposed the Latins with respect to their making use of unleavened bread in the eucharist, their observation of the sabbath, and fasting on Saturdays, charging them with living in communion with the Jews. To this Pope Leo IX. replied; and in his apology for the Latins de claimed very warmly against the false doctrine of the Greeks, and interposed at the same time, the authority of his see. He likewise by his legates excommunicated the patriarch in the church of Santa Sophia, which gave the last shock to the reconciliation attempted a long time after, but to no purpose; for from that time the hatred of the Greeks to the Latins, and of the Latins to the Greeks, became insuperable, insomuch that they have continued ever since separated from each other's communion.

The Greek church, which is now dependent on the patriarch of Constantinople, was not formerly so extensive as it has been since the emperors of the East thought proper to lessen or reduce the other patriarchates, in order to aggrandize that of Constantinople; a task which they accomplished with the greater ease, as they were much more powerful than the emperors of the West, and had little or no regard to the consent of the patriarchs, in order to create new bishoprics or to confer new titles and privileges Whereas in the western church the popes, by slow degrees, made themselves the sole arbiters in all ecclesiastical concerns; insomuch that princes themselves at length became obliged to have recourse to them, and were subservient to their directions on every momentous occasion. There are several catalogues or lists now extant of the different divisions of the Greek church which are dependent on that of Constantinople; but as most of them are very ancient, and do not sufficiently illustrate the vast extent of which that church at present boasts, they are not quoted in this place, it being enough to state that the number of metropolitans amounts to upwards of one hundred bishoprics.

The Greek church at present deserves not even the name of the shadow of what it was in its former flourishing state, when it was so remarkably distinguished for the learned and worthy pastors who presided over it; but now nothing but wretchedness, ignorance, and poverty are visible in it. It is indeed very surprising that in the abject state to which the Greeks at present are reduced, the Christian religion should maintain the least footing among them. Their notions of Christianity are principally confined to the traditions of their forefathers, and their own received customs; and among other things, they are much addicted to external acts of piety and devotion, such as the observance of fasts, festivals, and penances; they revere and dread the censures of their clergy, and are bigoted slaves to their religious customs, which have been irrefutably proved to be abused and ridiculous; and yet it must be acknowledged that, although these errors reflect a considerable degree of scandal and reproach upon the holy religion they profess, they nevertheless prevent it from being entirely lost and abolished among them.

The patriarch of Constantinople assumes the honorable title of *Universal Patriarch.* As he purchases his commission of the Grand Seignior, it may be easily supposed that he makes a tyrannical and simoniacal use of a privilege which he holds himself by simony. The patriarch and bishops are always single men; but the priests are indulged in marriage before ordination; and this custom, which is generally practiced all over the Levant, is very ancient. Should a priest happen to

marry after ordination, he can officiate no longer as
priest; the marriage, however, is not looked upon as
invalid; whereas, in the Latin church, such marriages
are pronounced void and of no effect, because the
priesthood is looked upon as a lawful bar or impedi-
ment.

CHAPTER XVI.

THE MIDDLE OF THE DARK AGES; OR, ROMAN SUPREMACY CONTINUED.

In this chapter the account of the church in Catholicism will be continued It would seem, judging from
the great darkness existing at that time, that there
were no true Bible Christians. But amid all the scandalous contentions that made the men of that day distinguished, piety, purity, and salvation were not
utterly lost in the world: some real Christians were
found in the retirement of private life, or inferior
stations of life; nor shall the solitary ones here and
there be excluded, even those in monastic seclusion,
who loved and served a pardoning God, perhaps with
much darkness of view or conformity to established
superstitions, but yet with sincerity and truth, maintaining the truth as it is in Jesus; and possessing the
life of God in their souls. One character of distinguished eminence, bishop of Turin, made a resolute
stand against many of the abominations of the Roman
pontiffs. His writings contain more evangelical truth

than perhaps any other of that day; and the vilest abuse and opposition which he received from Rome and her partisans, speak the fidelity with which he supported the doctrines which he believed.

The churches in Bohemia and Moravia by Cyril, renounced the jurisdiction of Rome, and worshiped God; if not without superstitious rites, yet more in spirit and in truth than others. Indeed, those most remote from the scenes of pride, contention, wealth, and ambition would probably be most preserved from evil, by their poverty and seclusion from the world. In Britain and the Cambrian mountains a trace of the true primitive religion could be found. Thither many Christians had resorted from the ravages of the Danes. One would suppose that when the great Alfred recovered the kingdom, restored order, and erected the University of Oxford, to revive religious knowledge and literature, fallen into the deepest decay, some sparks of truth still survived amidst the reign of ignorance and superstition The famous Ausgar manifested in his missionary zeal the flame that burned in his own bosom and those of his Anglo-Saxon associates; and there is every reason to conclude that among his numerous converts some real Christians would be found. Nor also could we doubt but among the persecuted Paulicians and their pastors men of real Christian simplicity would be found. The persecuted and the suffering professors of Christianity, to every man who knows its real nature, have many presumptive evidences in their favor.

Notwithstanding these sparks of primitive light, the professed church was descending deeper and deeper into the regions of darkness and primeval night; pursuing the history of a church without salvation; and receiving from the toil of investigation little else but disgust and disappointment.   Scarcely a feature remains of primitive simplicity and purity; but the advancing depravity of manners, according to the universal testimony, was great, as all the doctrines of truth were distorted by the superstitions, frauds, idolatry, and ignorance of the teachers.   During this century (the ninth) there was seemingly quite an outward growth produced by the labors of the monks   But it is really a sorrowful case that so much labor in these days went to so little purpose; the far greater part of these operations only contributed to the establishment of superstition and priestcraft, monkery and fraud.   A striking proof of this we have in the bitter contests between the bishops of Rome and Constantinople on the subject of dividing the fruits of these missionary labors.

The arms of Mohammed were still triumphant; they kept possession of all those countries they had gained on the Mediterranean, and threatened even the reduction of Rome itself.   The few Christians suffered considerably from a host of new adversaries—Normans, including Danes, Norwegians, and Swedes; who proved a great scourge to the maritime inhabitants of Germany, Gaul, Spain, and Britain.   They even penetrated the heart of Italy, carrying everything before them with fire and sword.   These pirates and plunderers miserably harassed the poor Christians, by pillaging their church buildings and laying waste their countries.

The internal state of the professed church exhibited a scene of every abomination; the Roman pontiff, at the head of all authority and rule, dealing out life and death, blessing and cursing. Next in order, bishops, who by their intrigue and love of the world had inveigled the great and the noble out of their estate to save their souls, assumed the title of dukes, counts, marquises; and uniting the regalia of their several domains with the priestly habiliment, they glittered in courts, vaunted in camps, and wallowed in luxury. Nor were the inferior orders of the clergy, in the spirit of their minds, a whit behind them—the religious houses shared in the plunder. While priests and monks could hold men's souls in bondage, they failed not to lavish the ill-gotten gain upon their depraved lusts.

As to the heresies and schisms of this age, one can hardly tell what to say of such things, as they have heretofore been understood in the church. A heretic in former centuries, was one that denied the faith, or brought in an erroneous doctrine; a schismatic was one that made a rent in the church, a division in the body of the faithful. It hardly appears possible to be guilty of either, as the church now stands; there are scarcely any good principles to deny, or any possibility of adding to the enormous mass of error and fraud, with which it is already overborne. The system is so far separated from anything like Christianity, that to break from it, and to teach others so to do, is rather a virtue than a crime. The course of historical events, however, furnishes us with a proof that the monstrous pile of error is capable yet of receiving addition. In this century was brought forth that absurd and gross doctrine, *Transubstantiation.* A monk named Paschasius Radbert was the profound originator of this mystery. It afforded in that day a matter for dispute, which controversy lasted till the thirteenth century, when it was dropped, and the doctrine incorporated with that august symbol, *the sacrament of the altar.* This doctrine asserts that the elements of bread and wine, after consecration by the priest, become the *real* body and blood of Christ, the *appearance* and *form* only of bread and wine being left.

The moral effect of all these superstitions upon the lives and common transactions of men was truly deplorable. The principles of right and wrong became equivocal, everything depended upon the sanction of the priesthood; hence cases between man and man, which ought to have been tried and determined in a court of justice, were brought to the trials of ordeal, both by fire and water, and also to the cruel and uncertain decision of single combat. That the clergy should preside at such barbarous practices, and even on such occasions celebrate the Lord's Supper, is really horrible, but not more horrible than true.

Before leaving this century some things about the lives of Frederic, bishop of Utrecht, and Claudius, bishop of Turin, should be noticed. Here is an incident in the life of Frederic which shows something of the character and life of the man. As he was dining one day with the emperor Lewis the Meek, he was exhorted by that prince to discharge the duties of the episcopal office with faithfulness and impartiality. The bishop, pointing to a fish on the table, asked whether it were better to take hold of it by the head or by the tail? "By the head, to be sure," replied the emperor. "Then I must begin my career of faithfulness," returned Frederic, "with your majesty." The emperor was at this time living in adultery and incest with the princess Judith. Frederic, like another John, said, "It is not lawful for thee to have her"; according to the teachings of Jesus Christ. Lewis little expected such a salutation, and was little inclined to part with his Herodias. This no sooner reached the ear of Judith than, she proceeded to act out the character of an adulteress, by plotting the death of the holy man; which purpose she found assassins ready enough to effect. Thus died Frederic, bishop of Utrecht.

The spirit of a reformer appears in the history of Claudius. He was by birth a Spaniard. In early life he was introduced to Lewis the Meek, and became his chaplain. About the year 817 he was appointed to the see of Turin. Here he exercised himself faithfully in destroying the worship of images. From his writings he appears to have embraced the grand truths of Christianity and to have been influenced with no small hatred to the reigning abominations of the times He asserts the equality of all the apostles with St. Peter, always owning Jesus Christ the only proper head of the church; he is severe against the doctrines of human merit, and human tradition; exposes the absurd practice of praying for and seeking the prayers of the dead. His reasoning against image worship is both ingenuous and just; and in his own department he was doubtless attended with success. Such a bishop, in the province of Piedmont, must have proved a great source of encouragement to those refugees in the valleys; indeed the Romish writers deplore this, and ascribe a great deal of the spirit of reformation which afterward appeared in the Waldenses to the heresy of Claudius. He lived to the year 839, and then through the good hand of God upon him, was suffered to die a natural death.

In the history of true religion the memorial of the Waldenses must be preserved, whose retreat furnishes a race of people with whom remain the scriptures, and who appear to make a good use of them. They hold the headship of Jesus, and his atonement; him they worship and him they serve. The beginnings of the Moravian denomination are to be traced to this century.

CHAPTER XVII.

THE CRUSADES.

CRUSADE may be applied to any war undertaken on pretense of defending the cause of religion, but has been chiefly used for the expeditions of the Christians against the infidels for the conquest of Palestine. These expeditions commenced A. D. 1096. The foundation of them was superstitious veneration for those places where our Savior performed his miracles and accomplished the work of man's redemption. Jerusalem had been taken, and Palestine conquered by Omar. This proved a considerable interruption to the pilgrims who flocked from all quarters to perform their devotions at the holy sepulcher. They had, however, still been allowed this liberty on paying a small tribute to the Saracen caliphs, who were not much inclined to molest them.   But in 1064 this city changed masters. The Turks took it from the Saracens, and, being much more fierce and barbarous, the pilgrims now found they could no longer perform their devotions with the same safety.   An opinion was about this time also prevalent in Europe which made these pilgrimages much more frequent than formerly: it was imagined that Christ was soon to make his appearance in Palestine to judge the world, and that consequently journeys to that country were in the highest degree meritorious, and even absolutely necessary.   The multitudes of pilgrims who now flocked to Palestine, meeting with a very rough reception from the Turks, filled all Europe with complaints against those infidels, who profaned the holy city, and derided the sacred mysteries of Christianity, even in the place where they were fulfilled.   As soon as the feelings of Europe had been sufficiently heated Urban openly took up the question. Two councils were held in 1095.   At the second, held at Clermont, in France, a crusade was definitely determined.   The pope himself delivered an address to a vast number of clergy and laymen, and as he proceeded, the suppressed emotions of the crowd burst forth, and cries of "God wills it" rose simultaneously from the whole audience.   The words "*God wills it,*" by the injunction of Urban, were made the war-cry of the enterprise, and every one that embarked in it wore, as a badge, the sign of the cross; hence the name Crusade (Fr. *Croisade,* from Lat. *Crux,* a cross).

First Crusade.   From all parts of Europe, thousands upon thousands hurried at the summons of the pope to engage in the holy war. "The most distant islands and savage countries," says William of Malmesbury, "were inspired with this ardent passion. The Welshman left his hunting, the Scotchman his fellowship with vermin, the Dane his drinking party, the Norwegian his raw fish." In the spring of 1096 thousands, and some say millions, were in motion toward Palestine. Previous to the setting out of the great host of European chivalry, four armies, amounting in all to 275,000 persons, had departed for Palestine. The first consisted of 20,000 foot, and was commanded by a Burgundian gentleman, Walter the Penniless. It marched through Hungary, but was cut to pieces by the natives of Bulgaria, only a few, among whom was Walter himself, escaping to Constantinople. The second, consisting of 40,000 men, women, and children, was led by Peter the Hermit. It followed the same route as its predecessor, and reached Constantinople greatly reduced. Here the two united, crossed the Bosporus, and were utterly defeated by the Turks at Nice, the capital of Bithynia. A third expedition of a similar kind, composed of 15,000 Germans, led by a priest named Gottschalk, was slaughtered or dispersed in Hungary; which also proved the grave of the fourth, a terrible horde, consisting of about 200,000 wretches from France, England, Flanders, and Lorraine, who had swept along through Germany, committing horrible ravages, especially against the Jews, whom they murdered without mercy.

Now, however, the real crusaders made their appearance: the gentry, the yeomanry, and the serfs of

feudal Europe, under chiefs of the first rank and
renown. Six armies appeared in the field, marching
separately, and at considerable intervals of time. The
respective leaders were Godfrey of Bouillon, Duke of
Lorraine; Hugh the Great, Count of Vermandois, and
brother of Philippe, king of France; Robert Curthose,
Duke of Normandy, son of William the Conqueror;
Count Robert of Flanders; Bohemond, Prince of
Tarentum, son of the famous Guiscard, under whom
was Tancred, the favorite hero of all the historians of
the crusade; and lastly, Count Raymond of Toulouse.
The place of rendezvous was. Constantinople   The
Greek emperor, Alexius, afraid that so magnificent a
host—there were in all not less than 600,000 men exclusive of women and priests—might be induced to
conquer lands for themselves, cajoled all the leaders,
excepting Tancred and Count Raymond, into solemnly
acknowledging themselves his liegemen. After some
time spent in feasting, the crusades crossed into Asia
Minor (accompanied by the unfortunate Peter the
Hermit). Here their first step was the siege and capture of Nice, the capital of Sultan Soliman, the 24th
of June, 1097. This monarch was also defeated by
Bohemond, Tancred, and Godfrey at Dorylæum.
Boldwin, brother of Godfrey, now crossed into Mesopotamia, where he obtained the principality of Edessa.
After some time, the crusaders reached Syria, and laid
siege to Antioch. For several months the city held
out, and the ranks of the besiegers, were fearfully
thinned by famine and disease. Many even brave
warriors lost heart, and began to desert Melancholy
to relate, among the list of cowards was the poor

enthusiast who had planned the enterprise. Peter was actually several miles on his way home when he was overtaken by the soldiers of Tancred and brought back to undergo a public reprimand. At length on the 3d of June, 1098, Antioch was taken, and the inhabitants were massacred by the infuriated crusaders, who were in turn besieged by an army of 200,000 Mohammedans sent by the Persian sultan. Once more famine and pestilence did their deadly work. Multitudes also deserted, and escaping over the walls carried the news of the sad condition of the Christians (so-called in that dark age) back to Europe.

But again victory crowned the efforts of the besieged. On the 28th of June, 1098, the Mohammedans were utterly routed, and the way to Jerusalem opened. It was on a bright summer morning (1099) that 40,000 crusaders, the miserable remnant of that vast array which two years before had laid siege to Nice, obtained their first glimpse of Jerusalem. The emotion was intense, the scene sublime. On the fifteenth of July, after a siege of rather more than five weeks, the grand object of the expedition was realized. Jerusalem was delivered from the hands of the infidel. Eight days after the capture of the city, Godfrey of Bouillon was unanimously elected king of Jerusalem. His kingdom at first comprising little more than the mere city of Jerusalem, was gradually extended by conquest until it included the whole of Palestine. A language resembling Norman French was established, a code of feudal laws drawn up—Jerusalem was erected into a patriarchate, and Bethlehem into a bishopric. The best part of Asia Minor was restored to the Greek empire,

while Bohemond became prince of Antioch.   For
nearly fifty years, the three Latin principalities or
kingdoms of the East—Edessa, Antioch, and Jerusalem
—not only maintained themselves against the attacks of
the Mohammedans of Egypt and Syria, but greatly
increased in size, power, and wealth.

Second Crusade.   In 1144 the principality of Edessa
was conquered by the Emir of Mosul, and the Christians slaughtered.   His son, Noureddin, advanced to
destroy the Latin kingdoms of Syria and Palestine.
Europe once more trembled with excitement.   A
second crusade was preached by the famous St. Bernard, abbot of Clairvaux, in Champagne; and early in
1147 two enormous armies, under the command of
Louis VII , king of France, and Conrad III , emperor
of Germany, marched for the Holy Land.   Their
united numbers were estimated at 1,200,000 fighting
men.   The expedition nevertheless proved a total
failure   The Greek emperor, Manuel Comnenus, was
hostile; and through the treachery of his emissaries,
the army of Conrad was all but destroyed by the Turks
near Iconium, while that of Louis was wrecked in the
defiles of the Pisidian mountains   After a vain
attempt to reduce Damascus, the relics of this mighty
host returned to Europe.

Third Crusade.   The death-blow, however, to the
kingdom of Jerusalem, and the power of the crusaders,
was given, not by Noureddin, but by Salah-Eddin,
commonly called Saladin, a young Kurdish chief, who
had made himself sultan of Egypt, and who aspired to
the presidency of the Mohammedan world.   He invaded Palestine, took town after town, and finally, in

October, 1187, compelled Jerusalem itself to capitulate, after a siege of fourteen days. The news of this led to a third crusade, the chiefs of which were Frederick I. (Barbarossa), emperor of Germany, Philippe Auguste, king of France, and Richard *Cœur-de-Lion*, king of England. Barbarossa took the field first in the spring of 1189, but accidentally lost his life by fever caught from bathing in the Orontes. His army, much reduced, joined the forces of the other two monarchs before Acre, which important city was immediately besieged. In vain did Saladin attempt to relieve the defenders; and after a beleaguerment of twenty-three months, the place surrendered. But the crusaders were not united among themselves Philippe soon after returned to France; and Richard, after accomplishing prodigies that excited the admiration of the Saracens, concluded a treaty with Saladin, by which the people of the West were to be at liberty to make pilgrimages to Jerusalem, exempt from the taxes which the Saracen princes had in former times imposed. This, as has been previously noticed, was all that had been claimed by the first crusaders. On the 25th of October, 1192, Richard set sail for Europe.

Fourth Crusade Crusading unfortunately now became a constituent of the papal policy; and in 1203 a fourth expedition was determined upon by Pope Innocent III., although the condition of the Christians was by no means such as to call for it. It assembled at Venice; but how entirely secular crusading had become will be seen from the fact that the army never went to Palestine at all, but preferred to take possession of the Byzantine empire. The leader of this host of *pseudo-*

crusaders, Baldwin, Count of Flanders, was seated on the throne of the East in 1204, where he and his successors maintained themselves for fifty-six years.

Fifth Crusade. This was commanded by Frederick II., emperor of Germany. It began in 1228, and terminated in a treaty between that monarch and the sultan of Egypt, by which Palestine was ceded to Frederick, who after being crowned king of Jerusalem returned to Europe, leaving his new possessions in a state of tranquillity.

Sixth Crusade. In 1244 a new race of Turks burst into Syria, and once more the Holy Land fell into the hands of these ferocious barbarians. Jerusalem was burned and pillaged. In 1249 Louis IX. of France (St. Louis) headed a crusade against them, but was utterly defeated, and taken prisoner by the sultan of Egypt. By the payment of a large ransom he obtained his liberty and that of the other prisoners. On his return to Europe he was regarded as a sort of martyr in the cause of Christ.

Seventh Crusade. This also was primarily undertaken by St. Louis, but he having died at Tunis in 1207, on his way to Palestine, Prince Edward of England, afterwards Edward I., who had originally intended to place himself under the command of St. Louis, marched direct for Palestine, where his rank and reputation in arms gathered round him all who were willing to fight for the cross. Nothing of consequence, however, was accomplished; and Edward soon returned to England, the last of the crusaders. Acre, Antioch, and Tripoli still continued in the possession of the Christians, and were defended for some time by the Templars and

other military knights; but in 1291 Acre capitulated,
the other towns soon followed its example, and the
knights were glad to quit the country, and disperse
themselves over Europe in quest of new employment,
leaving Palestine in the undisturbed possession of the
Saracens

Effects of the Crusades. Though these crusades were
effects of the most absurd superstition, they tended
greatly to promote the good of Europe. Great social
changes were brought about. A commerce between
the East and West sprang up, and towns—the early
homes of liberty in Europe—began to grow great and
powerful. The crusades indeed gave maritime commerce the strongest impulse it had ever received. The
united effects of these things, again, in predisposing
the minds of men for a reformation in religion have
often been noticed. Other causes undoubtedly co-
operated, and in a more direct and decisive manner,
but the influence of the crusades in procuring an audience for Luther, can not be overlooked.

Multitudes, indeed, were destroyed in the different
crusades. M. Voltaire estimates the number who
perished in the different expeditions at upwards of two
millions Many there were, however, who returned;
and these having conversed so long with the people who
lived in a much more magnificent way than themselves, began to entertain some taste for a refined and
polished way of life Thus the barbarism in which
Europe had been so long immersed began to wear off
soon after. The princes also who remained at home,
found means to avail themselves of the frenzy of the
people. By the absence of such numbers of restless

and martial adventurers, peace was established in their dominions. They also took the opportunity of annexing to their crowns many considerable fiefs, either by purchase, or the extinction of the heirs; and thus the mischiefs which must always attend feudal governments were considerably lessened. With regard to the bad success of the crusaders, it was scarcely possible that any other thing could happen to them. The emperors of Constantinople, instead of assisting, did all in their power to disconcert their schemes: they were jealous, and not without reason, of such an inundation of barbarism. Yet had they considered their true interests, they would rather have assisted them, or at least stood neutral, than enter into alliance with the Turks. They followed the latter method, however, and were often of very great disservice to the western adventurers, which at last occasioned the loss of their city. But the worst enemies the crusaders had were their own internal feuds and dissensions. They neither could agree while marching together in armies with a view to conquest, nor could they unite their conquests under one government after they had made them. They set up three small states; one at Jerusalem, another at Antioch, and another at Edessa. The states, instead of assisting, made war upon each other and on the Greek emperors; and thus became an easy prey to the common enemy. The horrid cruelties they committed, too, must have inspired the Turks with the most invincible hatred against them, and made them resist with the greatest obstinacy. They were such as could have been committed only by barbarians inflamed with the most bigoted enthusiasm. When

Jerusalem was taken, not only the numerous garrison were put to death by the sword, but the inhabitants were massacred without mercy and without distinction. No age or sex was spared, not even sucking children. According to Voltaire, some Christians (so-called) who had been suffered by the Turks to live in that city led the conquerors into the most private caves, where women had concealed themselves with their children, and not one of them was suffered to escape. What eminently shows the enthusiasm by which these conquerors were animated, is their behavior after this terrible slaughter. They marched over heaps of dead bodies toward the holy sepulcher, and while their hands were polluted with the blood of so many innocent persons, sung anthems to the common Savior of mankind. Nay, so far did their religious enthusiasm overcome their fury, that these ferocious conquerors now burst into tears. If the absurdity and wickedness of their conduct can be exceeded by anything, it must be what follows. In 1204, the frenzy of crusading seized the children, who are ever ready to imitate what they see their parents engaged in. Their childish folly was encouraged by the monks and schoolmasters; and thousands of those innocents were conducted from the houses of their parents on the superstitious interpretation of these words: "Out of the mouths of babes and sucklings hast thou perfect praise." Their base conductors sold a part of them to the Turks, and the rest perished miserably.

In the foregoing history of the crusades it is easy to see the mature fruit of superstition and ignorance, enthused by a religious fallacy. The atmosphere of

light, truth, and holiness in which we live, makes it
almost impossible for us to realize the dark mysteries
of idolatry, immorality, degrading slavery, barbarisms,
and awful sins that were practiced during the dark
ages. The superstitions and ridiculous things of the
middle ages were bred in the hot-beds of ignorance.
As soon as men got the word of God and let the light
shine into their hearts and minds, superstition and the
horrid wickedness of the dark ages began to disappear.
The account given of the unhappy issues of the crusades will be sufficient to suggest a lively idea of the
melancholy condition to which the professed Christians
were reduced in Asia, which is a good sample of the
condition of the church in all parts of the world at
that time.

CHAPTER XVIII.

CONNECTING LINK BETWEEN THE PAPACY AND THE REFORMATION.

THE year 1300, during the pontificate of Boniface
VIII., may be regarded as marking the highest eminence to which the papal power ever attained. From
this period, firm and lasting as the dominion of the
Roman pontiffs seemed to be, it appears to have been
gradually undermined and weakened, partly by the pride
and rashness of the popes themselves, and partly by several unexpected events. A circumstance here falls under
notice, which in its relation and tendency contributed

in no small degree to weaken the power of the papal supremacy. And this is said to have been the first to weaken this power and to aid in the establishing of the Reformation principles. Philip of France, surnamed the Fair, was a man of a bold and enterprising spirit— a man worthy to wear a crown. To check such a spirit in every popish monarch was the true interests of St. Peter. Boniface VIII. therefore thought it advisable to let Philip understand that the tiara was superior to the diadem, and that France as well as all other kingdoms was subject to the pope, both in spiritual and temporal matters. Such arrogance was despised by Philip, who replied to the holy father, "We give you to understand that in temporal affairs we are subject to no'one." The great prelate being insulted at such insolence, took greater measures to check the blasphemous monarch, declaring him a heretic, and as such given over to perdition. Philip treated all this pontifical fury with the contempt it deserved, and remained safely enthroned in the hearts of the people. Philip in the meantime took measures to depose the pontiff, by a general council, and in anticipation of the meeting of such a council, caused Boniface to be seized. The person intrusted with this business treated the pope most rudely, inflicting a severe wound upon his head. His friends, however, secured his rescue; but the mortification occasioned by his insults soon after caused his death. The successor of this unfortunate pontiff, Benedict XI., had learned by these things to behave with moderation toward such a man as Philip.

Benedict soon died, and Philip succeeded in getting

a French pope to succeed him, and also the removal of
St. Peter's chair from Rome to Avignon, in France,
where it continued seventy years. This contributed
greatly to the weakening of the authority and influence
of the papal dominion, while it added new vigor to the
measures of the aspiring French monarch Terrible
were the effects of the change of the papal residence,
especially as the pontiff was now generally a French-
man. Some attempts were made to restore the holy
chair to its former and original standing, but the issue
produced a complete schism in papacy, in the year
1378, which lasted forty years Rome was the seat
of Urban VI., and Avignon that of Clement VII. The
rival pontiffs forgot not to hurl thunder at each other's
head. nor were the people less confused, they knew
not which to obey—both could not be legitimate—and
therefore, while they were thus undermined, and the
popes mutually resolved to hold their respective posts,
the French entered into a determination to acknowledge
neither; and the Avignon father was, by order of the
king, thrown into prison Thus the papal authority,
which had been long viewed with enthusiasm and
devotion, began to sink into contempt; at least it was
most fully proved that the papal throne was not like
mount Sinai at the giving of the law, which even a
beast might not touch with impunity. Philip and his
successors gave such a grievous stab to the papal
power, that it never afterwards reached that height
which had distinguished it for ages before.

While the Roman see was roaring and tossing and
lashing its furious waves against the rocks and threatening death on every hand, there were a few gleams of

light springing up here and there, indicating the approaching dawn of the Reformation The proper place has now been reached to give a short sketch of some of these lights, or forerunners of reform..

CHAPTER XIX.

FORERUNNERS OF THE REFORMATION.

THE WALDENSES.

THE Waldenses, a community of Christians who inhabit a mountain tract on the Italian side of the Cottian Alps, southwest from Turin, were among the first to protest against papal authority, and to attempt to lift up a higher standard than the doctrines of the church of Rome. The religious doctrines of the Waldenses are now similar to those of the Reformed churches. There is a minister in each parish, called a *barba*, and the synod is presided over by an elected moderator. The Waldenses had at one time bishops, but that was when the sect was more widely spread than it now is The history of this people from the days of Claudius to the time of Peter Waldo (1160) is involved in much obscurity. They seem to have had no writers among them capable of recording their proceedings, during this period; but it is well known that they existed as a class of Christians, separate from the erroneous faith and practice of the Catholic church; and at length became quite numerous. From the time of Peter Waldo the Waldenses, or Vaudois church, as it is called, was much increased by his labors.

The attempts of Peter Waldo and his followers were neither employed nor designed to introduce new doctrines, nor to propose new articles of faith to Christians. All they aimed at was to reduce the form of ecclesiastical government, and the manners both of the clergy and people, to that amiable simplicity and primitive sanctity that characterized the apostolic ages, and which appear so strongly recommended in the precepts and injunctions of the Divine Author of our holy religion. In consequence of this design, they complained that the Roman church had degenerated, under Constantine the Great, from its primitive purity and sanctity. They denied the supremacy of the Roman pontiff, and maintained that the rulers and ministers of the church were obliged, by their vocation, to imitate the poverty of the apostles, and to procure for themselves a subsistence by the work of their hands They considered every Christian as, in a certain measure, qualified and authorized to instruct, exhort, and confirm the brethren in their Christian course; and demanded the restoration of the ancient penitential discipline of the church; that is, the expiation of transgressions by prayer, fasting, and alms, which the newly-invented doctrine of indulgences had almost totally abolished They at the same time affirmed that every true Christian was qualified and entitled to prescribe to the penitent the kind or degree of satisfaction or expiation that their transgressions required; that confession made to priests was by no means necessary, since the humble offender might

12

acknowledge his sins and testify his repentance to any true believer, and might expect from such the counsel and admonition which his case demanded. They maintained that the power of delivering sinners from the guilt and punishment of their offenses belonged to God alone; and that indulgences, of consequence, were the criminal inventions of sordid avarice. They looked upon the prayers and other ceremonies that were instituted in behalf of the dead, as vain, useless, and absurd, and denied the existence of departed souls in a purgatorial state of purification; affirming that they were immediately, upon their separation from the body, received into heaven, or thrust down to hell. These and other tenets of a like nature, composed the system of doctrine propagated by the Waldenses. Their rules of practice were extremely austere; for they adopted as the model of their moral discipline the sermon of Christ on the mount, which they interpreted and explained in the most rigorous and literal manner; and consequently prohibited and condemned in their society all wars, and suits of law, and all attempts towards the acquisition of wealth, the inflicting of capital punishment, self-defense against unjust violence, and oaths of all kinds.

During the greater part of the seventeenth century, those of the Waldenses who lived in the valleys of Piedmont, and who had embraced the doctrine, discipline, and worship of the church at Geneva, were oppressed and persecuted in the most barbarous and inhuman manner by the ministers of Rome. The persecution was carried on with peculiar marks of rage and enormity in the years 1655, 1656, and 1696, and

seemed to portend nothing less than the total extinction of that unhappy people.   The most horrid scenes
of violence and bloodshed were exhibited in this theater
of papal tyranny; and the few Waldenses that survived
were indebted for their existence and support to the
intercession made for them by the English and Dutch
governments, and also by the Swiss cantons, who solic-
ited the clemency of the duke of Savoy on their behalf.

JOHN WYCLIFFE.

John Wycliffe, the greatest of the reformers before
the Reformation, was born in 1324, and is supposed to
have been a native of the parish of the same name,
near the town of Richmond in Yorkshire.   He studied
at Oxford; but of his early university career nothing
is known.   He is deservedly called the Father of the
Reformation, not only because by his numerous writings he fearlessly and successfully exposed the wicked
and unchristian pretensions of the popes and prelates,
and the extreme corruption of the Romish church;
but especially as he first rendered the scriptures into
the English tongue.   Wycliffe was a prodigy of learning in that dark age.   He was professor of divinity at
Oxford, which university he defended against the
insolent pretensions of the mendicant friars.   He
boldly remonstrated with the pope, on account of his
exorbitant exactions, which upon various pretenses, it
is said, amounted to a great deal more than was paid
by the nation in taxes to the king.   Wycliffe rendered
to the church the greatest service which was possible
in the order of instrumentality.   Besides restoring the
true doctrine of a sinner's justification by faith in the
atonement and righteousness of Christ, he translated

the whole Bible into English; by the circulation of which, especially the New Testament, the word of God was spread open to the people, and a permanent foundation was laid for the future destruction of the Romish idolatry, superstition, and tyranny, by the diffusion of the pure doctrine of the gospel of Christ. Every possible effort was made, both by the popes and the prelates, not only to silence Wycliffe, but to destroy him; but he was protected by the powerful Duke of Lancaster, son of the aged king. He spent the latter years of his life in the discharge of his pastoral duties, as rector of Lutterworth, in Leicestershire, where he died in peace in A. D. 1384.

The principles of this reformer were too sacred to perish at the death of their advocate; though, by his zealous opposition to popery and prelacy, he created many enemies, who labored to extirpate his doctrine and blast his memory. His doctrines were condemned in a popish council at Constance; and, by order of Pope Martin V., his books were burned; his bones were also dug up and burned to ashes by the same order, under the direction of Fleming, bishop of Lincoln, in A. D. 1428 These proceedings were insufficient to extinguish the divine light which his ministry had kindled. His numerous writings rendered him famous; and they were sought, copied, and circulated all over Europe—recommended not a little by a public testimony borne by the doctors of the University of Oxford, to the character of that great man.

The followers of Wycliffe, during his lifetime, were considerably numerous; but after his death, they greatly increased, both in England and other countries.

They were called Wycliffites, and, by a vulgar term of reproach brought from Belgium into England, Lollards. The increase of the Wycliffites filled the clergy, and the other friends of popery, with alarm; and a most spirited persecution of them was commenced. Many were imprisoned, and others were suspended by chains from a gallows, and burned alive. Among the sufferers who perished in this manner, was Lord Cobham, a man who by his valor and loyalty had raised himself high in the favor of both the king and the people.

JOHN HUSS.

From England the writings of Wycliffe were carried by an officer of Oxford into Bohemia, where they were read by John Huss, rector of the University of Prague. These writings opened the mind of Huss, who, having great boldness and decision of character, began vehemently to declaim against the vices and errors of the monks and clergy, and was successful in bringing Bohemia, and especially the university, to the adoption of the sentiments of Wycliffe. The introduction of Wycliffe's writings into the university gave great offense to the archbishop of Prague. Between him and Huss a controversy arose, which was at length carried to the pope, who ordered Huss to appear before him at Rome. This Huss declined to do, and was excommunicated. He continued, however, boldly to propagate his sentiments, both from the pulpit and by means of his pen.

In the year 1414 was convened the Council of Constance, the object of which was to put an end to the papal schism, which was accordingly effected, after it

had continued nearly forty years. Before this council
Huss was cited to appear, and at the same time,
Jerome of Prague, the intimate friend and companion
of Huss. By the council both these eminent men were
condemned, the former of whom was accordingly
burned in 1415, and the latter in the following year.
Here it was also that the writings and bones of
Wycliffe were ordered to be burned.

John Huss raised his voice in Bohemia a hundred
years before Luther offered to speak in Saxony. He
appeared to have dipped deeper than his predecessors
into the real essence of Christian truth. He begged of
Christ to grant him the grace whereby he might be
enabled to glory in nothing save in his cross and in the
inappreciable shame of his sufferings. The flames
which rose from his funeral pile kindled a fire that
through dense darkness spread a distinct light, the in-
fluences of which were not readily extinguished. John
Huss from the bottom of his dungeon, sent forth to
the world words of prophetic import   He foresaw the
need of an absolute reformation. When driven from
Prague, he wandered an outcast among the fields of
Bohemia, where many crowded anxiously to listen to
his words.   He began to declare: "The wicked have
commenced by preparing for the goose perfidious nets;
but if even the goose, which is no more than a domestic
bird, a peaceable creature, and whose flight carries it
but a short way into the air, has nevertheless broken
through their meshes, other birds, whose flight will
bear them boldly towards the heavens, will yet break
through them with much more force   Instead of a
silly goose, the truth will hereafter send forth eagles

JOHN HUSS.

and falcons with piercing looks." This was fulfilled
in the reformers a hundred years later. When Huss
was brought to the stake and the fagots were piled up
around him he said to those doing it, "You are
now going to burn a goose [Huss signifying goose in
the Bohemian language]: but in a century you will
have a swan, whom you can neither roast nor boil."
This surely was fulfilled in Martin Luther. Scarcely
had the councils of Constance and Basel, in which
Huss and his pupils had been condemned, terminated
their meetings, when the witnesses against Rome again
commenced with yet greater vigor, a few of whom will
be mentioned.

OTHER TESTIMONIES AGAINST POPERY PRIOR TO THE REFORMATION.

Thomas Conecte, Carmelite, made his appearance in
Flanders. He declared the practice of abominations
in Rome, that the church stood in need of reformation, and that, in observing the worship of God, it
was not necessary to fear excommunication by the
pope.

Andreas, the archbishop of Crayn, and a cardinal,
finding himself at Rome as ambassador from the emperor, was horror-stricken upon discovering that the
papal sanctity in which he had so devoutly believed
was no more than a fable; and in his simplicity, he addressed to Sixtus IV. certain evangelical representa-
tions. These were answered in terms of derision and
with acts of persecution. He declared the whole church
to be shaken with divisions, heresies, crimes, vices, injustice, and errors, and evils innumerable, so that it
was ready to be swallowed up in the ravenous abyss of

condemnation." For these sayings he was cast into prison, and died in a dungeon.

Jerome Savonarola also suffered death at the stake in 1497 because he believed God forgives men their sins, and justifies them in mercy.

John Vitrarius of Tournay, the gray friar, whose monastic spirit did not appear to be of a very high order, spoke in very strong terms against the corruptions of the church. "It would be better," said he, "to cut the throat of a child than to rear him in a religion not reformed."

John Lallier, teacher of Sorbonne, rose up in 1484 against the tyrannical domination of the hierarchy.

John de Vesalia, a teacher of theology in Erfurt, a man of strong mind and quick perceptions, attacked the errors upon which the hierarchy rested, and declared the holy scriptures to be the only ground of faith. This good old man was left by the Inquisition to die in one of the dungeons of that institution in the year 1482.

John Wessel, undoubtedly the most remarkable of these forerunners of the Reformation, was a man full of courage and love of the truth, who was a teacher of theology, successively at Cologne, Louvain, Paris, Heidelberg, and Groningen, and of whom Luther decared, "If I had sooner read his writings, my enemies might have been able to think that Luther had drawn all his ideas out of Wessel, so much is his mind and mine in complete accord." "St. Paul and St. James," said Wessel, "relate different, but not contrary things. Both believe that the just live by faith, but by a faith which acts through charity. He who, listening to the gospel, believes, desires, hopes, trusts in the good news, and loves him who justifies and blesses him, giving himself afterwards entirely over to him who loves him, attributes nothing to himself, since he knows that out of his own funds he has nothing to give. The sheep must distinguish the things given him to eat, and avoid poisonous food, even though offered by the shepherd himself. The people ought to follow the pastors in the pastureground, but when it is no longer in the pastureground they lead them, they are no more pastors; and then since they are beyond their province, the people are no longer bound to obey their call. Nothing works more surely for the destruction of the church than a corrupt body of clergy. It is not necessary to fulfill the precepts of the prelates or teachers beyond the limits prescribed by St. Paul. We are the servants of God and not of the pope, as it is said, 'Thou shalt worship the Lord thy God, and him only shalt thou serve.' The Holy Spirit has promised to strengthen, to vivify, to preserve, and to increase the unity of the church, and he will not leave the church to the care of the pontiff of Rome, who often takes no care of it. Nor does the mere sex prevent a woman even, if she be faithful and prudent and have the spirit and charity spread abroad in her heart, from feeling, judging, approving, and resolving, by a judgment which God ratifies.''

Thus as the Reformation draws near, the testimonies against popery increase. The Reformation had an existence within the hearts of the people before the appearance of Luther. The doctrines of Wycliffe, issuing from the colleges of Oxford, had spread rapidly over the whole extent of Chistendom, and had secured adherents in Bavaria, Swabia, Franconia, Prussia, and Bohemia.

MARTIN LUTHER AND HIS WIFE.

PERIOD III.

CHAPTER XX.

LUTHER AND THE REFORMATION.

This third period of history embraces (1) the Reformation by Martin Luther in the sixteenth century, and the decline of the Roman supremacy, and (2) other reformers and sect-making in the sixteenth, seventeenth, eighteenth, and nineteenth centuries.

Martin Luther was born at Eisleben on Nov. 10, 1483. His father was a miner in humble circumstances; his mother, as Melanchthon records, was a woman of exemplary virtue, and peculiarly esteemed in her walk of life. Shortly after Martin's birth, his parents removed to Mansfield, where their circumstances ere long improved by industry and perseverance. Their son was sent to school; and both at home and in school his training was of a severe and hardening character. His father sometimes whipped him, he says, "for a mere trifle, till the blood came," and he was subject to the scholastic rod fifteen times in one day. Scholastic and parental severity was the rule in those days; but whatever may have been the character of Luther's schoolmaster at Mansfield, there is no reason to believe that his father was a man of exceptionally stern character. While he whipped his son soundly, he also tenderly cared for him, and was in the habit of carrying him to and from school in his arms with gentle solicitude. Luther's schooling was

completed at Magdeburg and Eisenach, and at the
latter place he attracted the notice of a good lady of
the name of Cotta, who provided him with a comfortable home during his stay there.

When he had reached his eighteenth ʾyear, he entered the University of Erfurt, with the view of qual-
ifying himself for the legal profession.   He went
through the usual studies in the classics and the school-
men, and took his degree of doctor of philosophy, or
master of arts, in 1505, when he was twenty-one years
of age.   Previous to this, however, a profound change
of feeling had begun in him.   Chancing one day to
examine the Vulgate in the university library, he saw
with astonishment that 'there were more gospels and
epistles than in the lectionaries.   He was arrested by
the contents of his newly found treasure.   His heart
was deeply touched, and he resolved to devote himself
to a ʾspiritual life.   He separated himself from his
friends and fellow students, and withdrew into the
Augustine convent at Erfurt.   Here he spent the
next three years of his life—years of peculiar interest
and significance; for it was during this time that he
laid, in the study of the Bible and of Augustine, the
foundation of those doctrinal convictions which were
afterwards to rouse and strengthen him in his struggle
against the papacy. ·He describes very vividly the
spiritual crisis through which he passed, the burden
of sin which so long lay upon him, "too heavy to be
borne"; and the relief that he at length found in the
clear apprehension of the doctrine of forgiveness of
sins through the grace of Christ

In the year 1507 Luther was ordained a priest, and

in the following year he removed to Wittenberg, destined to derive its chief celebrity from his name. He became a teacher in the new university, founded there by the elector Frederick of Saxony. In 1509 he became a bachelor of theology, and commenced lecturing on the holy scriptures. His lectures made a great impression, and the novelty of his views already began to excite attention. "This monk," said the rector of the university, "will puzzle our doctors, and bring in a new doctrine." Besides lecturing he began to preach, and his sermons reached a wider audience, and produced a still more powerful influence.

In 1510 or 1511, he was sent on a mission to Rome, and he has described very vividly what he saw and heard there. His devout and unquestioning reverence, for he was yet in his own subsequent view "a most insane papist," appears in strange conflict with his awakened thoughtfulness and the moral indignation beginning to stir in him at the abuses of the papacy. On Luther's return from Rome, he was made a Doctor of the Holy Scripture, and his career as a reformer may be said to have commenced. He became indignant against the different sins and abominations that were practiced and urged upon the people, and his bold steps against these things were all that was necessary, to awaken a wide-spread excitement. Many were the combats and narrow escapes of Luther during his life.

In the year 1525 he was married to Catharine von Bora, one of nine nuns, who, under the influence of his teaching, had emancipated themselves from their religious vows. His marriage rejoiced his enemies, and

even alarmed some of his friends.   But it greatly contributed to his happiness, while it served to enrich and
strengthen his character.   All the most interesting
events of his life were in connection with his wife
and children.   He died in the end of February, 1546.

Luther's works are very voluminous, partly in Latin,
and partly in German.   Among those of more general
interest are his "Table-talk," his "Letters," and his
"Sermons."   De Wette has given to the public a copi-
ous and valuable edition of his "Letters," which, along
with his "Table-talk" are the chief authority for his
life.   Many special lives of him, however, have been
written, by Melanchthon, Audin, and others.   The
reader will see the growing fruits of Luther's labor
as he proceeds with the following short history of the
Reformation.

CHAPTER XXI.

THE REFORMATION OF THE SIXTEENTH CENTURY.

SINCE the introduction of the gospel to mankind,
sixteen hundred years have elapsed, a small portion
of which exhibits Chistianity in its native simplicity
and glory.   But the mystery of iniquity, which had
been working from the apostle Paul's time, slowly
gathering strength, soon matured under the smiles of
a civil establishment.   From the time of the papal
usurpation to the Reformation, was a long and gloomy

period—a dark day of twelve hundred sixty years—
from which we have emerged during the century now
under consideration. The evils arising from papal
domination were, in their moral and political character, of the worst kind that could possibly befall the
human race: all civil government was prostrate before
the chair of St. Peter. Before the period of the Reformation, the pope had in the most audacious manner
declared himself the sovereign of the whole world.
The wealth of nations could not be legally possessed
by its right owners, but a large proportion was thrown
into the coffers of the pope and priests. A vast part
of the population in every Christian country, instead
of being employed in useful avocations, were leading
an idle and disorderly life in caves and convents or
wandering all the world over, circulating the most
abominable falsehoods, and committing the worst
crimes. Nonsense and superstition were the summit
of learning; and the glory of man consisted in his
living and dying in the faith and favor of the Catholic
church. This vast fabric, with all its appendage of
strength and of splendor, was set on fire and consumed
by the truth. "And then shall that Wicked be revealed, whom the Lord shall consume with the spirit
of his mouth, and shall destroy with the brightness of
his coming."—2 Thess. 2:8.

The Reformation began by Luther in the city of
Wittenberg, in Saxony, but was not long confined
either to that city or that province. In 1520 the Fran-
ciscan friars, who had the charge of promulgating the
indulgences in Switzerland, were opposed by Zwingli,
a man not inferior in understanding and knowledge to

Luther himself.   He proceeded with the greatest
vigor, even at the very beginning, to overthrow the
whole fabric of popery; but his opinions were declared
erroneous by the universities of Cologne and Louvain.
Notwithstanding this, the magistrates of Zurich approved of his proceedings; and that whole canton,
together with those of Bern, Basel, and Schaffhausen
embraced his opinions.

In Germany, Luther continued to make great ad-
vances, without being in the least intimidated by the
ecclesiastical censures which were thundered against
him from all quarters, he being continually protected
by the German princes, either from religious or political motives, so that his adversaries could not accomplish his destruction, as they had done that of others.
Melanchthon, Carlstadt and other men of eminence
also greatly forwarded the work of Luther; and in all
probability the popish hierarchy would have soon come
to an end, in the northern parts of Europe at least, had
not the emperor Charles V given a severe check to the
progress of the Reformation in Germany.

During the confinement of Luther in a castle near
Wartburg, the Reformation advanced rapidly, almost
every city in Saxony embracing the Lutheran opinions.
At this time an alteration in the established forms of
worship was first ventured upon at Wittenberg, by
abolishing the celebration of private masses, and by
giving the cup, as well as the bread, to the laity in the
Lord's Supper.   In a short time, however, the new
opinions were condemned by the University of Paris, and
a refutation of them was attempted by Henry VIII of
England.   But Luther was not to be thus intimidated,

He published his reproofs with as much determination as if he had been refuting the meanest adversary. And while the efforts of Luther were thus everywhere crowned with success, the divisions began to prevail which have since so much agitated the reformed body. The first dispute was between Luther and Zwingli concerning the manner in which the body and blood of Christ were present in the eucharist. Both parties maintained their tenets with the utmost obstinacy, and, by their divisions, first gave the adversaries an argument against them, which to this day the Catholics urge with great force; namely, that the Protestants are so divided that it is impossible to know who are right or wrong, and that there can not be a stronger proof than these divisions that the whole doctrine is false. To these intestine divisions were added the horrors of civil war, occasioned by oppression on the one hand, and enthusiasm on the other. These proceedings, however, were checked.

Luther and Melanchthon were ordered by the elector of Saxony to draw up a body of laws relating to the form of ecclesiastical government, and the method of public worship, which was to be proclaimed by heralds throughout his dominions. This was *the first Protestant discipline.* While confined by his friend Frederick of Saxony in the old castle of Wartburg, to protect him from seizure by order of the pope or the emperor Charles V., Luther completed his translation of the New Testament into German. This was published in September, 1522. When it was read the people were greatly astonished to find how different the laws of Christ were from those which had been imposed by the

pope, and to which they had been subject. The
princes and people saw that Luther's opinions were
founded on truth   They openly renounced the papal
supremacy, and the happy morn of the Reformation
was welcomed by those who had long sat in superstitious darkness.

In the year 1530 Charles V. assembled the famous
diet of Augsburg, which was opened in the month of
June. At this diet, the emperor determined, if possible, to bring all subjects in dispute between the papists
and Protestants to a final termination.   In view of
such a determination, Luther drew up a summary of
the Protestant doctrines to be presented to the diet.
This was rewritten and polished by the scholarly
Melanchthon, and is known to the present day as the
Confession of Augsburg. This confession dates the close
of the dark night of the papacy, and the beginning
of the cloudy day of sectism.   After toiling through a
long dismal night of papal darkness, a beam of gospel
day, as the morning spread upon the mountains, re-
vives the fainting spirit of Christianity.   During the
twelve hundred sixty years of papal reign the darkness
was total.   Most all the grand features of primitive
Christianity were lost.   But now the gospel began to
shine, and men saw the awful darkness from which
they were emerging. but because of division and sect-
making the full gospel light was not permitted to shine
even in Protestantism.   The scripture was fulfilled in
Zech. 14.6, 7—"And it shall come to pass in that day,
that the light shall not be clear, nor dark: but it shall
be one day which shall be known to the Lord, not day
nor night."

On the opening of the diet, this Confession was presented, and on being read, was listened to by the emperor and assembled princes with profound attention.
After it had been read in the diet of Augsburg, it
was subscribed to by many German princes, who had
not before heard a clear statement of the position of
the reformers.   Such was the impression made upon
the minds of the members that strong hopes were indulged that the diet would consent that Protestantism
should be tolerated.   But these hopes were not destined at this time to be realized.   Strongly pressed by
the papacy, the emperor at length agreed to the passing of a decree, commanding all his subjects to acknowledge the supremacy of Rome in all matters
ecclesiastical, upon pain of the imperial wrath.   On
the breaking up of the diet the Protestant princes saw
that nothing remained for them but to unite in measures of mutual defense of their cause.   Accordingly
in the latter part of the same year, they assembled at
Smalkald, and entered into a solemn league, commonly
known by the name of the *League of Smalkald*, for the
support of their religious liberties, and resolved to
apply to the kings of France, England, and Denmark
for protection.   These preparations for defense made
no small impression upon the emperor; besides, he was
at this time considerably perplexed in consequence of
an attack upon his dominions by the Turks, which
rendered a rupture with the Protestant princes extremely unpleasant.   Hence he was induced to conclude a treaty of peace with them at Nuremburg, in
1532, by which the decrees of Worms and Augsburg
were revoked, and the Lutherans were left to enjoy

their rights till the long promised council should assemble, and decide the mighty controversy. This inspired all the friends of the Reformation with vigor and resolution. It gave strength to the feeble, and perseverance to the bold. The secret friends of the Lutheran cause were induced to come forward; and several states openly declared on the side of Protestantism, to the great mortification of the Roman pontiff and the papal advocates

In 1534 the overthrow of the papal power in England, and the founding of the *Church of England* happened, under peculiar circumstances. Henry VIII., reigning monarch of England at that time, a man of distinguished abilities, but notorious for his violent passions and beastly vices, in consequence of the pope's refusal to grant him a divorce from his wife, in order that he might marry another woman, shook off the papal yoke and declared himself head of the church in England; and from this time the papal authority in England in a great measure ceased. The progress of reformation in England, during the life of Henry, was slow. The principle alteration consisted in the removal of the supremacy from the pope to the king; the dissemination of the Bible, and the suppression of the monasteries. In most other respects the Romish superstition remained untouched; and great severity was exercised against such as attempted to advance the reformation beyond what the king prescribed.

Happily for the cause of truth, Henry elevated to the see of Canterbury Thomas Cranmer, a man of distinguished learning. His mind being opened to a just view of the great doctrines of the Bible, he labored to forward the cause of the Reformation. And in this he was assisted by the new queen, Anne Boleyn. Convinced of the importance of a general dissemination of the Scriptures, Cranmer persuaded the king to authorize their publication, which was accordingly effected, and the Bible was read in many of the assemblies, by which multitudes were caused to hear it.

Cranmer also directed the king's attention to the suppression of the monasteries. These were at this time exceedingly numerous, and possessed immense wealth. They extended no small influence in respect to learning and religion; and while they existed it was evident that ignorance and superstition would exercise a lordly power over the land. To Cranmer's suggestion Henry acceded. The monks were his enemies and, under the pretext of their immorality, he was willing to lay hold of their wealth. In the year 1535 Cranmer commenced the visitation. The result of this investigation was very unfavorable to these institutions; they were represented as nurseries of idolatry, cruelty, intemperance, and incontinence, and worthy only to be broken up. Immediately an order was issued for the suppression of the lesser convents; three hundred seventy-six of which were destroyed, by which Henry acquired £10,000 in plate and movables, and an annual income of £30,000. About ten thousand ejected friars were thrown upon the government to support, many of whom were introduced, from economy, into vacant benefices; and these hosts of disquieted papists—enemies of innovation—became connected with the Church of England. Another inquiry was not long after instituted into the character of the larger monasteries, and their suppression followed. From 1537 to 1539 six hundred forty-five monasteries were destroyed, besides ninety colleges, more than two thousand chantries, five chapels, and ten hospitals; and all their wealth—including lands, silks, and jewels—flowed into the royal coffers. The conduct of Henry was no sooner reported at Rome, than he was denounced as an opponent of Christ's vicar on earth. He was excommunicated, his kingdom laid under an interdict, and he himself cited to appear at Rome. To the lofty spirit of Henry, these ravings of the pope were only as an idle wind. Henry died in the year 1547.

In order to see how far reform had advanced at this time, it is necessary only to look at the principal grounds of dispute, and the light in which they then stood. These were (1) papal supremacy, (2) infallibility, (3) reading the scriptures in an unknown tongue, (4) indulgences, (5) image worship, (6) transubstantiation, and (7) the denial of the cup to laymen. The first four were corrected; the fifth was modified; but the last two were still corrupting the national creed.

CHAPTER XXII.

THE REFORMATION CONTINUED.

WHEN the sun is up, who can hinder its shining? The light of reformation was risen upon the benighted souls of men, and it was impossible to prevent the

impulse it was calculated to produce.   In spite of all
the united efforts of popes and princes, France was
added to the scenes of heretical pravity.   The state of
politics between France and Germany rendering the
affairs of the Reformation very precarious, it was to the
interest of Francis I. sometimes to tolerate and at
other times to persecute.   The queen of Navarre was a
zealous Protestant, and sister to the French monarch.
Her influence often prevailed in favor of the glorious
cause; but Francis himself was a bigoted papist, and
desired the total extirpation of Lutheranism.   He was
heard to say that if he thought the blood in his arm
was tainted with the Lutheran heresy, he would have
it cut off; and that he would not spare even his own
children, if they entertained sentiments contrary to
those of the Catholic church.

It was under the reign of this persecuting prince
that the famous John Calvin began his career.   Calvin
was born at Noyon, in Picardy, in the year 1509.   In
the year 1534 he forsook the fellowship of Rome, and
in 1536 was made teacher of theology at Geneva.   His
genius, learning, eloquence, and piety, rendered him
respectable even in the eyes of his enemies.

The name *Calvinist* seems to have been given at first
to those who embraced not merely the doctrine, but
the church government and discipline established at
Geneva, and to distinguish them from the Lutherans.
But since the meeting of the Synod of Dort, the name
has been chiefly applied to those who embrace his
leading views of the gospel, to distinguish them from
the Arminians.   The leading principles taught by
Calvin were the same as those of Augustine.   The

main doctrines by which those who are called after his name are distinguished from the Arminians, are reduced to five articles; and which, from their being the principal points discussed at the Synod of Dort, have since been denominated the five points. These are· predestination, particular redemption, total depravity, effectual calling, and the certain perseverance of the saints.

The character of Calvin stands high among the reformers. Next to Luther he accomplished more for the Reformation than any other individual　He early exhibited specimens of mental greatness, and as his intellectual powers developed themselves it was apparent that he was destined to take a high rank among his contemporaries　The ardor with which he pursued his studies was unremitted; and at the age of twenty-two, Scaliger pronounced him to be "the most learned man in Europe." The reformed churches in France adopted his confession of faith, and were modeled after the ecclesiastical order of Geneva. The liturgy of the English church was revised and reformed by his means. In Scotland and Holland his system was adopted, and by many churches in Germany and Poland; indeed, every country in which the light of the Reformation had made its way, felt the influence of his powerful mind. But at Geneva, as a central point, he was the light of the church. the oracle of the laws, the supporter of liberty, the restorer of morals, and the fountain of literature and the sciences. He died in the year 1564.

The principles which underlay Calvin's theological and ecclesiastical system have been a powerful factor in the growth of civil liberty. Wherever Calvinism spread—in England, Scotland, Holland, or France— men learned to defend their rights against the tyranny of civil rulers. Moreover, the separation of church and state was the first step in the development of religious freedom.

Calvin's doctrine. Though Calvin was an active and energetic worker in the Reformation, yet some of his opinions were foreign to the real meaning of the gospel. "We assert," says Calvin, "that by an eternal and unchangeable decree God hath determined whom he shall one day permit to have a share in eternal felicity, and whom he shall doom to destruction. In respect of the elect the decree is founded in his unmerited mercy, without any regard to human worthiness; but those whom he delivers up to damnation are by a just and irreprehensible judgment excluded from all access to eternal life." From the doctrine of "election" follows that of "particular redemption"; i. e., that Christ died only for the elect, and not for all men. A full statement of these opinions may be found in the "Westminster Confession of Faith" set forth by the "Westminster Assembly of Divines" (1643-1649), which is still the authoritative confession of the Kirk of Scotland, and is recognized as more or less authoritative by all Calvinistic sects. Great controversies have arisen among Calvinists respecting the divine decree, and they are divided into two parties: one holding that those imagined decrees were positively issued, and thus "absolute"; the other that they were only God's foresight of the fall. Whitefield also separated from Wesley on account of the determined opposition which the latter offered to the Calvinism of the former. The Calvinists were called to experience the most severe trials from the persecuting spirit of the Roman Catholics.

ANABAPTISTS.

At this period in history a class of people denominated Anabaptists may properly be mentioned. They seem to be considered by some historians as a low and degraded class of people. Anabaptists are those who maintain that baptism ought always to be performed by immersion. The word is compounded of two Greek words signifying "anew" and "a baptist," and practically means that those who have been baptized in their infancy ought to be baptized anew. It is a word which has been indiscriminately applied to Christians of very different principles and practices. The English and Dutch Baptists do not consider the word as at all applicable to their sects; because those persons whom they baptize they consider as never having been baptized before, although they have undergone what they term the ceremony of sprinkling in their infancy. During the dark ages of papacy the apostolic mode of baptism had been almost lost, but it was maintained by a few; and during the period of the Reformation a few practiced baptism by immersion, but they were classified among the fanatics.

The Anabaptists of Germany, besides their ideas concerning baptism, believed in a perfect church establishment, pure in its members, and free from the institutions of human policy. Some of them considered it possible by human industry and vigilance, to purify Roman Catholicism; and seeing the attempts of

Luther to be successful, they hoped that the period had arrived in which the church was to be restored to this purity. Others not satisfied with Luther's plan of reformation undertook a more perfect plan, or, more properly, a visionary enterprise to found a new church, entirely spiritual and divine. This sect was soon joined by great numbers, whose characters and capacities were very different. Their progress was rapid; for in a very short space of time their discourses, visions, and predictions excited great commotions in various parts of Europe.

The most fanatic faction of all these was that which pretended that the founders of this new and perfect church were under a divine impulse, and were armed against all opposition by the power of working miracles. It was this faction that, in the year 1521, began their fanatical work under the guidance of Munzer, Stubner, Stork, etc. These men taught that among Christians who had the precepts of the gospel to direct and the Spirit of God to guide them, the office of magistracy was not only unnecessary, but an unlawful encroachment on their spiritual liberty; that the distinction occasioned by birth, rank, or wealth should be abolished; that all Christians, throwing their possessions into one stock, should live together in that state of equality which becomes members of the same family; that as neither the laws of nature, nor the precepts of the New Testament had prohibited polygamy, they should use the same liberty as the patriarchs did in this respect. They employed at first the various arts of persecution in order to propagate their doctrines, and related a number of visions and revelations, with which they pretended to have been favored from above; but when they found that this would not avail, and that the ministry of Luther and other reformers was detrimental to their cause, they then madly attempted to propagate their sentiments by force of arms.

Munzer and his associates, in the year 1525, put themselves at the head of a numerous army and declared war against all laws, governments, and magistrates of every kind, under the chimerical pretext that Christ himself was now to take the reins of all government into his hands; but this seditious crowd was routed and dispersed by the elector of Saxony and other princes, and Munzer, their leader, put to death. Many of his followers, however, survived, and propagated their opinions through Germany, Switzerland, and Holland. In 1533 a party of them settled at Munster, under two leaders of the names of Matthiesen and Bockhold. Having made themselves masters of the city, they deposed the magistrates, confiscated the estates of such as had escaped, and deposited the wealth in a public treasury for common use. They made preparations for the defense of the city, and invited the Anabaptists in the Low Countries to assemble at Munster, which they called mount Sion, that from thence they might reduce all the nations of the earth under their dominion. Matthiesen was soon cut off by the bishop of Munster's army, and was succeeded by Bockhold, who was proclaimed by a pretended special designation of heaven, as the king of Sion, and invested with legislative powers like those of Moses The city of Munster, however, was taken after a long siege, and Bockhold punished with death.

It must be acknowledged that the true rise of the insurrections of this period ought not to be attributed to religious opinions. The first insurgents groaned under severe oppressions, and took up arms in defense of their civil liberties; and of these commotions the Anabaptists seem rather to have availed themselves than to have been the prime movers. That a great part were Anabaptists seems indisputable; at the same time it appears from history that a great part also were Roman Catholics, and a still greater part were those who had scarcely any religious principles at all. Indeed, when one reads of the vast numbers that were concerned in these insurrections, of whom it is reported that 100,000 fell by the sword, it appears reasonable to conclude that they were not all Anabaptists. It is but just to observe also, that the Baptists in England and Holland, and all countries at the present day are to be considered in a different light from those above mentioned.

CHAPTER XXIII.

THE REFORMATION CONCLUDED.

Huguenots. The origin of the term *Huguenot* is extremely obscure. It is supposed to have had its rise in 1560, but authors are not agreed as to the origin and occasion of it. It is said to have been applied first to the Protestants of France by way of contempt, or nickname, and that like the Geux of Flanders, they assumed and bore it with pride. Some suppose the term to be derived from *hugon*, a word used in Touraine to signify persons who walk at night in the streets —the early Protestants, like the early Christians, having chosen that time for their religious assemblies. Others are of the opinion that it was derived from a French and faulty pronunciation of the German word Eidgenossen, or Confederates, the name given to those citizens of Geneva who entered into an alliance with the Swiss cantons to resist the attempts of Charles III., Duke of Savoy, against their liberties. The Confederates were called Eignots, and hence, probably, the derivation of the word Huguenots. A third surmise is that the word was derived from one Hugues, a Genevese Calvinist. The persecution which the Huguenots have undergone has scarce its parallel in the history of religion. During the reign of Charles IX., on the 24th of August, 1572, happened the massacre of St. Bartholomew's day, when more than thirty thousand of them throughout France were butchered with circumstances of aggravated cruelty.

In each country of Europe the Reformation had its distinctive features. In France it was peculiarly a national movement. France had already witnessed two movements for reform before the rise of Protestantism. In the fifteenth century the Gallican theologians had sought to remove ecclesiastical abuses and to check the encroachments of the papacy. Two centuries before the rise of the Gallican reformers, a movement of a much more radical character began in southern France. Here the anti-sacerdotal sects—the Waldenses, of which an account has already been given, and the Catharists—flourished for a time. But only a small remnant survived the terrible persecutions to which they were subjected, and continued to cherish the simple faith of their ancestors. France it seems was in reality opposed to any reformation which struck at the foundations of the Roman Catholic system. It had no sympathy with attack on the sacraments and the hierarchic body. Protestantism, which was first introduced into France under the Lutheran form, soon became Calvinistic through the influence of Geneva; for from the Genevan printing-offices there were sent forth Bibles and many other books. This means of spreading the truth had become in the hands of the reformers at this time a great power, not only in France but all over Europe.

Printing, one of the greatest blessings that God ever bestowed upon the world, had been invented about a century before this, but had slowly come into use. Until the invention of printing, the most profound thinker saw his influence limited to his immediate circle of friends, but the new art made it possible for men to speak to and act upon the world at large. It enabled books to be multiplied rapidly, in such numbers and at such moderate cost that all mankind were brought into nearer and more intimate relation with each other. It is not the author's purpose to describe the discovery or the gradual growth of the art, but merely to speak of the influence which it exercised upon the minds of men with regard to matters of religion. The early printers confined themselves chiefly to printing and publishing great numbers of copies of the Bible; and they had ready sale for all that they

14

could print, at prices sufficient to pay them for all their labor. The demand was more than they could supply. The effect of the study of the scriptures by these first readers was wonderful. They at once began to see the glorious way of life as pointed out by Jesus Christ and the apostles. Men in different countries at once set about to translate the Bible into the language of their respective tongues. These translations were given to the public by the printers. In 1448 a Bohemian version of the Bible appeared It was followed by an Italian version in 1471, a Dutch version in 1477, a French version in 1477, and a Spanish version in 1478. Thus at the opening of the sixteenth century, the Bible was accessible to many persons in all the principal countries of Europe.

At first it was not permitted to be read by the public, but only priests had a right to read it to the people But as the art of printing increased and improved, Bibles became so numerous that the people could take them to their homes and read them in secret. People of the present time, who have the Bible upon their tables, and in their pockets, and have the liberty to read it when they please, have no conception of the feverish eagerness with which the people of the sixteenth century turned to the blessed Book for information and relief. They found the teaching of God's Holy Word one thing, and the claims and practices of the Roman church another. The Bible gave no license to extort money from the people by the sale of indulgences or to inflict tortures upon heretics; neither did it teach the supremacy of the pope, the praying to the Virgin Mary or the saints, or the worship of images and relics. But it taught that men are saved by believing in Jesus Christ and the atoning efficacy of his blood. A perusal of the scriptures satisfied men that the simple teachings of Christ and his apostles were a very different thing from the faith and practice of the Roman church. The people who had so long walked in darkness now saw light—"the true light that lighteth every man that cometh into the world."

Bible-readers wonderfully increased, and the great work of improvement and reformation went on, until it seemed that France was on the eve of a great moral and social as well as a religious regeneration. Rome now took alarm. It made but little difference to the priests and monks whether the manners and morals of the people were bettered or not. They saw only that their own power was at stake. The mass was neglected, and the amount of revenue lessened. Their tyrannical grasp upon humanity was being loosened, and they resolved to put a stop to a practice so dangerous to the church as reading the Bible. As soon as the news reached the ears of the pope, that the reading of the Bible was bringing about such a great change, he immediately ordered a stop put to the reading, and also a destruction of all the Bibles in France. From that time it was determined by the papal power to exterminate the supporters of the Reformation in France. In 1525 Clement VII. established, or enlarged, the Inquisition in France, conferring upon it "apostolic authority" to try and to condemn heretics. The king, also, urged on by the clergy, became the enemy of the reformed Royal edicts were issued commanding the extermination of heretics in every part of the kingdom.

See the account of the persecution in France as given in the next chapter.

The pope and the clergy denounced the Bible as being the vilest of all publications and the cause of all the trouble. Wherever the Bible was found printed in the common tongue it was burned. All that were suspected of printing, selling, or circulating the Bible were seized and burned. In Paris alone, during the first six months of the year 1534, twenty men and one woman were burned for this cause. The art of printing also suffered vengeance from the Romanists. They denounced it as of the devil, and endeavored to destroy it, and printers suffered everywhere, as well as the venders of the Bible. All efforts, however, to destroy the Bible or the art of printing, or even to stop its progress, proved to be in vain. Printing had become a necessity to men, and it was impossible to destroy it. Germany, Holland, and Switzerland were full of printing-presses sending forth Bibles and the literature of Luther and Calvin more rapidly than their enemies could destroy it. English, French, Dutch, and German Bibles came pouring from these fruitful presses. Effort after effort, and edict upon edict went forth to stop the progress of the Reformation. But persecution could not check the spread of the truth. The Huguenots increased in strength in spite of the cruel laws against them. Men and women suffered death at the stake and in many other ways, rather than give up their faith. The curiosity of the unbelieving was aroused; they desired to learn what was in the forbidden Bible to inspire such zeal and endurance, and they too read the Bible, and many of them also became converted to the salvation of Jesus.

On Jan. 17, 1562, appeared an edict, giving noble-men the right of the free exercise of their religion on their own estates. It seemed that France was about to extend justice to the reformed. But the pope and priests were determined if possible to quash the cause of the reformers. The Huguenots availed themselves of this liberty for a short time and held their meetings of worship for a while. On Christmas day, 1562, a congregation of three thousand Huguenots assembled for religious worship at the town of Vassy. On Sun-day, March 1, 1563 they assembled again in a large barn near the same town. They numbered about twelve hundred persons, having come in from all parts of the surrounding country. It happened that while they were assembled the Duke of Guise, accompanied by his wife, and his brother, the cardinal of Lorraine, and a company of armed men on their way to Paris were passing through Vassy. Being informed of the meeting of the Huguenots, he immediately marched his men to the barn where they had assembled. The duke's men at once began to abuse the peo-ple of the congregation as "heretics, dogs, and rebels." Two shots were fired at persons on the plat-form, others followed, and three persons were killed and several wounded. The Huguenots were unarmed, and unable to make any resistence. They therefore endeavored to shut the doors of the building, but these were broken open by Guise's men, who rushed in and continued their assault. Guise's orders were to put all the heretics to the sword, and to spare none. His orders were faithfully executed. About fifty were

killed on the spot, and two hundred wounded; many
of the wounds were mortal. The rest escaped from
the building and sought safety in flight.

After the murdering was ended and the Duke was
walking about viewing the awful work of which he
had been the leader, some one handed him a book that
had been picked up in the barn. He examined it curi-
ously, having never seen anything like it before.
Handing it to his brother, the cardinal of Lorraine,
he exclaimed. "Here is one of the cursed Huguenots'
books!" The cardinal glanced at it, and smiled:
"There is not much harm in it, he said, "for it is the
Bible of the Holy Scriptures." The duke was confused, but burst out angrily· "What! The Holy Scriptures! It is fifteen hundred years since Jesus Christ
suffered death and passion, and but one since that
book has been printed. Do you call it the Gospel?
By God's death it is worth nothing." "My brother is
in the wrong," quietly observed the cardinal as he
turned away The duke then marched on to Paris,
where he was received with great joy and pomp, and
was praised by loud cheers, hailing him as the defender
of the faith and the savior of the country.

About this time all the Catholics in France rose
up against the Huguenots. Urged on by the pope and
Catherine the queen-mother, a civil war ensued,
lasting about ten years and resulting in much bloodshed and also in the defeat of the Catholics. The
treaty of peace at this time did not stop the persecution of the Huguenots by the papacy. The Jesuits
went about their work using the Inquisition as a
mighty battering-ram against the ranks of the Hugue-

nots. Certain it is, that these poor people suffered in greater numbers in France than in any other part of the continent. At one time twelve hundred were beheaded under the imputation of rebellion; at another, three thousand were slain; and during three months the papists were allowed to murder Huguenots at their pleasure, in which time two thousand fell victims to the Catholics.

But the crowning scenes were on *St. Bartholomew's day*, August 24, 1572. The extreme unparalleled wickedness of this day was effected by a deep-laid scheme. Catherine de' Medici, queen-mother of King Charles IX., after many fruitless attempts to extirpate heresy by force of arms, determined now by deception to win the Huguenots to her confidence so as to disarm them of any suspicion, in order to arrange to strike the blow that would wipe the Huguenots out of France. In order to make things appear more flattering, a marriage was agreed upon between the king's sister and Henry of Navarre. The marriage was accordingly solemnized at Paris, August 18, and a great number of the Protestants were present. During the afternoon of the 23d, the king rode through the streets of Paris accompanied by the Chevalier d'Angouleme; and the queen-mother, to disarm suspicion, held her court as usual. Neither gave any outward indication of the dreadful crime they had in contemplation. On the morning of the 24th of August, 1572, the awful work of death began. Sunday morning being St. Bartholomew's day, as the bells were ringing for morning prayers, a great number of soldiers appeared suddenly in the streets, and began to murder the Huguenots. The massacre continued three days, during which seven hundred houses were pillaged, and more than five thousand people perished. One man boasted to the king that he had killed one hundred fifty in one night. From Paris the bloody orders were sent to the surrounding provinces, where many thousand more were added to the inhuman account. The entire number of the victims of this dreadful persecution has been variously estimated from 30,000 to 100,000. This sad affair, so disgraceful to the annals of France, must be laid chiefly to the charge of Rome; for the Vatican resounded with rejoicing, and the court of Spain publicly recognized the deed. It appears from authentic records, that between the years 1530 and 1580 not less than a million French Protestants lost their lives through the mad zeal and savage cruelty of blind infatuated papists. If such were the slaughters among the people, what must have been the whole number of Protestants? It is said that in the year 1571 they had two thousand one hundred fifty congregations, in many of which were ten thousand members; and yet this vast body at length saw the predominance of the Roman hierarchy, and their own cause reduced to a state the most degrading and hopeless.

CHAPTER XXIV.

PERSECUTIONS ENDURED BY THE REFORMERS.

PERSECUTION has been the means in the providence of God of strengthening and spreading the very principles which at times seemed to expire with the martyr. In the days of the primitive church, when persecution was strong against them they increased in numbers, faith, and favor with God; but when peace was declared, Christians became proud, careless, and weak in faith. The grandest and most fruitful achievements of Christians were won at the stake, on the cross, in the arena, and on the scaffold. All the pagan kings and powers, and also the Jewish powers, were arrayed agianst the poor unarmed Christian. We see him expiring in the flames at the stake; we see him devoured by the wild beasts; we see him dying on the gallows; we see him hewn down by the sword; we see him languishing in prison; we see him stoned, mocked, scourged, sawn asunder, tempted, and wandering about in sheepskins, and goatskins, being destitute, afflicted, tormented, and wandering in deserts, and in mountains, and in dens, and caves of the earth. Yet in the midst of all these sufferings and persecutions, we see the stone that was cut out without hands which smote these powers, and we see the kingdom which the God of heaven set up, a kingdom which shall never be destroyed—we see it break in pieces and consume all these kingdoms. Yes, we see it standing

yet to-day and forevermore; and it will stand throughout all eternity.

As primitive Christianity won its crown of glory
through the awful fires of persecution, so did Protestant Christianity.   Rome had taken away the Bible
and hidden its truths away, as she supposed, forever
from the people.   But when Martin Luther and other
reformers began to uncover the truth, papal Rome,
following the example of her pagan predecessors,
struggled fiercely to crush the truths which the reformers, after much labor, succeeded in rescuing from
the dungeons of superstition and ignorance, to which
they had been consigned.   Thank God that they did
succeed in rescuing the blessed charter of our salvation, and made it free to all men.   In defense of a free
Bible they went to the stake gladly, counting themselves happy to suffer persecution and death so that
those who survived or came after them might enjoy the
rights purchased with their blood.   In all the countries of Europe the fires blazed, and the groans of the
martyrs went up to God, but everywhere the principles
for which they died have triumphed.

The loss which the Roman power sustained by the
Reformation was severely felt by her.   She had been
successfully attacked, and her wide-spread influence
was narrowing down.   A still deeper depression
awaited her, unless means could be devised by which
her authority could be sustained.   Under this conviction, the Roman pontiffs were continually on the alert,
and ready to take advantage of every facility by which
their power might continue as it was; or, if possible,
be restored to its former lordly state.   The first means

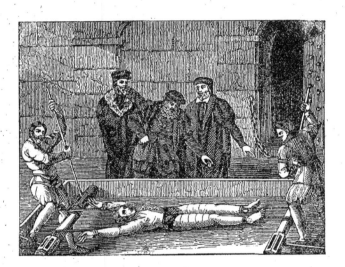

CRUELTIES OF THE INQUISITION—RACK.

adopted for this purpose was the employment of the order of Jesuits, whose business it was to go forth, as the advocates of the papal power, to teach the world the propriety of submission to its authority, and its superior claims upon their respect and patronage. A second means employed by the papacy to secure and enlarge its declining authority was an attempt to Christianize the heathen in several parts of Asia and South America. A third means employed by the Roman church to sustain and increase its authority consisted in the better regulation of its internal concerns. Accordingly, the laws and procedures in the courts of Inquisition were revised and corrected; colleges and schools of learning were established; youths were trained up in the art of disputing, and in defending the doctrines of the Catholics; books of a pernicious tendency were revised or suppressed; and high and honorable distinctions were conferred on the most zealous defenders of the faith. In short, every plan which ingenuity could suggest or which wealth and influence could carry forward, was adopted to maintain the authority of the Roman pontiff.

A fourth plan adopted by them to advance their cause and maintain their power, was their persecution of the Protestants. A full account of the calamities caused by the papists, even in a single country, would greatly exceed the limits of this volume. Scarcely a country in which Protestants were to be found was exempted from cruelties, which equaled and often exceeded in severity, those which had been experienced at an earlier day under Nero and Domitian. It has been computed that during these persecutions not less than fifty millions of Protestants were put to death. The countries which suffered most severely were Italy, the Netherlands, Spain, France, parts of Germany, and England.

The following brief account of the persecutions of the sixteenth century in different parts of Europe, is taken from Buck's Dictionary. The friends of the Reformation were anathematized and excommunicated, and the life of Luther was often in danger, though at last he died on the bed of peace. From time to time innumerable schemes were suggested to overthrow the reformed church, and wars were set on foot for the same purpose. The Invincible Armada, as it was vainly called, had the same end in view. The Inquisition, which was established in the thirteenth century against the Waldenses, was now more effectually set to work. Terrible persecutions were carried on in various parts of Germany, and even in Bohemia, which continued about thirty years, and the blood of the saints was said to flow like rivers of water. The countries of Poland, Lithuania, and Hungary, were in a similar manner deluged with Protestant blood.

HOLLAND.

In Holland and in the other Low Countries, for many years the most amazing cruelties were exercised under the merciless and unrelenting hands of the Spaniards, to whom the inhabitants in that part of the world were then in subjection. Father Paul observes that the Belgic martyrs were 50,000, but Grotius and others observe that there were 100,000 who suffered by the hand of the executioner. Herein, however, Satan and his agents failed of their purpose; for in the issue a

great part of the Netherlands shook off the Spanish
yoke, and erected themselves into a separate and independent state, which has ever since been considered
as one of the principal Protestant countries.

FRANCE.

No country, perhaps, has ever produced more martyrs than France.   After many cruelties had been
exercised against the Protestants, there was a most
violent persecution of them in the year 1572, in the
reign of Charles IX., of which an account has already
been given in Chapter xxiii   But all these persecutions
were, however, far exceeded in cruelty by those which
took place in the time of Louis XIV.   It can not be
pleasant to any man's feelings, who has the least
humanity, to recite these dreadful scenes of horror,
cruelty, and devastation; but to show what superstition, bigotry, and fanaticism are capable of producing,
and for the purpose of holding up the spirit of persecution to contempt, they are here detailed, though as con-
cisely as possible.   The soldiers and dragoons went
into the Protestant houses, where they marred and
defaced their household stuff; broke their looking-
glasses and other utensils; threw about their corn and
wine; sold what they could not destroy; and thus, in
four or five days, the Protestants were stripped of
above a million of money.   But this was not the
worst: they turned the dining-rooms of gentlemen
into stables for horses, and treated the owners of the
houses where they were quartered with the greatest
cruelty, lashing them about, not suffering them to eat
or drink.   When they saw the blood and sweat run
down their faces, they would dash water upon them,

HERETICS ON THE WAY TO EXECUTION.

and, putting over their heads kettles and pans turned upside down, they made a continual din upon them till these unhappy creatures lost their minds. At Negreplisse, a town near Montauban, they hung up Isaac Favin, a Protestant citizen of that place, by his armpits, and tormented him a whole night by pinching him and tearing off his flesh with pincers. They made a great fire round about a boy, twelve years old, who, with hands and.eyes lifted up to heaven, cried out, "My God! help me!" and when they found 'the boy resolved to die rather than renounce his religion, they snatched him from the fire just as he was on the point of being burned. In several places the soldiers applied red-hot irons to the hands and feet of men, and the breasts of women. At Nantes, they hung up several women and maids by their feet, and others by their arms, and thus exposed them to public view stark-naked. They bound mothers, that gave suck, to posts, and let their sucking infants lie languishing in their sight for several days and nights, crying and gasping for life. Some they bound before a great fire, and, being half-roasted, let them go—a punishment worse than death. Amidst a thousand hideous cries, they hung up men and women by the hair, and some by their feet, on hooks in chimneys, and smoked them with wisps of wet hay till they were suffocated. They tied some under the arms with ropes and plunged them again and again into wells; they bound others, put them to the torture, and with a funnel filled them with wine till the fumes of it took away their reason, when they made them say they consented to be Catholics. They stripped them naked, and, after a thousand indignities, stuck them with pins and needles from head to foot. In some places they tied fathers and husbands to their bed-posts, and before their eyes ravished their wives and daughters with impunity. They blew up men and women with bellows till they burst them. If any, to escape these barbarities, endeavored to save themselves by flight, they pursued them into the fields and woods where they shot them like wild beasts, and prohibited them from departing the kingdom upon pain of confiscation of effects, the galleys, the task, and perpetual imprisonment—cruelties worse than ever was practiced by Nero or Diocletian. With these scenes of desolation and horror the popish clergy feasted their eyes and made only matter of laughter and sport of them!

ENGLAND.

England has also been the seat of much persecution. Though Wycliffe, the first reformer, died peacably in his bed, yet such was the malice and spirit of persecuting Rome, that his bones were ordered to be dug up and cast upon a dunghill. The remains of this excellent man were accordingly dug out of the grave, where they had lain undisturbed forty-four years. His bones were burned, and the ashes cast into an adjoining brook. In the reign of Henry VIII. Bilney, Bainham, and many other reformers were burned; but when Queen Mary came to the throne the most severe persecutions took place. Hooper and Rogers were burned in a slow fire. Saunders was cruelly tormented a long time at the stake before he expired. They put Taylor into a barrel of pitch, and set fire to it. Eight illustrious persons, among whom was Farrar, Bishop of St.

15

David's, were burned by the infamous Bonner. In 1555, sixty-seven persons were burned, among whom were the famous Protestants Bradford, Ridley, Latimer, and Philpot. In the .following year, 1556, eighty-five persons were burned. Women and children suffered in the flames for heresy O God, what is human nature when left to itself! Alas, dispositions ferocious as infernal then reign and usurp the heart! The queen erected a commission court, which was followed by the destruction of nearly eighty more The whole number that suffered death for the reformed faith during the reign of Queen Mary were not less than two hundred seventy-seven persons, of whom were five bishops, twenty-one clergymen, eight gentlemen, eighty-four tradesmen, one hundred husbandmen, laborers, and servants, fifty-five women, and four children Besides these there were fifty-four more under prosecution, seven of whom were whipped, and sixteen perished in prison.

Nor was the reign of Elizabeth free from this persecuting spirit. If any one refused to consent to the least ceremony in worship, he was cast into prison, where many of the most excellent men in the land perished Two Protestant Anabaptists were burned, and many perished She also, it is said, put two Brownists to death; and though her whole reign was distinguished for its political prosperity, yet it is evident that she did not understand the right of conscience; for it is said that more sanguinary laws were made in her reign than under any of her predecessors, and her hands were stained with the blood both of papists and of Puritans.

BISHOPS RIDLEY AND LATIMER, 1555.

James I. succeeded Elizabeth: he published a proclamation, commanding all Protestants to conform strictly, and without any exception to all the rites and ceremonies of the Church of England. About five hundred clergy were immediately silenced, or degraded, for not complying. Some were excommunicated, and some banished. Two persons were burned for heresy; one at Smithfield, and the other at Litchfield. Worn out with endless vexations, and unceasing persecutions, many retired into Holland, and from thence to America. It is witnessed by a judicious historian that in this and in some following reigns 22,000 persons were by persecution banished from England to America.

In the reign of Charles I. arose the persecuting Laud. A single trait of Laud's character, drawn from his own diary, will delineate the man better than could any painter. Dr. Leighton, one of the Puritans, was by the archbishop's instigation, condemned in the star-chamber for writing a book against the hierarchy. When sentence was pronounced in court, Laud, pulling off his cap and lifting up his eyes to heaven, gave thanks to God, who had enabled him to behold this vengeance on his enemies; and he thus records the execution of the sentence: "1630, Nov. 6.—1st. He was severely whipped, and then placed in the pillory; one of his ears cut off; one side of his nose slit; branded on the cheek with a red-hot iron, with the letters S. S.; a fortnight afterward, before the sores upon his back, ear, nose, and face were healed, he was whipped a second time, and placed in the pillory, the other ear cut off, the other side of his nose slit, and the other cheek branded." He continued in prison till the long parliament set him at liberty. Of what a spirit must that man have been, that could with apparent satisfaction, record in a private diary such an act of cruelty, injustice, and malignity, perpetrated under the cloak of law and religion! About four years afterwards, William Prynne, a barrister, for a book he wrote against the sports on the Lord's day, was deprived from practicing at Linclon's Inn, degraded from his degree at Oxford, set in the pillory, had his ears cut off, was imprisoned for life, and fined five thousand pounds.

Nor were the Presbyterians, when their government was in the ascendancy in England, free from the charge of persecution. In 1645 an ordinance was published, subjecting all who preached or wrote against the Presbyterian directory for public worship to a fine not exceeding fifty pounds; and imprisonment for a year, for the third offense in using 'the Episcopal Book of Common Prayer, even in a private family. In the following year the Presbyterians applied to Parliament, pressing them to enforce uniformity in religion, and to extirpate popery, prelacy, heresy, and schism, but their petition was rejected; but in 1648 the Parliament, ruled by them, published an ordinance against heresy, and determined that any person who maintained, published, or defended the following errors should suffer death. These errors were: 1. Denying the being of a God. 2. Denying his omnipresence, omniscience, etc. 3. Denying the Trinity in any way. 4. Denying that Christ had two natures. 5. Denying the resurrection, the atonement, the

Scriptures. In the reign of Charles II. the Act of
Uniformity passed, by which two thousand clergymen
were deprived of their benefices. Then followed the
Conventicle Act, and the Oxford Act, under which it
is said that eight thousand persons were imprisoned
and reduced to want, and many to the grave. In this
reign also the Quakers were much persecuted, and
numbers of them imprisoned. Thus we see how England
has bled under the hands of bigotry and persecution;
nor was toleration enjoyed until William III.
came to the throne, who showed himself a warm
friend to the right of conscience. From this time
on persecution in England practically ceased.

IRELAND.

Ireland has likewise been drenched with the blood
of the Protestants, forty or fifty thousand of whom
were cruelly murdered in a few days, in different parts
of the kingdom, in the reign of Charles I. It began
on the 23d of October, 1641. Having secured the
principal gentlemen and seized their effects, they murdered
the common people in cold blood, forcing many
thousands to fly from their homes and settlements
naked into the bogs and woods, where they perished
with hunger and cold. Some they whipped to death,
others they stripped naked, and exposed to shame, and
then drove them like herds of swine to perish in the
mountains. Many hundreds were drowned in rivers,
some had their throats cut, others were dismembered.
With some the execrable villains made themselves
sport, trying who could hack the deepest into a Protestant's
flesh; wives and young virgins were abused in
the presence of their nearest relations; nay, they taught

HORRIBLE CRUELTIES INFLICTED ON THE PROTEST-
ANTS IN IRELAND, IN 1641.

their children to strip and kill the children of the
Protestants, and dash out their brains against the
stones. Thus many thousands were massacred in a
few days, without distinction of age, sex, or quality,
before they suspected their danger, or had time to provide for their defense.

SCOTLAND, SPAIN, AND OTHER COUNTRIES.

Besides the persecutions named above, there have
been several others carried on in different parts of the
world. Scotland for many years together was the
scene of cruelty and bloodshed, till it was delivered by
the monarch of the revolution. Spain, Italy, and the
valleys of Piedmont, and other places, have been the
scenes of much persecution. Popery has had the
greatest hand in this diabolical work. It has to answer, also, for the lives of millions of Jews, Mohammedans, and barbarians.

When the Moors conquered Spain, in the eighth
century, they allowed the Christians the free exercise
of their religion; but in the fifteenth century, when the
Moors were overcome, and Ferdinand subdued the
Moriscoes, the descendants of the Moors, many thousands were forced to be baptized or burned, massacred,
or banished, and their children sold for slaves; besides
innumerable Jews, who shared the same cruelties,
chiefly by means of the infernal courts of Inquisition.
A worse slaughter, if possible, was made among the
natives of Spanish America, where fifteen millions are
said to have been sacrificed to the genius of popery in
about forty years.

It has been computed that fifty millions of Christians have at different times been the victims of the

CRUELTIES PRACTICED ON THE PROTESTANTS IN SCOT-
LAND, IN 1543.

persecution of the papists, and put to death for their
religious opinions.   Who can not help dropping a tear
of sympathy and emotion when he reads the foregoing
accounts of suffering for Christ's sake, and of the
madness of depraved humanity?

> Avenge, O Lord! thy slaughtered saints, whose bones
> Lie scattered on the Alpine mountains cold;
> Even them who kept thy truth so pure of old,
> When all our fathers worshiped stocks and stones,
> Forget not: in thy book record their groans
> Who were thy sheep, and in their ancient fold
> Slain by the bloody Piedmontese that rolled
> Mother with infant down the rocks.   Their moans
> The vales redoubled to the hills, and they
> To heaven.   Their martyred blood and ashes sow
> O'er all the Italian fields, where still doth sway
> The triple tyrant; that from these may grow
> A hundredfold, who having learned thy way
> Early may fly the Babylonian woe.
>
> —*Milton.*

Never was there a more decided enemy to persecution on account of religion, than Milton.   He appears
to have been the first in that darkened age who understood the principles of toleration.   He took a great
interest in his time, in effecting the reformation, and
his name deserves to be handed down to the remotest
ages of the world.   Why should we not remember the
names, and dwell upon the memory of those who
have been heroes in the cause of Christ?   We erect
statues and monuments to the memory of those who
by their lives gave to us our civil freedom, and we are
never weary of recounting their deeds.   Why, then,
should we not tell the story of the brave and patient
Christian men and women who died for our religious
freedom, who gave us the Bible at the cost of their
lives, and who brought Christ back to us as our personal Savior and friend?   A nobler, sweeter, and more

solemn story is not to be found in all the range of history, or one which appeals to us more directly or powerfully.

CHAPTER XXV.

SECT-MAKING, OR DENOMINATIONALISM.

At a diet held in Augsburg in 1555, opened by Ferdinand in the name of the emperor, the subjects of dispute were discussed, and a treaty was formed, called the *Peace of Religion,* which established the Reformation, inasmuch as it secured to the Protestants the free exercise of their religion, and placed this inestimable liberty on the firmest foundation. From that time the power of the Roman pontiff has, on the one hand, been on the decline, and the principles of the Reformation have, on the other hand, been advancing.

The state of Europe at this time or a few years later, in respect to religion, stood thus: Italy, Spain, Portugal, and the Belgic provinces under the Spanish yoke continued their adherence to the Roman pontiff. Denmark, Norway, Sweden, Prussia, England, Scotland, Ireland, and Holland, became Protestant. Germany was about equally divided. In Switzerland the Protestants claimed a small majority. For a season it was to be hoped that France would forsake the fellowship of Rome; but at length she became decidedly papal, although she retained several million Protestants within her limits.

Since the establishment of the Reformation, the body of professing Christians has been divided into several distinct communities or denominations and called by different names.   Consequently it will be necessary in the remainder of this work to treat the Protestant church as divided, and under different names.   A view of these religious names will present a melancholy account of the apostasy.   It will evince the nature and the effects of that apostasy, and thus confirm the scriptural narrative on the subject   It will exemplify the great fact of human degeneracy in a form and manner calculated to convince every candid reader that original, deep, and wide-spread corruption, in which the fall of man consists, appears in dark lines in the history of the various religions which mankind have embraced.   Indeed, the most disgusting exhibitions of man's apostasy are found in many of the religions he has contrived, with a view to superseding the religion derived from heaven.   A view of these religions, so far as they are departures from the truth, will furnish a sad detail of the extent and power of Satan's empire in the world.   Mankind having apostatized from God, have, in every nation and in every period of time, been successively brought under the dominion of Satan.   They have been subject to his influence, obeyed his laws, and in their religious rites often directly paid him homage.   In reality, they have been his slaves and he has claimed them as his property.   The wickedness in which he delights they have, in innumerable instances, practiced.   Before proceeding with the short history of these divisions, the reader's attention is called to the following comparison of their doctrines with the doctrine of the Bible.

It is undoubtedly true that the Bible teaches oneness. All the doctrines which it inculcates agree with each other. They have a mutual dependence and connection; they give one another a reciprocal support and influence; they grow out of each other, and all hang together, alike deriving their ripeness, freshness, and flavor from the same parent stalk. Let any person take a copy of the Scriptures with a good concordance, and undertake to collect from all parts of the Bible upon any one doctrine or moral duty, all that it says upon the subject, and he will be surprised at the uniformity of the teaching of the different writers. They never speak for and against the same doctrine; they never bear witness on both sides of any question, nor is there an instance in which they affirm and deny the same thing. That which in reality has any scripture in its favor, has all scripture in its favor. There is not one scripture in the Bible that favors division among God's children. But why there is division among professed Christians is not the purpose in this book to explain. We know that in the best and purest age of the church it was one. It was one fold under one Shepherd. It is true that, at the beginning, there were a great number of churches, but each was distinguished by a name descriptive of its locality. There was a church of Jerusalem, of Antioch, of Ephesus, of Smyrna, of Corinth, and of Rome, besides many others. There was not a church consisting of the followers and defenders of the doctrine of Paul, and another of those of John, and another of those of Peter. There were then no such sects as Luther-

ans, Calvinists, and Wesleyans, nor such names as
Congregationalist, Presbyterian, Methodist, Episcopalian, or Baptist.   Agreement in fundamentals was the
only doctrinal unity then demanded, and the united
band of Christ's disciples assembled around the same
table, declaring by their actions, "We, being many,
are one bread and one body, for we are all partakers of
that one bread " Disciples, Christians, or saints, were
their grand distinctive names; and when spoken of as a
church, it was designated the church of God.   Nor
did any one of the apostles or their fellow laborers
establish any sects in the church of God.   The bare
supposition of the contrary is absurd and revolting to
every mind acquainted with the inspired record   So far,
indeed, were they from forming sects, that they firmly
resisted the introduction of divisions and parties.
Thus, for example, when in the Corinthian church
(1 Cor. 1 10) there was an attempt to introduce different leaders, such as Paul, Apollos, Peter, Luther,
Calvin, Zwingli, or Wesley, we find the apostle saying,
"Now I beseech you, brethren, by the name of our
Lord Jesus Christ, that ye all speak the same thing,
and that there be no divisions among you; but that ye
be perfectly joined together in the same mind and in
the same judgment " Read also verses 11-17.   Thus
evident is it that the church is one.   God, her God, is
one, Christ, her Redeemer, is one; the Holy Spirit,
her sanctifier, is one; the Holy Scriptures, the rule or
discipline of her faith and worship and obedience, are
one, the faith of her true members is one precious
faith, and their privileges, interests, objects, and des-
tination, are one.   "There is," says the apostle, "one

body, and one Spirit, even as ye are called in one hope
of your calling; one Lord, one faith, one baptism, one
God and Father of all, who is above all, and through
all, and in you all."

Notwithstanding all the persecution, and division
among Protestants, the truth, the light of the gospel,
has spread rapidly; yet not so rapidly, and in so clear
a form as it would have been if Protestants had kept
in the one body of Christ. All through the dark
ages, and during the Reformation, and later, the Bible
had to struggle against opposition, visible and latent,
artful and violent. It has had to contend with the
prevalence of error, the tyranny of passion, and the
cruelty of persecution. And as it could not be destroyed by fire, men have endeavored to destroy its
influence by argument. Infidelity and skepticism
have risen up with great fluency and power against it.
Celsus and Porphyry hurled arguments in ancient times
against it, and more modern times have exhibited the
philosophy of Hobbs, the skeptic doubts of Boyle, the
polished sarcasm of Bolingbroke, the subtlety of
Hume, the learning of Gibbon, the mockery of Voltaire, the vulgarity of Paine, the empty caviling of
Strauss, the shallow sophistry of Renan, and the ridi-
cule of Ingersoll. But from all these assaults God's
word has been preserved. And how marvelous has
been its preservation! The Book at which kings, emperors, generals, philosophers, statesmen, and legisla-
tors have all aimed in vain, still holds its enemies in
derision. It has flourished, while its adversaries have
been blasted one after another, and never did the
Bible, the Book of books, bid so fair as at present to

be the book of the whole family of mankind.   It has
spread open its pages in almost every land.   It is
printed in Chinese camps, pondered in the red man's
wigwam, sought after in Benares, a school-book in
Figi, eagerly bought in Constantinople, loved in the
kloofs of Kafir-land, while the voice of the dying from
Assyria to Egypt has been lifted up to bear it witness.   No book has taken such a hold on the world.
It goes into the literature of the scholars, and colors
the talk of the street.   The ship or boat of the merchant can not sail the sea without it; no ship of war
goes to conflict but the Bible is there.   It enters men's
closets and mingles in all the grief and cheerfulness
of life   The Bible attends them in their sickness, and
they are helped by its words in their afflictions.

The Bible brings both peace and judgment.   'If we
measure to its truths, it is peace and life; but if we do
not, it is judgment and death.   The apostle says,
"The word of God is quick and powerful, and sharper
than any two-edged sword, piercing even to the divid·
ing asunder of soul and spirit, and of the joints and
marrow, and is a discerner of the thoughts and intents
of the heart."   The prophet said, "Then I turned, and
lifted up mine eyes, and looked, and behold a flying
roll.   And he said unto me, What seest thou?   And I
answered, I see a flying roll; the length thereof is twenty cubits, and the breadth thereof ten cubits.   Then
said he unto me, This is the curse that goeth forth
over the face of the whole earth: for every one that
stealeth shall be cut off as on this side according to it;
and every one that sweareth shall be cut off as on that
side according to it.   I will bring it forth, saith the

Lord of hosts, and it shall enter into the house of the thief, and into the house of him that sweareth falsely by my name, and it shall remain in the midst of his house, and shall consume it with the timber thereof and the stones thereof."

CHAPTER XXVI.

SECT-MAKING, OR DENOMINATIONALISM.

IN this chapter the history of the divisions of Protestantism will be taken up. The purpose is to give a concise summary of the denominations that are the nearest orthodox; as this work is designed to trace a history of the true church, and not all the divisions and superstitions in the world. God has a people to-day, and a goodly number of his people are scattered into the different denominations. It is not the profession that makes the child of God, but the new birth. And any one who hears enough of the word of God to know how to become a child of God and is born of the Spirit, belongs to the family or church of God, whether he belongs to a denomination or not.

LUTHERANS.

The Lutherans derive their name from Martin Luther, of whom a short account has already been given. Their faith or creed was drawn up by Luther and Melanchthon, and presented to the emperor Charles V., in 1530, at the Diet of Augsburg, and hence called the Augsburg Confession. To the end of Luther's life,

perfect harmony existed between him and his friend
Melanchthon, but after that time things changed, and
the gentle, peace-loving spirit of Melanchthon led him
to various concessions, both to the Reformed and to
the Roman Catholics, which finally produced a wide-
spread fear that the distinctive doctrines of Luther
would be sacrificed, and the Reformation itself per-
iled.   Even the most devoted friends of Melanchthon
were at last forced to the conviction that his mediating
spirit was attended with the most serious danger to the
great work which had been wrought.   And while the
great body of the Lutherans looked with regretful tenderness on the mistakes of Luther's bosom friend,
there was a small extreme class thoroughly embittered
against him.   In this case as in every other the effort
at premature peace added strength to the animosity.
Melanchthon's gentleness led to a fiercer conflict than
had been called forth by Luther's firmness.   No controversy was ever conducted with more bitterness than
the *Sacramentarian Controversy*, so called because the
principal dispute was about the Lord's Supper.   Lutheranism prevails principally on the Continent of Europe,
and is the principal form of religion in Prussia, Sweden,
Norway, Denmark, Hanover, Saxony, and some of the
other German states.   In the United States this denomination is known as the *Evangelical Lutheran
church.*

The establishment of Lutherans in America was
made a little more than a century after the discovery
by Columbus, and within a few years of the landing of
the Pilgrims at Plymouth (1620).   The earliest settlements were made in New York by people from Hol-

land. Following this came that of the Swedes, on the banks of the Delaware, in 1636. The third was that of the Germans, which gradually spread over Pennsylvania, Maryland, Virginia, and the interior of New York and the western states.

The chief doctrinal difference between the Lutherans and the Reformed is as to the real presence of Christ in the sacrament of the Lord's Supper; the Lutherans holding what is often—though very incorrectly—styled the doctrine of consubstantiation. They hold a supernatural, or sacramental presence, though rejecting transubstantiation, while many of their theologians have asserted not only the presence of the human nature of Christ in the Lord's Supper, but, as Luther did, the personal omnipresence of his human nature. Other points of difference relate to the allowance in Christian worship of things indifferent; and many of those things at first retained by Luther and his fellow reformers have become favorite and distinguishing characteristics of some of the Lutheran societies—as images and pictures in places of worship, clerical vestments, and such like. Though the Lutherans were the first to come out of papal Rome, yet to-day in formality they are as near like them as any other denomination. In some Lutheran congregations the doctrines of Luther and of their symbolical books have given place in a great measure to Arminianism, and to a system of religion very inconsistent with Luther's doctrine of justification by faith.

CHURCH OF ENGLAND.

The Church of England dates its origin from the time of the Reformation, when Henry VIII. shook off

the pope's authority and took upon himself the title of
"Head of the Church," as has been mentioned in a
preceding chapter. The term "Episcopal Church" is
usually applied to the Established Church of England,
and its branch, Protestant Episcopal Church, in the
United States of America. These two organizations
constitute one and the same church in all points of
faith and doctrine, and differ only in those ideas of
church government which are required by the different political organizations of the countries in which
they exist   The doctrines of the Episcopal Church are
stated in the Thirty-nine Articles, to be found in their
Book of Common Prayer.

KIRK OF SCOTLAND.

The Church of Scotland was not firmly established
until 1689 in the reign of William and Mary, when
episcopacy was totally abolished in Scotland. The
Westminster Confession of Faith was then received as
the standard of the national creed; to which all ministers and principals and professors in universities are
obliged to subscribe as the confession of their faith
before receiving induction into office. The Church of
Scotland is remarkable for its uncommon simplicity of
worship: it possesses no liturgy, no altar, no instrumental music, and its services are all of the simplest
kind   It observes no festival days   Its ministers are
all equal   It acknowledges no earthly head, and is
quite distinct from and independent of the state. Its
government is Presbyterian, and properly it is the
mother of all Presbyterian societies   The name *Presbyterian* is appropriated to a large denomination of
dissenters in England who have no attachment to the

Scotch mode of church government; and therefore to them the term in its original sense is improperly applied. The different factions of Presbyterianism will not be taken up.

The Pesbyterian denomination of the United States is a daughter of the Church of Scotland. In 1689 Presbyterians from Scotland and the north of Ireland began to emigrate to America. They settled principally in Maryland and Pennsylvania, and soon began to establish their church organizations similar to those to which they had been devoted in their own countries. Later, Francis Makemie, from Ireland, and John Hampton, from Scotland, were sent over to preach the gospel in the middle and southern colonies. They were successful. In 1689 the first Presbyterian Church was organized in Philadephia, and about the same time congregations were organized in New Jersey, Maryland, Delaware, Virginia, and South Carolina. About the year 1705 the Philadelphia Presbytery, consisting of seven ministers, was formed, and by 1716 the society had grown so rapidly that it was found necessary to organize the Philadelphia Synod, in which four presbyteries were represented. From this time their growth has been rapid and steady, and to-day they are a very rich and populous denomination.

BAPTISTS.

This appellation signifies a denomination of Christians who maintain that baptism is to be administered by immersion, and not by sprinkling. They observe that the word *baptize* signifies immersion, or dipping, only; that John baptized *in* Jordan; that he chose a place where there was much water; that Jesus came

up out of the water, that Philip and the eunuch went
down both into the water; that the terms *washing,
purifying, purging* in baptism, so often mentioned in
scripture, allude to this mode; that immersion *only* was
the practice of the apostles and the first Christians;
and that one of the reasons why it was laid aside was
the love of novelty.   These positions they believe to
be so clear from scripture and history that they stand
in need of but little argument to support their views.

Baptists claim to have a history previous to the
Reformation.   Indeed, they claim that the advocates
of their views of the church and of the ordinances may
be traced back through the Vaudois, the Waldenses
("Poor Men of Lyons"), the Albigenses, the Cathari,
the Paulicians, and the Patarenes, the Donatists, the
Novatians, the Messalians, the Euchites, and the Montanists of the second century, to the apostles.   It is no
doubt true that immersion was practiced all along
down to the present time, but there is no account of a
people characterized as Baptists until 1638.   There
were, however, baptists — *immersers* — among the
Albigenses, the Waldenses, and the followers of Wycliffe, but it does not appear that they were known
by the name *Baptists*.   The Anabaptists, of whom
an account has been given (See Chapter xxii.), must
not be confounded with Baptists.   In this connection
the following quotation from the International Cyclo-
pædia will serve to make the matter clear   "The Baptists of Great Britain and America reject the name of
Anabaptists, as expressing only an accidental circumstance of their tenets—viz., the rebaptizing of converts
from other sects, who happen to have been baptized in

infancy—and also as associating them with the scan-
dals of the German Anabaptists of the sixteenth century, from whom they claim to be historically distinct.
From the same feeling, the modern sect in Germany
and Holland style themselves *Taufgesinnte.*"

About 1644 they began to make a considerable figure
in England, and spread themselves into several separate
congregations. After they had separated from the
Independents (about the year 1638) and set up for
themselves under a pastor, having renounced their
former baptism, they sent over one of their number to
be immersed by one of the Dutch Mennonites of
Amsterdam, that he might be qualified to baptize his
friends in England after the same manner. The Baptists subsisted for a long time under two denominations; viz., the *Particular*, or *Calvinistical*, who preach
predestination, and the *General*, or *Arminian*, who
teach that salvation is offered to all mankind. Some of
them observe the seventh day of the week as the
Sabbath, not apprehending the law that enjoined it to
have been repealed by Christ. At the present time
Baptists are divided into many factions.

In America the Baptists were chiefly Calvinistic, and
held occasional fellowship with the Particular Baptists
in England. But of late years the Arminian side has
flourished and increased more rapidly. The name of
Roger Williams must have the honor of being placed at
the head of every account of the introduction of Baptists into America, and of the establishing of the Baptist Church in this country. Roger Williams was born
in Wales. In his youth he came to London, and attracted the attention of Sir Edward Coke by his short-

hand notes of sermons, and speeches in the star-chamber, and Coke assisted him to a university education. He was a member of the Church of England, and was designed for the priesthood. But he became a Puritan, and emigrated to America in 1630, settling at Salem, Massachusetts. He was not there long before his liberal views on the question of conscience in matters of belief rendered him obnoxious to the Puritan settlers of the colony. He contended against religious persecution in all forms. He protested against the union of church and state, which then and long after existed in both Massachusetts and Connecticut. He was not then a Baptist, though in advocating these views he was defending principles of which Baptists had ever been the representatives. This the authorities of the colony would not tolerate. He was therefore condemned, and for no other reasons than holding those opinions which now none think of questioning, but all love. In the enjoyment of civil and religious liberty, one might be inclined to think it was always so. But it was not. This freedom cost much heroic suffering, and noble sacrifice. To none are Americans more indebted than to Roger Williams.

The Salem Puritans sentenced Williams to banishment, and expelled him in 1635 from the colony. In the spring of 1636 he settled in what is now the state of Rhode Island, on the site where the city of Providence stands. Here he founded a colony, obtaining a charter from the king. A fundamental principle of this colony was, that there should be no persecution for conscience' sake in matters of religion, but that every man was to have perfect freedom to worship God

after his own conviction of truth and duty. It was
not *toleration* he established, which implies the right to
punish, but magnanimously withholds it. It was *perfect freedom, which denies the right.* This is just the
difference between Rhode Island colony, and that of
Lord Baltimore in Maryland. The latter granted
toleration only as a privilege that they retained power
to revoke at any time. The former incorporated
religious liberty into the fundamental law of the commonwealth. It was the first time the world ever beheld
such a sight. The little colony of Rhode Island was
the first government that every was based upon it.
The Puritans who fled from religious intolerance knew
not how to be tolerant. Roger Williams fled from
their intolerance and established a colony in which perfect freedom was guaranteed by the law to all its
inhabitants.

It was after he arrived in Rhode Island, but before
he obtained the charter, that he was baptized, though
in theory he was a Baptist before he was banished.
"He was the first person in modern Christendom to
assert in its plenitude the doctrine of religious liberty
of conscience, and the equality of all before the law,
and in its defense he was the harbinger of Milton, and
the precursor of Jeremy Taylor His philanthropy
compassed the earth. Williams would permit the persecution of no religious opinion, of no religion, leaving
heresy unharmed by law, and orthodoxy unprotected
by penal enactments." Such was Roger Williams, the
first of American Baptists. Possibly a few were in the
other colonies before he avowed himself one, but the
first mention of Baptists in this country is in connection with him.

The principles that Williams advocated were destined to spread, and have exerted a mighty influence in
molding the free institutions of this nation.   All now
defend religious liberty, but American Baptists claim
to have been its first and staunchest defenders.   In
England they stood alone as representatives of the
right of all men to worship God according to the dictates of their own conscience.   The same was true of
them for a time in America, though soon after their
appearance the Quakers became their zealous co-
operators in this good cause, now so triumphant, but
which the colonists were so slow to accept, and of
which to give others the benefit.   Dr. Bushnell says of
the Pilgrim Fathers· "They as little thought of raising a separation of church and state as of planting a
new democracy.   In New England the Congregation-
alists remained by statute law the standing order, for
support of which all others were taxed.   Nor was this
unjust law repealed in Connecticut until 1838.   In
Virginia the Church of England was not established by
law until some years after the Revolution   As late as
1785, through the influence of Episcopalians, the leg-
islature of Georgia enacted a law on the subject of
religion, against which Baptists protested, and it was
repealed at the next session.   At length the principle
triumphed in every one of the original thirteen colonies in which church and state had been united in
any form, so that now the constitution of every state
in the Union accords with the amendment to the
national constitution passed, as is claimed, through
the influence of the protest of the Virginia Baptists
in 1789.

It is remarkable what barbarous cruelties and persecutions were carried on by those who themselves had fled from these things to this land of freedom. As has been noted, Roger Williams was banished from Massachusetts colony in the midst of the rigors of a New England winter, and compelled to track his way across the wilderness in search of a home for himself and followers, which home he found on the banks of the Narragansett—seeking an asylum among savages, when banished from the civilization of Christian men who had themselves fled from persecution. The laws of Massachusetts colony against Baptists and Quakers were severe. The more their principles prevailed the more violent became the laws. The penalties inflicted were the severest the spirit of the age would allow; banishment, whipping, fine, and imprisonment, beside being taxed to support the clergy of the "Standing Order." For failure or refusal to pay this tax, regarding it as unjust, they "oftentimes had their bodies seized upon and thrown into the common jail as malefactors, and their cattle, swine, horses, household furniture, and implements of husbandry, forcibly taken from them and shamefully sold, many times at not a quarter of their first value." In Connecticut Baptist ministers were put in the stocks, and afterward thrown into prison for preaching the gospel contrary to the law. In Virginia Dr. Hawks, an Episcopalian, says, "No dissenters experienced for a time harsher treatment than the Baptists. They were beaten and imprisoned, and cruelty taxed its ingenuity to devise new modes of punishment and annoyance." The spirit of persecution long lingered after the strength of popular feeling had bound it hand and foot, and the laws enacted remained unrepealed on the statute-books of the New England colonies and of Virginia years after public sentiment had made their execution impossible.

Just here, however, another incident of persecution must be noticed In Virginia on June 4, 1768, three Baptist ministers, John Walker, Lewis Craig, and James Childs, were brought before the magistrates in Spottsylvania county, and bound over for trial as "disturbers of the peace," charged with preaching the gospel, their accusers saying they could not meet a man "without putting a text of scripture down his throat." This trial has been made memorable in history because of the part taken in it by the eloquent Patrick Henry, who on hearing of their arrest, rode sixty miles that he might be present at their trial, and volunteer in their defense. Seating himself in the court-room, he listened to the reading of the indictment. The words "for preaching the gospel of the Son of God" caught his ear. Rising immediately on the concluding of the reading, he stretched out his hand, received the paper, and then addressed the court He dwelt on the charge "for preaching the gospel of the Son of God." He asked at the close of a most eloquent appeal, "What law have they violated?" And then, for the third time, in a slow, dignified manner, he lifted his eyes to heaven, and waved the indictment about his head. The effect was electrical. The court and audience were at the highest pitch of excitement. The prosecuting attorney and the witnesses against the three men grew pale and trembled.

The judge shared in the excitement, now becoming extremely painful, and with tremulous voice gave the authoritative command, "Sheriff, discharge those men." In New England the persecutions were longer in duration, because commencing at an earlier period, and they were also much more severe. In 1649 John Clark, Obadiah Holmes, and John Crandall were arrested and imprisoned in Boston, each well whipped, and fined, in the order in which their names are here given, twenty, thirty, and five pounds each. About this time Dr. Dunster, President of Harvard College, an able preacher, and learned in Hebrew, Greek, and Latin, became a Baptist. He was not only removed from his presidency, but the feeling against him in the colony was so bitter that he was compelled to go to Plymouth colony, where he died in 1659. Many other accounts of persecution might be given.

The first Baptist church in America was organized in 1639 in Providence, Rhode Island. Since that time Baptists have greatly increased in America. *Baptists* as here used means all Christian denominations that practice immersion for baptism. In concluding this chapter mere mention will be made of a few of the principal factions of this denomination.

Free-will Baptists, one of the smallest of those societies in the United States coming under the general classification "Baptist," is one of the most active in the promotion of spirituality of personal religious character. They appeared for the first time as organized and distinctive in the year 1780. They are Arminian in doctrine. The founder of this body was Benjamin Randall. He was an uneducated man, but of sound sense and fervent piety. He was converted at New Castle, New Hampshire, under the preaching of the celebrated Geo. Whitefield, when twenty-two years of age. About four years after his conversion, in 1776, he united with the Calvinistic Baptist Church in Berwick. Afterwards imbibing Arminian notions, he dissented from the body with which he had connected himself. His case was considered and the hand of fellowship withdrawn from him. The first church organized was at New Durham, New Hampshire. As with all new sects, terms of reproach were used in describing them. They were called Randallites, General Provisioners, New Lights, and Free-willers, the last of which has clung to them, and which they have accepted, being known now as Free-will Baptists.

Campbellite Baptists, or Disciples. They regard the title "Campbellite Baptists" as a reproach. They are sometimes known by the name *Christians.* This society was founded by Alexander Campbell about the year 1827. The Disciples claim that their object is simply to bring back Christianity to its early simplicty. They reject all symbols of faith except the Bible, and object to all technicalities in theology. They claim to require faith in Christ and deep repentance before baptism is administered, but they seem to attach to this ordinance more than due efficacy. Unlike some Baptists, they invite Christians of all denominations to commune with them at the table of the Lord's Supper, which service they celebrate every Lord's day. They have had a rapid growth, and in many sections of the United States, and in parts of the British provinces, they are now numerous and influential.

Some of the minor Baptist denominations are *Wine-brennerians*, *Dunkards*, *Mennonites*, and *Sabbatarians*, or *Seventh-day Baptists*.

CHAPTER XXVII.

SECT-MAKING, OR DENOMINATIONALISM, CONTINUED.

METHODISTS.

THE term *Methodists*, as the distinctive appellation of a religious sect, owes its origin to John Wesley, a native of England, who was born in the year 1703. Wesley, while a student of Lincoln College, Oxford, about the year 1729, became impressed with the conviction of the importance of a deeper and more earnest zeal in spiritual things. He began to hold meetings with several of the students, among whom was the celebrated Whitefield. Their meetings caused considerable stir, in which the students began to notice the difference in the lives of Wesley and his associates, that their conduct was much superior to the generally licentious lives of the members of the university. They not only held their meetings, but they visited the poor of the town and those that were in prison in the castle. The gospel as preached by Wesley and his companions seemed to have a wonderful impression upon the people. He appealed with peculiar force to the intelligent common sense of all unconverted men. He struck a powerful blow against Calvinism, to de-

stroy the unreasonable and unscriptural doctrine which
it sets forth, and to show how God could be just and
yet the justifier of every believing soul that in real
penitence accepts the Lord Jesus Christ; and also,
how God can save all infants and irresponsible persons,
and how in every nation all who fear God and work
righteousness, are accepted by him. He presented the
word of God in such a way as to throw wide open the
door of hope to every soul.   Wesley held the standard
of Christian perfection higher than any other minister
during the Protestant reformation, up to his time.
Justification, sanctification, holiness, and perfection,
were familiar topics for him. We also notice, by reading his writings, that he makes a distinction between
regeneration and sanctification.   He teaches two distinct works of grace: (1) justification by faith; (2)
sanctification, or Christian perfection.   He teaches
that the work of sanctification is wrought instantane-
ously, though it may be approached by slow and gradual steps; he also teaches that it is impossible to remain in a justified state, and be guilty of known sin.
He avoids most carefully, and condemns most emphat-
ically, all fanaticism and spiritual pride and foolish-
ness, and shows how easily the experience may be lost

In the year 1739 Wesley acquired an old building
known as "The Foundry" as a meeting-place for himself and a few of his followers. This was the first society under the direct control of Wesley, and the existence of the Methodist Church can be dated from this
time. It was not, however, till 1743 that Wesley published the rules of his society. By that time not a few
other local societies had been added to that at "The

JOHN WESLEY.

Foundry," the three chief centers being London, Bristol, and Newcastle. Hence Wesley called his society, when he published the "Rules" in 1743, the "United Societies." Methodism from this time increased very rapidly in Europe and spread into other countries.

It was not until thirty years later, in 1769, that their first missionaries were sent to America. Although some Methodists had sailed from Ireland to America previous to this, not much work had been done until in 1769 Robert Williams, one of Wesley's preachers, came to America and gave himself up wholly to the work of an evangelist, and labored with great success in Petersburg, Norfolk, and through eastern Virginia and North Carolina. John King, a local preacher, came from England in the same year and began his labors in the Potter's Field, now Washington Square, Philadelphia, and extended them through Delaware, Maryland, and New Jersey. On the third of August, 1769, Wesley announced in their conference in England the cry that came from America for help, and asked, "Who is willing to go?" Richard Boardman and Joseph Pilmoor responded to the call, and were set apart and returned on the conference journal as missionaries to America. They arrived in Philadelphia in 1769, and were warmly welcomed by George Whitefield, who was then laboring in that city. They set themselves at once to systematize the work, and in 1770 "America" appears for the first time on Wesley's printed minutes, with four preachers, Boardman, Pilmoor, Williams, and King; and the following year records 316 members. On July 14, 1773 the first

American Methodist conference was held at Philadelphia, consisting of ten preachers, with a membership of 1,160.

Until 1779 Wesley had enjoined in England and in America the necessity of loyalty to the Church of England. No ordinances were received or administered by them outside of the established church. Wesley now foresaw that an independent society was necessary, and he at once set to work to arrange for the important movement that was assuming definite shape in the new republic. John Wesley himself assumed the office of bishop, and, assisted by other presbyters of the Church of England, he set apart and ordained Thomas Coke, already a presbyter of the Church of England, as general superintendent of the American societies. He arrived in America Nov. 3, 1784, and summoned all the preachers to meet him at Baltimore on the 24th of December. They assembled on that day in a conference and agreed to form a "Methodist Episcopal Church." Here the Methodist Episcopal Church of America was launched forth as a separate and distinct society, with superintendents, elders, and deacons.

Although the Methodists endured severe struggles in later years, and there were several secessions from the Methodist Episcopal body, its progress has been steadily onward in numbers and riches of this world, but in spirituality, it is sad to say, there has been retrogression. This is well shown by the following language of the late Bishop R. S. Foster concerning the spiritual condition of the Methodist Episcopal Church. Some Methodists may dislike so plain a picture of their denomination, yet it was drawn by the pen of their own bishop. He says:

"The church of God is to-day courting the world. Its members are trying to bring it down to the level of the ungodly. The ball, the theater, nude and lewd art, social luxuries, with all their loose moralities, are making inroads into the sacred enclosure of the church; and as a satisfaction for all this worldliness, Christians are making a great deal of Lent and Easter and Good Friday, and church ornamentation. It is the old trick of Satan. The Jewish church struck on that rock; the Romish church was wrecked on the same, and the Protestant church is fast reaching the same doom.

"Our great dangers as we see them, are assimilation to the world, neglect of the poor, substitution of the form for the fact of godliness, abandonment of discipline, a hireling ministry, an impure gospel, which summed up is a fashionable church. That Methodists should be liable to such an outcome, and that there should be signs of it in a hundred years from the 'sail loft' seems almost the miracle of history; but who that looks about him to-day can fail to see the fact?

"Do not Methodists, in violation of God's word and their own discipline, dress as extravagantly and as fashionably as any other class? Do not the ladies, and often the wives and daughters of the ministry, put on 'gold and pearls and costly array'? Would not the plain dress insisted upon by John Wesley and Bishop Asbury, and worn by Hester Ann Rogers, Lady Huntingdon, and many others equally distinguished, be now regarded in Methodist circles as fanaticism? Can any one going into the Methodist Church in any of our chief cities distinguish the attire of the communicants from that of the theater and ball goers? Is not worldliness seen in the music? Elaborately dressed and ornamented choirs, who in many cases make no profession of religion and are often sneering skeptics, go through a cold artistic or operatic performance, which is as much in harmony with spiritual worship as an opera or theater. Under such worldly performance spirituality is frozen to death.

"Formerly every Methodist attended class and gave testimony of experimental religion. Now the class-meeting is attended by very few, and in many churches abandoned. Seldom the stewards, trustees, and leaders of the church attend class. Formerly nearly every Methodist prayed, testified, or exhorted in prayer-meeting. Now but very few are heard. Formerly shouts and praises were heard; now such demonstrations of holy enthusiasm and joy are regarded as fanaticism.

"How true that the Methodist discipline is a dead letter! Its rules forbid the wearing of gold or pearls or costly array; yet no one ever thinks of disciplining its members for violating them. They forbid the reading of such books and the taking of such diversions as do not minister to godliness; yet the church itself goes to shows and frolics and festivals and fairs, which destroy the spiritual life of the young as well as the old. The extent to which this is now carried on is appalling. The spiritual death it carries in its train will be known only when the millions it has swept into hell stand before the judgment. The early Methodist ministers went forth to sacrifice and suffer for Christ. They sought not places of ease and affluence, but of privation and suffering. They gloried not in their big salaries, fine parsonages, and refined congregations, but in the souls that had been won for Jesus. Oh, how changed! A hireling ministry will be a feeble, a timid, a truckling, a time-serving ministry, without faith, endurance, and holy power. Methodism formerly dealt in the great central truth. Now the pulpits deal largely in generalities and in popular lectures. The glorious doctrine of entire sanctification is rarely heard and seldom witnessed in the pulpits."

Since the formation of Methodism as a distinct sect there have been many factions or divisions forming into separate bodies. Of these the following are of sufficient note to be mentioned here. The *New Connection* separated under the leadership of Alexander Kilham, on the questions of the sacraments and lay influence, in the year 1797. The *Primitive Methodists* separated in the year 1810. They claimed, but were forbidden, the right to use the original exciting methods of promoting conversion. The *Bible Christians*, or *Bryanites*, formed a sect in Cornwall in 1815. The *Wesleyan Methodist Association* was formed in 1835, and the *Wesleyan Methodist Reformers* in 1839; both of which have since been united in one sect called *United Free Church Methodists*. The *Methodist Reformed Church*. This sect of American Methodists separated from the main body in the year 1814, giving up the form of episcopacy and reverting to the original characteristics of Methodism. *African Episcopal Methodists.* This is an offshoot of the original sect, formed by the secession of its black members in Philadelphia and Baltimore in the year 1816.   They profess to hold precisely the same doctrines, and to practice the same discipline as the body from which they seceded, their only reason for separation being the contemptuous treatment which they received from their white brethren.   Of the colored faction there is also the *African Methodist Episcopal Zion Church*.   Of the minor Methodist bodies, the *Methodist Protestant Church* is the most numerous.   This was organized in 1830.   Its creed is not different from that of the principal Methodist body.   The *Free Methodist* sect, though small compared to the Methodist Episcopal Church, has considerable zeal and demonstration of power, and does considerable evangelistic work.

UNITED BRETHREN IN CHRIST.

This is a religious organization having a near affinity to the Methodists.   Its founder was William Otterbein, a missionary of the German Reformed Church, and a native of Germany, who came to America in 1752. While preaching at Lancaster, Pennsylvania, an awakening in his own mind of religious fervor, which he felt to be really a new birth, moved him to hold meetings in different places.   Among the attendants from different denominations there came, on one of these occasions, Martin Boehm, a Mennonite preacher, who delivered an impressive discourse.   At the close of his sermon, Otterbein grasped his hand in token of fraternal fellowship, saying, "We are brethren."   This suggested the name of the society, which, by their joint labors, acquired a stable form.   The United Brethren are Arminian in their creed, and their organization

resembles that of the Methodists.   In reference to the
ordinances they are about the same as Methodists.
They believe that the ordinances of baptism and the
remembrance of the sufferings and death of our Lord
Jesus Christ are to be in use, and practiced by all
Christian societies; and that it is incumbent on all the
children of God particularly to practice them; but
the manner ought always to be left to the judgment
and understanding of every individual   Also the example of washing feet is left to the judgment of every
one to practice or not.   They have not been wanting
in active exertions for the building up of institutions
of learning and the diffusion of religious knowledge
They were a unit until about twelve years ago, when
they split on the subject of secret societies.   The
division was the cause of two distinct parties—*Radicals*
and *Liberals;* the former holding to the old discipline,
and the latter receiving into its membership persons
belonging to secret societies.

QUAKERS

George Fox is considered the founder of the Quaker
sect.   He was born in Leicestershire about the year
1624.   It is said of him that he was of a thoughtful
temper, and loved to be alone.   While yet young he
learned the shoemaker's trade.   While in this business
he devoted all his spare moments to the study of the
scripture, very often exhorting his fellow shoemakers.
Though Fox is regarded as the founder of the Quaker
faith, Penn and Barclay, after the Restoration, remod-
eled their principles, and reduced them to a more reg-
ular form.   The name *Quaker* was given to them in
derision, but afterwards became their distinguishing

name. Quakerism took its rise in England about the middle of the seventeenth century, and from there spread to America. They believe in the doctrine of the Trinity. They also believe that we obtain salvation through the atoning merits of the death of Christ; that man was created a free and responsible agent; that he forfeited his right to the blessings of the Creator by his fall, and will-owe his restoration to his lost estate to the mercy of God and the blood of Christ; that the Holy Scriptures are the work of inspiration, and a good rule of life and faith. Both sexes have general meetings, which may be called classes, colloquies, and synods.

The manners and customs of the Quakers, as well as those of other denominations, have changed somewhat in the last few years. Some of their peculiar notions and manifestations have been dispensed with. Primitively their devotion consisted in a profound contemplation, while some one of them, man or woman, would rise up, either with a sedate and composed motion or in a kind of transport, as if actuated by an irresistible power, and often with sighs, groans, and tears. This variety of behavior, said they, was caused by the impressions of the "spirit," which often dictated to the person speaking. Sometimes the "spirit" would dictate a sermon two or three hours long, often a deep silence of an equal duration. Sometimes they were seized with tremblings and shakings, and frequently it happened that a meeting would close without any sermon, exhortation, or public prayer. War is opposed by them as contrary to the spirit and teachings of the gospel, and oaths of all kinds are forbidden. Temper-

ance and the utmost simplicity in all things are enjoined. They do not practice any of the ordinances,
claiming that the baptism which saves the soul is not
dipping or sprinkling with water, but that of the
Spirit, and that the Lord's Supper is inward and spir-.
itual.   Some years ago the Quakers were divided into
two branches—the *Orthodox* or those maintaining the
doctrine stated above, and the *Hicksites*, whose leader
was Elias Hicks, about the year 1830.   He advocated
doctrines of a decidedly Socinian tendency, and caused
a very great discord among the Quakers, many of
whom adopted his tenets.   The physical manifestations and convulsions which followed the preaching of
the Quakers excited persecution.   But none of the
extravagances into which many of the early Quakers
fell, much less their refusal to pay tithes and to com-
ply with other ecclesiastical demands, furnish an excuse for the merciless persecution which pursued these
eccentric but devout people.   They were shut up in
pestilential cells; at one time, four thousand of them
are said to have been in prison in England.   Many of
the early preachers died in prison   Women as well as
men were attacked by savage mobs.   Their meeting-
houses were pulled down, sometimes by the order of
the established church.

In 1656 Quakers came to the United States, settling
in Massachusetts, Virginia, and other colonies, but persecution did not cease here.   Several of them, including one woman, were hanged, and many others were
harassed in different ways.   Very severe laws were
framed against them.   Persecution against them did
not cease until after the Declaration of Indulgence

by James II. After that they shared in the disad-
vantages which other dissenters had to endure. In the
course of time by their active labors of philanthropy,
prejudice and bitterness against them ceased. William
Penn, with a large company of Quakers, reached the
shores of America in 1682. The next year he laid out
on the Delaware the fine city of Philadelphia. The
Puritans were a moral and industrious people, but
stern and formal. They cropped their hair close to
their heads, and were opposed to wigs and veils. They
thought it wicked for women to wear lace, silk hoods,
or flowing sleeves. They observed Sunday strictly and
commenced it on Saturday evening. They liked very
long prayers and sermons, and punished those who
stayed away from religious services. They had fled
from England to escape persecution. Yet when they
got the power in this country they persecuted others.
The Puritans of Massachusetts, it must be remembered, drove out Roger Williams. They treated
Quakers still worse, fining and whipping such as were
found within the limits of the colony. At last, they
even put several Quakers to death. How could professing Christians think such cruelty was of God?

This chapter, as was explained in its commencement,
was not designed to give a history of all the Protestant
denominations, but only a short account of a few of the
leading ones. From these leading ones all others have
sprung, and to write a concise history of all would
make many volumes. To-day Protestantism is the
controlling influence in the world, but because it con-
trols the world is no reason why it should be divided
into so many factions and under so many heads, and

governed by so many different kinds of laws and rules, or creeds. *Protest* means a solemn declaration against, and the true meaning of *Protestant* is, a Christian who protests against the doctrines and practices of the Roman Catholic Church. The great powers, including our own free land, which control the destinies of the world are Protestant; but how much more powerful would be these powers if all these professed Protestants were a unit in Christ. The nations whose ships cover every sea, and bring the countries of the earth into closer and more binding relationship with each other are Protestant; but how much more successful would have been the missionaries in converting the heathen and bringing the nations of the earth together, if they all had preached the same doctrine, the Bible. The nations whose institutions are freest and most substantial, and in which the greatest amount of individual comfort and happiness is experienced, are Protestant; but how much greater and more substantial would these institutions be, and the happiness how much more heavenly, and the glory how much brighter it would shine, if produced from the great source of unity and love. The intellect of the world is Protestant, and if it was all used by the "one spirit" and the one mind, which is the "mind of Christ" and the spirit of unity, what an intellectual power would be manifest to-day. Civil and religious freedom are Protestant, and if they were exercised by the spirit of freedom that Christ taught, viz., "Whomsoever the Son maketh free is free indeed," the freedom would be perfect. The printing-press is Protestant, but if the printing-presses of to-day were all sending forth pure literature, and teaching no other doctrine than that which Christ and the apostles taught, the good could not be estimated. But on the other hand, the devil is using the press as a great sow-sack in his hands, from which to spread division and discord. Protestants may boast of all these things which go to make up what men call the glories of the nineteenth century, the great era of progress and enlightenment, which is all right and true. But if Protestants, after they had shaken off the shackles that had bound them down so long in papal superstition and darkness, had taken the New Testament as their creed, and unity and love as their theme, instead of manufacturing so many systems, their glory and power would be a million times greater.

CHAPTER XXVIII.

DISTINGUISHED CHARACTERS IN THE PROTESTANT PERIOD.

IN this chapter will be given short biographical notices of a few of the most noted teachers and Christians of the Protestant age. Since the establishment of the Reformation the number of eminent leaders of religious thought has greatly increased. But a few, however, will be taken up in this chapter.

WILLIAM TYNDALE was born in Gloucestershire, England, about 1484. He was a student first at Oxford and afterward at Cambridge. He began his work of translation of the New Testament at London, but the priests of Rome finding out his sympathy with the Reformation by his bold speeches, he was compelled to flee, and located in Hamburg, where he continued for one year. The first ten pages of his New Testament were printed at Cologne, and in 1525, at Worms, two editions were published without his name. These were the first English printed copies of the New Testament. In spite of the great opposition by the clergy, people were anxious to procure a copy of it. Tyndale suffered great abuse and opposition by such men as Sir Thomas More, who wrote seven books against him The fifth edition of his New Testament was published in 1530, and in 1534 a revised edition came out with his signature. He also translated the first five books of the Bible. After the first issue of his New Testament, many efforts were made by the English government to arrest him, which at last succeeded in having him taken at Antwerp, where he was imprisoned for more than a year, and then executed, by strangling and burning, at Vilvoorden, Oct 6, 1536.

The common English Testament was based largely on Tyndale's translation. His translation of the New Testament was the true primary version. The versions that followed were either substantially reproductions of Tyndale's translation in its final shape, or revisions of versions that had been themselves almost entirely based on it. Three successive stages may be recognized in this continuous work of authoritative revision: first, the publication of the *Great Bible* of 1539-41, in the reign of Henry VIII.; next, the publication of the *Bishops' Bible* of 1568 and 1572, in the

WILLIAM TYNDALE.

reign of Elizabeth; and lastly, the publication of *King James's Bible* of 1611, in the reign of James I. Besides these there was the *Geneva Bible,* of 1560, itself founded on Tyndale's translation; which, though not put forth by authority, was widely circulated, and largely used by King James's Translators. Thus the form in which the English New Testament has now been read for 289 years was the result of various revisions made between 1525 and 1611, and all based largely on Tyndale's two editions published at Worms.

JOHN ROGERS was a zealous English preacher who suffered martyrdom at Smithfield in 1555, in the persecuting reign of Mary.

THOMAS CRANMER, archbishop of Canterbury, was a great friend of King Henry VIII. He aided the king in obtaining his divorce. After the king turned Protestant he also drifted in that way. The king found in Cranmer a pliable tool. Cranmer was active in having the Bible translated, and became a strong publisher of the truth. The dying Edward VI. won him over to signing the paper that was to make Lady Jane Grey queen instead of Mary. He was condemned for treason, then retried as a heretic. From Oxford jail he saw Latimer and Ridley die at the stake. Before his execution he wrote several recantations, but when he found that he must burn, he took back all these, declaring that when he came to the fire the hand that had written them should first be burned. Accordingly he went to the stake cheerfully, and thrusting his right hand into the flame, kept it there, saying, "This hand hath offended—this unworthy hand."

HUGH LATIMER, bishop of Worcester, for his zeal in

THREE ENGLISH REFORMERS AND MARTYRS.

the Protestant cause was burned at Oxford, in 1555.

NICHOLAS RIDLEY, bishop of London, was burned at the same time with Latimer and for the same cause.

OLIVER CROMWELL, protector of the Commonwealth of England, greatly favored the cause of the dissenters in that country, and promoted the faithful preaching of the gospel. Died in 1658.

JAMES USHER, archbishop of Armagh, in Ireland, was a prelate of distinguished learning and religious principles, author of "Annals of the Old Testament." Died in 1655.

ISAAC WATTS was the author of several treatises on philosophical subjects, but he is still better known for his sermons and his metrical version of the Psalms. Died in 1748.

PHILIP DODDRIDGE was an English dissenter distinguished as a theological instructor, and for several valuable works, among which were his "Course of Lectures," and "The Family Expositor," and "The Rise and Progress of Religion in the Soul." He died in 1751.

TIMOTHY DWIGHT, a well-known American theologian and educator, was born in 1752, at Northampton, Massachusetts, and was a grandson of Jonathan Edwards. He was a student of Yale College, was a chaplain in the American army during the Revolution, and later was settled as a minister at Greenfield, Connecticut, where he also conducted an academy with great success. In 1795 he became president of Yale College. He died in 1817. His grandson Timothy Dwight was a member of the American Committee for the revision of the English version of the Bible,

DR CHARLES CULLIS.

BARTHOLOMEW ZIEGENBALG was the first Protestant missionary to India. He was sent out by Frederick IV., king of Denmark, in 1706; and died at Tranquebar, in 1719. He was indefatigible and successful in his labors.

CHRISTIAN F. SCHWARTZ was a most eminent and devoted missionary to India. He entered the field of his labors in 1750, under the government of Denmark, and labored at Tanjore and other stations in its vicinity until his death in 1798. It is said that he reckoned two thousand persons converted through his instrumentality.

J. T. VANDERKEMP was missionary to South Africa. He labored with success among the Kafirs and Hottentots.

HENRY MARTYN was an English missionary to Hindustan and Persia. He engaged in the work of evangelizing the heathen with the ardor and zeal of an apostle, but in 1812 he sunk under the severity of his labors and the destructive influence of the climate. He lived, however, to complete a translation of the New Testament and the Psalms into the Persian language.

HESTER ANN ROGERS, who lived in England during the latter half of the eighteenth century, presented one of the holiest lives in history. It demonstrates in the most striking manner how one can not serve two masters, and that it is possible to attain to that perfection in holiness that is set forth in the New Testament.

DR. CHARLES CULLIS was born in Boston, Massachusetts, March 7, 1833. "Have faith in God" is his

Yours truly
C. H. Spurgeon

life-motto   Some of the great fruits of his faith were
the building of the Consumptive Home, Children's
Home, Spinal Home, Faith Cure at Boston, and other
institutions of importance.   He commenced this great
work on a small scale, with no capital, only the great
confidence he had in God verifying his promise,
"What things soever ye desire when ye pray, believe
that ye receive them, and ye shall have them."   With
the blessing of God the work rapidly enlarged until his
work is known even to the uttermost parts of the earth.

C. H. SPURGEON was born in Essex, England, June
19, 1834.   His education was somewhat limited, but
his natural abilities were great.   He was a member of
the Baptist denomination.   When only eighteen he
became the pastor of a Baptist congregation at Water-
beach, and the small congregation was soon doubled.
He went to London in 1850, his church building there
being twice enlarged to accommodate the crowds that
flocked to hear him, until in 1861 the great "Tabernacle," seating 6,000, was built for him.   At one service
in the Crystal Palace he preached to an audience of
24,000.   His sermons were issued in weekly numbers
and translated into many languages.   He preached
without writing his sermons, which were taken down
by shorthand as they were delivered, and carefully
revised by himself.   The weekly circulation averaged
30,000, but that of particular sermons was much
larger.   His publications reached nearly 100 volumes.
Besides preaching he has conducted a training-school
for ministers, an orphanage and almshouse, and built
thirty-six chapels in London.   He died at **Mentone**,
France, Jan. 31, 1892.

ALFRED COOKMAN was born about 1828, and at the age of ten was converted, and shortly after that experienced the great work of sanctification. He dedicated himself to God, surrendered all that was doubtful, and accepted Christ as a Savior from all sin, and realized the witness of the Spirit to his entire sanctification. It is stated that Bishop Foster said that of all men he had ever known he was the most sacred. An account of his premature death may be interesting to the reader. Upon his dying bed he confessed that he had known for years what it was to be washed in the blood of the Lamb. When he realized that the moment of his death was near at hand he called his wife and friends to his bedside and said to his wife, "My dear, if the Lord should take me away, can you then say, 'Lord, thy will be done'?" In reply she said, "Oh, but how can I live without thee?" He replied, "Jesus will be all to thee. He has been with us always, and he will not forsake thee now. The Bible is full of precious promises for the widow and orphans. Live by faith every moment, and when thy earthly pilgrimage is done, I will be the first to meet thee at the pearly gates." Then his aged mother kissed him for the last time. "Mother," said he, "besides Jesus, I owe it all to you. Your holy influence, your godly example, and your wise counsels have made me the Christian and minister that I am." To his brother he said, "I am not afraid to die. Death is the gate to endless glory; I am washed in the blood of the Lamb." While dying he often repeated, "Oh, I am so sweetly washed in the blood of the Lamb" He died Nov. 13. 1871.

D. L. MOODY was born at Northfield, Massachusetts,
Feb. 5, 1837. He became an earnest Christian worker
in early life. Being bold and of great enthusiasm and
energy, he made his mark wherever he went in the
Christian cause. Wishing to be independent, and
mark out a new path for himself, he went to Chicago.
Here he was successful in whatever he set himself to.
He was very successful in hunting up the ragged children of Chicago, and winning them to the Sunday-
school and to a good life. A deserted school-building
was hired for a Sunday-school, which Moody built into
a great mission. In 1861, at the recruiting camp near
Chicago he carried on a great revival among the soldiers. Soon a call came from the field in the interest
of the sick and wounded. Back and forth between
Chicago and the various camps and battle-fields Moody
toiled and traveled; he was on the field after the battles of Shiloh and Murfreesboro, and was one of the
first to enter Richmond. Moody was one of the
world's greatest evangelists, and his success as a revivalist has been seldom equaled. His charge in Chicago
as pastor of a congregation there could not keep him
from carrying on those great revivals in all parts of
the country, which were so successful and which will
always hold his name in remembrance. His trips to
England in 1870 and in 1883 in company with Ira D.
Sankey were as successful as his labors had been in
America. Many other fields of labor and institutions
in which he was engaged during his life might be
mentioned. At the present writing this great man's
voice has been but recently hushed, he having died
Dec. 22, 1899. Several lines of work built up by him
are to be continued in his honor.

DWIGHT L. MOODY.

T. De Witt Talmage, the world's most popular preacher, lecturer, and author, was born in Bound Brook, N. J., Jan. 7, 1832. He graduated at the New York University, and at the New Brunswick Theological Seminary. As a Presbyterian he held positions as pastor in several different cities, and in the time of the war was chaplain of a Pennsylvania regiment. Beginning with 1869, he was for over twenty years pastor of the Central Presbyterian Church of Brooklyn, N. Y., during which time his church building burned three times. He is at present a pastor in Washington, D. C. He is a speaker of great expression, and he always draws and interests great audiences as a preacher or lecturer. His lectures are delivered with dramatic elocution and spiced richly with anecdotes. He is plain and outspoken against error. His sermons are said to be published weekly in 600 journals, and translated into five languages.

CHAPTER XXIX.

DAWN OF THE FOURTH PERIOD.

The holiness reformations from the close of the Civil war in the United States of America to A. D. 1880 were only rays of light from the great source of all light, signaling the approaching time predicted by the prophet when he said, "At evening time it shall be light." Holiness associations were being formed in all parts of the country, and the subject of holiness

T. De Witt Talmage

was sharply discussed in most every denomination.
But on account of a spirit of opposition against holiness, manifested by many in the denomination, it was
thought best to organize into associations where all
those that desired the benefits of holiness could belong
and yet be members of their respective denominations.
No one could become a member of one of these associations unless he was a member of good standing in
some denomination.   The ministers, a great many of
them, seemed to think that holiness, or sanctification,
was a Bible doctrine, but that it would not do to teach
it in the denomination.

A great many ministers professed sanctification and
belonged to the association but. were not allowed to
preach the doctrine to the congregations of which they
were pastors.

An incident that came under the writer's observation
about twenty years ago, in a yearly meeting held in
Auglaize county, Ohio, by the United Brethren in
Christ will. illustrate the general spirit.   On Sunday
morning after the principal discourse was over liberty
was given to any who desired to testify.   During the
testimonies an old sister arose and testified that she
was "both justified and sanctified."   Just then one of
the leading elders arose and beckoning with his hand,
commanded her to be seated, and also said that he
wanted to hear no more of that kind of stuff.   There
were several of the United Brethren ministers at that
meeting that professed sanctification, but because some
others opposed it, contrary to the word of God, they
were compelled to keep quiet.   This is only a sample of
the spirit that prevailed everywhere at that time.   The

denominations claimed to be the church of Jesus Christ. Jesus prayed that his disciples might be sanctified, but the preachers said it would not do to preach it. The apostle said, "This is the will of God, even your sanctification"; but the big preacher said, when one of his congregation claimed sanctification, "Stop that, sit down there, we do not want to hear such stuff as that." But notwithstanding all this opposition many accepted the doctrine and professed a holy and sanctified life. No one supposed, however, during this period of time that he could live a holy life except he belonged to or was identified with some religious denomination.

PERIOD IV.

CHAPTER XXX.

THE CHURCH OUTSIDE OF DENOMINATIONS.

IN this work the reader has seen first the church in the morning of the Christian era, or First Period, embracing the time from Christ to A. D. 270. During this time the church was a unit and Christ was the head. Next was presented a view of the church in the middle or dark ages of the Christian era, or Second Period, which embraced the time from A. D. 270 to 1530. During this period none were considered Christians except those that were subject to the pope; all others were classed as heretics, and adjudged worthy of death. In the Third Period the church in its Protestant, or cloudy age, has been shown, embracing the time from A. D. 1530 to 1880, during which the church was out from under the supremacy of the pope. But instead of coming out clear, and being a unit for God, and holding to the one name, and the one body, they began to divide and subdivide, and took upon themselves many names. This was, as has already been noticed, a general reformation; not only in religion, but in everything else.

The peculiar difference between the Roman Catholic age and the Protestant age in reference to the idea of church relationship was in this: that every one in the Catholic age was compelled to be a Catholic or suffer death or perpetual imprisonment; while in the Protestant age toleration prevailed, and a man could profess or not, as he felt disposed. But if he professed, it was supposed that he could not be a Christian unless he was identified with some Protestant denomination, and the prevailing and universal thought was that these different denominations constituted the church of God, not perceiving the language of the apostle: "For as the body is one, and hath many members, and all the members of that one body being many, are one body · so also is Christ. For by one Spirit are we all baptized into one body, whether we be Jews or Gentiles, whether we be bond or free; and have been all made to drink into one Spirit"; and again, "That there should be no schism in the body; but that the members should have the same care one for another. And whether one member suffer, all the members suffer with it; or one member be honored, all the members rejoice with it." To the Ephesians he also says, "There is one body, and one Spirit, even as ye are called in one hope of your calling; one Lord, one faith, one baptism, one God and Father of all, who is above all, and through all, and in you all." To fulfill and obey these scriptures would be impossible under the different creeds and isms of Protestantism.

In this Fourth Period it remains to notice the church coming out of these divisions and isms into the one body, which is the one church, "the body of Christ," which is his church. In Chapter xxix. it was seen that there was in the latter part of the Protestant period a reformation in holiness, which only indicated the approach of the Evening Light, or Fourth Period of church history, which embraces the gathering of God's people into *the one church.*

D. S. Warner, who was an active and energetic worker in those Holiness Associations at that time, and also a member of the so-called Church of God, or Winebrennerian sect, began to see the corruption of the different denominations, and that division of God's people into sects was detrimental to spirituality and contrary to the word of God; and that true Bible holiness would lead God's children into the unity of the Spirit, and one body.

In the year 1879 he was editor of the holiness department of a paper called *The Herald of Gospel Freedom.* The following quotation from that paper will give an idea of what then existed in his heart against denominational division. "We have lived," says he, "to see the false notion exploded, that the human family have so far improved that there is no more need of persecution. The fact is the devil has not reformed, nor unholiness ceased to hate holiness. Darkness and light are the same antipodes they ever have been, and the preacher or church that elicits no persecution simply works no harm to the devil's kingdom. We see in the October number of *The Herald of Purity,* a precious holiness monthly published at Moundsville, W. Va., that the editor of that magazine, J. P. Thatcher, has had his character arrested in his conference, and his case is referred to an investigating committee. The real cause of this is, we understand, his devotion to the cause of holiness. He will doubtless follow T. K. Doty and others who have gone out of the M. E. synagogue with Christ bearing his reproach." When the foregoing was written,

D. S. Warner had not yet openly declared himself free from sectism, but in the latter part of 1880 he, with several others, denounced the Eldership and declared themselves outside and clear from all straps and bands of men, and all man-made religion. About this time he changed the name of his paper to *The Gospel Trumpet.* (See account of *The Gospel Trumpet.*) From this time he began to preach and write boldly against sect names and denominational partyism, and to set forth the true church of God, by preaching holiness and purity of heart, and that we can attain to this only through sanctification, a second definite work of grace, subsequent to regeneration; and that instead of joining some denomination, God's children at conversion already belonged to his church, and all these denominational names were unscriptural, and manufactured by men.

In *The Gospel Trumpet* of 1881 he again makes mention of J. P. Thatcher, of Moundsville, W. Va., to the effect that he was no little surprised to receive a tract from Thatcher, announcing the formation of a new sect by him in that place Jan. 30, called the "Evangelistic Holiness Church." He quotes from this tract the following: "Since the great awakening on the subject of entire sanctification in the past score of years, conscientious, clear-headed, devoted persons have had fears that the various church organizations extant were so fossilized, so unscripturally formed and churchly, that the leaven of holiness would be so restrained and arrested in its working as to necessitate an organization that would be an improvement upon all others." "The above description of existing

sects," says Warner, "we think is about correct, but
instead of furnishing an excuse for another, methinks
it ought to be enough to lead us to the conclusion that
sect-building is a very poor business, and ought to be
abandoned entirely." "Is it not safe to abide in the
one church into which God puts every soul at conversion, use the name 'the mouth of the Lord' has given
her, and accept the word of God alone for our discipline?" "Should we not respect the counsel of J.
Wesley? He says, 'There are already too many sects
and parties in the family of God. Would to God the
time would come that we would abandon all party
names and divisions and sit meekly at the feet of Jesus
to learn his will and imbibe his loving Spirit."

D. S. Warner, with a few others, at this time began
to cry out mightily against sectism, proving by the
Word that it was wrong, and that the sects constituted
spiritual Babylon, and exhorting God's people to come
out of her, that ye partake not of her plagues. This
was a wonderful stroke, like a great thunderbolt from
heaven upon the sectarian world. The devil and all
sectism became stirred with prejudice, and moved
with envy against the few that were preaching this
new and strange doctrine; though it was as old as the
Bible, it was strange to the people that were blinded by
sectish darkness. They were persecuted, tried, afflicted,
and tormented; but God's grace was sufficient and enabled them to stand up and declare the whole truth.
They were advertised in the secular and religious
papers of the country as come-outers and a very low
set going about tearing down churches and turning the
world upside down, but notwithstanding this they in-

creased with zeal and energy, and great grace was upon them. Numbers increased and men and women consecrated their lives, means, time, and talent to the work. Evangelistic companies were formed, going from place to place, suffering deprivement and persecution to preach and declare the gospel. Indiana, Ohio, and Michigan were the first fields of labor for these reformers. During the first six years Warner had been preaching in this way, only a very few had accepted his teaching. There was a congregation of about eighty at Beaver Dam, Indiana. But during the winter of 1886 the work began to move on more encouragingly. Revival meetings were held in different parts of Indiana, Ohio, and Michigan, and congregations of saints were established in different localities in these states. From these different congregations went forth ministers and helpers in the gospel work to all parts of the Union and part of Canada, until in a very short time the number of believers increased to thousands. During the summer seasons grove and camp-meetings were held in different localities and largely attended. The oldest established camp-grounds were at Jerry City, Ohio; Bangor, Michigan; and Beaver Dam and Deerfield, Indiana. Since that time several others have been established and carried on with great success. The wonderful power of God was manifested in these camp-meetings, in the saving of souls from sin, sanctifying believers, and also in healing the sick, opening the eyes of the blind, and in many other miraculous ways.

In the latter part of the year 1892 the missionary spirit began to loom up in the hearts of some of the

ministers, and in January, 1893 two brethren set sail
for England, and soon after this a number of others
went to England and Germany, and this truth was
established in the hearts of some across the Atlantic.
G. Tufts, Jr., also set sail for India July 10, 1897, to
carry the liberalities of the Lord's people in America
to the starving in dark India, to which reference will
be made again in another place.   Missions are also
being opened up in different cities of the United States,
with no little success.

CHAPTER XXXI.

PERSECUTION AND SOME OF ITS CAUSES.

DURING every reformation in the Christian era
there has been more or less persecution. There are
different reasons why persecution comes upon those
that profess to be Christians. The apostle said, "Yea,
and all that will live godly in Christ Jesus shall suffer
persecution."   But persecution has not been confined
to those that were just strictly godly and in perfect
harmony with the word of God.   Fanaticism and
crooked living have often been the cause of persecution. Often perverted people console themselves with
the thought that they are right because they are persecuted. The promise of the blessing is to those that
are right. Jesus says, "Blessed are they which are
persecuted for righteousness' sake."   "Blessed are ye
when men shall revile you, and persecute you, and

shall say all manner of evil against you falsely, for my sake." If one is in the fault and is persecuted, there is no blessing for that.

Fanaticism, one of the greatest causes for persecution, is often found in company with zealous holiness work. The more life and vigor there is, the greater the devil's efforts to bring in fanaticism. Fanaticism knows no bounds. When zealous children of God see by the Word that it is their duty to dress plain, the devil pushes them over the mark, and they become slovenly and slouchy in their appearance—this is fanaticism. Any extreme in obeying and fulfilling the scripture is fanaticism. Fanaticism is always intensely in earnest. But this is not saying that one can not be in earnest and be in harmony with God. God loves a zealous and earnest people, but he wants them to keep in the bounds of decency and order. Paul says that charity "doth not behave itself unseemly." Fanaticism is stone-blind to discouragement, but it has no judgment to discern the bounds that God has set for his work. We believe it safe to say that fanaticism is one of the counterfeits of reformation. It runs parallel with reformation, but is not part of it. The world sometimes mistakes the one for the other. From this fact great persecution sometimes is brought upon the church. The history of all holiness reformations is full of importance on this line. This reformation has not been free from persecution, neither has it been free from the effects of fanaticism. Though at present fanaticism has been mostly exposed and quelled, yet it is liable to break out in a new form. Let the saints watch and pray.

A few cases of persecution in this reformation are worthy of mention. Persecution in this age does not seem to be as bad as it was in the sixteenth and seventeenth centuries, but in spirit it is just as bad. The law of the land is the only thing that holds it in restraint. The persecuting spirit of Catholicism only lies dormant because of restraint, and the same spirit in the breasts of many Protestants and ungodly persons is only kept in check by the ruling power. Rome is in constant conspiracy against the rights and liberties of men, all over the world. Liberty of conscience is declared by all the popes and councils of Rome to be a most Godless, unholy, and diabolical thing, which every good Catholic must abhor and destroy, at any cost. They declare that independence is an impiety and a revolt against God, and that the pope alone can know and say what man must believe and do; and claim the right to inflict the penalty of death upon those who differ in faith from the pope. They also hold that all government must rest upon the foundation of the Catholic faith, with the pope alone as the legitimate and infallible source and interpreter of the law. If Catholics ever gain a sufficient majority to hold the ruling power, religious freedom is at an end. The present pope, Leo XIII., requires the doctrine of St. Thomas to be taught in all their colleges all over the world, which is this: "Though heretics must not be tolerated because they deserve it, we must bear with them, till, by a second admonition, they may be brought back to the faith of the church. But those who after a second admonition, remain obstinate in their errors, must not only be excommunicated, but

they must be delivered to the secular power to be ex-
terminated.'' Pope Gregory VII. decided it was no
murder to kill excommunicated persons.   This rule
was incorporated in the Canon Law.   During the revision of the code, which took place in the sixteenth
century, and which produced a whole volume of cor-
rections, the passage was allowed to stand.   It appears
in every reprint of the *Corpus Juris*.   It has been for
over 700 years, and continues to be, part of the ecclesiastical law.   These bloody and anti-social laws were
written on the banners of the Roman Catholics when
slaughtering 100,000 Waldenses in the mountains of
Piedmont, and more than 50,000 defenseless men,
women, and children in the city of Bezieres.   It was
under the inspiration of those diabolical laws of Rome
that 75,000 Protestants were massacred the night and
following weeks of St. Bartholomew.   It was to obey
those bloody laws that Louis XIV. revoked the Edict
of Nantes, caused the death of half a million of men,
women, and children, who perished in all the highways
of France, and caused twice that number to die in the
land of exile, where they had found refuge.   Those
anti-social laws to-day are written on her banners with
the blood of ten millions of martyrs.

The persecutions of the present reformation have
not been to the stake and gibbet, as in former times,
but principally by slander, false-accusing, disturbing
worship and public meetings, by hallooing, cursing,
and swearing, and by throwing eggs, apples, and even
stones into congregations assembled for worship.
About the year 1886 or 7 while the saints near Rising
Sun, Ohio, were assembled in the home of Brother

Roush, a masked mob of several men assaulted them.
It being night the mob pushed the door open, and two
of them stepped in and took hold of the minister
(D. S. Warner) and attempted to take him out. When
they reached the door he braced himself against the
sides of the door, and also two of his company holding
on to him, the mob was prevented from succeeding in
their effort. While they were struggling to force him
through the door some of the congregation struck one
of the mob on the head with a cane, knocking him
down. The mob determined not to leave one of their
number a prisoner, and they grabbed up the unlucky
man and bore him away; so ended the riot. The
saints went on with their worship, singing and praising
God. The next morning revealed the fact that the
mob had prepared themselves with whips, and a preparation to besmear and whip the victim, should they
have succeeded in getting him out.

About this time, or it may have been a year earlier,
the church at Beaver Dam, Indiana, while assembled
in a schoolhouse for worship, were mobbed; the windows were broken in with clubs; and bottles, eggs,
and clubs were hurled into the crowd of innocent
women, children, and worshipers of God. During
the whole time of the mobbing they continued to sing
and shout the praises of God, and God protected them
from receiving a single hurt.

The church at New Pittsburg, Indiana, also suffered
great persecution about the year 1888 and later on,
being assaulted at different times with eggs, stones,
clods, and clubs. The house of worship was stoned a.
different times, the windows and doors were crushed

in, shots were fired into it, and in many ways it was
defaced. Injuries were also inflicted upon the property and persons of the saints; such as destroying
fruit-trees, throwing down fences, waylaying some in
the dark, knocking them down and then running, and
many other things. Such was the condition of things
until the authorities of Randolph county were able to
arrest the guilty parties and inflict upon them the
penalty due them according to the law of that state.
Judge Monks, a notable judge of that county at that
time, is understood not to have been a professor of
religion; yet his name should be commemorated for
the hand of justice shown to the cause of Christ. The
cause also suffered much in Missouri and Kansas by
annoying disturbances similar to the foregoing.

In the year 1891 as the truth began to be preached
in the southern states it also met with some opposition. As the saints were assembled at Beach Springs
schoolhouse in Mississippi, while the minister was
preaching the gospel, brick and clubs came crashing
through the window, all doubtless hurled in wrath at
the speaker. Nearly half of the sash was broken in,
and the glass flew all over the house. The speaker
stood about seven feet from the window, and nearly
opposite, but the hand of God protected him from
serious harm. At Spring Hill, in the same state, was
another scene of persecution, which it might be of interest to note. D. S. Warner, B. E. Warren, and
others were conducting meetings in this neighborhood
in the month of February, 1891. We will give an
extract from a report of that meeting published in the
Gospel Trumpet, March 15, 1891. "The first night

of meeting three souls came to the altar; two consecrated for entire sanctification, and one was gloriously
pardoned. The next night, the fierce powers of hell
being fully awakened from their brief slumber occasioned by our absence, a couple of lead balls, called
buckshot, were thrown through the open window, by
means of a rubber concern that we are told is even
dangerous to life. These wicked wretches also threw
stones with slings at some of God's saints that night
on their way home, even regardless of women and
children in the crowd. One woman was also hit.
That was a little the lowest and most cowardly work
we have ever yet met with. The next day four of
Satan's chief servants rode out in four directions, five
and seven miles, to enlist by his lies and slanders such
as were base enough to join in a great mob to assault
us that night. During the day we learned all about
the movement, and at a meeting at a brother's house
we recalled the meeting for the night, seeing no possible chance of doing good. . . . There being no
meeting at which the mob could assault us, they beset
the house where we stayed until about twelve o'clock
at night. They reported their number between
seventy-five and one hundred. They were armed with
guns and revolvers. . . . They state that their object
was only to give us orders to leave the country the
next day. A brave army gathered from several miles
around, about a hundred strong, to tell a few little
children of God to leave the next day! The mob hung
about until about midnight clamoring for us to come
out, stating they would not hurt us, etc. But when
men are low down enough to fling buckshot into a con-

gregation, and rocks into a promiscuous crowd, you might as well tell us that wolves and hyenas do not care for fresh meat, as to say that such did not want to hurt us. Hence our absence was doubtless the best thing to avoid trouble. Oh, may God show mercy to all of that crowd who are in the reach of mercy, that we may meet them at last among the redeemed! After all left the house, not a great way off, they fired off their pieces, which, for a few seconds, mimicked the din of war."—*Warner.* As late as the year 1898, a camp-meeting at Hartsells, Alabama was dispersed and the ministers driven out of the country by the same spirit of mob.

Just think! in the nineteenth century, and in this beautiful country of ours, claiming to be the land of the free! a country for which our forefathers bled and died that we might have free speech, and worship God according to the dictates of our conscience—now disgraced with such accounts as the above, which have not been exaggerated!

CHAPTER XXXII.

BIOGRAPHICAL SKETCHES OF A FEW OF THE OLDEST AND MOST EARNEST WORKERS OF THIS PERIOD.

D. S. WARNER.

D. S. WARNER was born in Bristol, Wayne County, Ohio. When but a young man he began the preaching

of the gospel of Christ. He was a member of the so-
called Church of God, or Winebrennerians, until the
year 1880, when, being fully convicted of the corruption of sectism, he began to cry out mightily against it,
and leaving the Eldership of that sect he stood clear
from all sects, and took the word of God as his only
creed. The radical stand he took in defense of the
pure gospel, was the occasion of much bitter persecution. Before this he was in good standing with many
editors and sectarian holiness workers, but because of
his decided stand for the truth, he was denounced in
their papers, set at naught by the ministry, and rejected by his former friends. Many were the severe
fiery trials of his life, through which he had to pass in
defense of the truth, but God crowned him with
success.

His education was somewhat limited, but he had
what was termed a common-school education, and
taught a few terms of district school. He was very
industrious and energetic in whatever he undertook
to do. He was converted when about twenty-two
years of age. A few weeks later he joined the Union
army as a substitute, to save his brother from going,
who was a man of a family and had been drafted.
After serving a short term for his country, he returned
home and entered into the ministerial work, in which
capacity he labored faithfully with tongue and pen
until his death. His pen was always at work, the
fruit of which was the production of several books and
tracts. "Bible Proofs of the Second Work of Grace,"
"Poems of Grace and Truth," and "Salvation, Present, Perfect, Now or Never" were his chief produc-

tions. His editorial work will be noticed more particularly in another chapter. He was among the first in
the nineteenth century to preach full salvation outside
of sectism. Being fluent in speech and having a good
understanding of the scriptures, by the aid of the Holy
Spirit, he was enabled to do much effective work for
the Master, and to give spiritual food to multitudes of
starving souls. Although he possessed a frail body all
his life, few men put in more hours for the Lord than
he did during his years of ministerial labor. Thursday, Dec. 12, 1895 he passed into eternity after an ill-
ness of only a few days. Funeral services were held in
Michigan at the Grand Junction camp-ground, Sunday, Dec. 15, conducted by Wm G. Schell. See
Chapters xxx. and xxxiii.

MOTHER SMITH.

Mother Sarah Smith, the oldest of the workers and
ministers of this reformation, was born Sept 20, 1822,
near Manchester, Ohio. She has been a very energetic
and faithful servant of Christ, and enabled by her exemplary life and words of comfort and admonition to
lead many souls to the cross of Christ, where they have
found deliverance from sin, and sweet peace. This
dear old mother, who is yet living, has presented us
with a written account of her Christian experience
with some other facts, which is here inserted.

Autobiography.

I was catechized and taken into the Lutheran sect at
the age of fourteen, without the experience of salvation. I had no knowledge of what it was to pray, because the preacher did all the praying himself. When

God saved me and I began to let my light shine by
praying and testifying to what Jesus had done for me,
I became a reproach to the Lutherans, and I could no
longer be a member with them.   Praise God! he had
something better in store for me.   On Friday, in
March, 1842, the Lord permitted a terrible wind-storm
to sweep through the country, which caused me for the
first time in my life to see myself a sinner in the sight
of God.   I had never heard a sermon preached on justification.   While seeking for my conversion I had a
few rings on my fingers, and the first impression upon
my mind was that in order to obtain peace to my soul
I must take those rings from my fingers, and never
put them on again.   As I opened the stove-door to
throw them into the fire, the devil stayed my hand,
supposing to persuade me to put them on again: but
the devil always made a fool of himself in my case—
they never went on again.   I continued to offer myself
to the Lord until the following Monday evening at
nine o'clock the Lord for Christ's sake pardoned all
my sins.   Oh, what peace and joy filled my soul! it
was unspeakable and full of glory.   Truly the first
verse of the fifth chapter of Romans, and also Jno.
10:9, were fulfilled in my conversion.   Christ says, "I
am the door; by me if any man enter in, he shall be
saved."   When I received the Spirit that bore witness with my spirit, I became his child.

I was not conscious then that God had taken me
into his church.   The church question had always
been a mystery to me.   I could not understand it; it
was hid away under the rubbish of sectism.   I had
been taught that the denominations were the church.

But why God's people should be so divided, I would
often wonder. As far as I knew my heart, I never had
a party, or sect, spirit; for I was at home with God's
people wherever I met them. I lived to all the light
I had. But after I had been saved from my sins, and
knew that I was a child of God, I discovered an element
in me that was warring against the Christ nature;
"for when I would do good, evil was present." I was
very timid and bashful, had a man-fearing spirit, and
the devil tried every possible way, by persecution and
by other means, to discourage me, but I prayed much
in secret, and oh, how I longed to get rid of that inward foe—such a hungering for a pure heart! But for
the lack of proper teaching I was compelled to struggle on for seventeen years, during which time I kept
my justification, and walked in all the light that I
had, taking the Bible for my guide. I found in 1
Jno. 4:18 that the apostle says, "Perfect love casteth
out fear," which caused me to seek for that perfect
love. Indeed God was leading me in a mysterious
way; for I had not in all these seventeen years heard a
single sermon preached on sanctification. I did not
know that I could have the old man crucified and the
cause of sin removed from my heart; but I wanted
perfected love. In a woods near by I erected an altar
of prayer, where I daily went and besought the Lord
for perfect love. For three months I attended this
altar daily, pleading and dying before the Lord, until
at last I thought I could stand it no longer, and that
I could not live without it. Then the devil tempted
me and tried to make me believe that I was losing
what I had: but I said, "How can this be when I am

seeking for perfect love?" And I said, "Lord, I have come for the last time, and I must feel better or die." I had given up all my friends, and all this world, and now I must have it. Praise God! I looked up to heaven and said, "Lord, what more can I do than I have done?" Then the Lord talked with me, and I could say Yes to everything, until the Lord said, "Will you work for me?" Then the devil said, "If you promise to do that, you know your husband will not let you go." Ah, there was a struggle between life and death; between heaven and hell; but when I got victory over the devil I said, "Yes, Lord." Praise God! I said it, and I felt it, and I meant it from the depths of my soul. And then and there in that woods in the month of August, 1859, the Lord did the work for me. The old man was crucified and the works of the devil cast out, and the baptism of the Holy Ghost was upon me, and I was filled with the power of God. I realized then what perfect love meant. All fear and doubts were taken away, and what boldness! I was made fearless of men and devils.

The Holy Spirit led me in a mysterious way. I began to understand that when I was born of the Spirit, I was born into the church of God, of which Christ is the head; and I was satisfied. But the sect preachers were not satisfied. The Evangelical preacher, without my knowledge, put my name on his class-book. They would say, "We must have a home"; but it was a poor home for me. It made no difference to me where I labored, but the preachers got jealous. A Methodist Episcopal preacher offered to see that I got license to preach, and a circuit, if

I would join that church. I said I did not want to be
bound. I wanted to be free to go where God wanted
me. God kept me from joining any conference, and
showed me step by step that these denominations were
not the church that Christ built. Finally the holiness people of that country joined themselves together
into a Holiness Association. They were taken in
from different denominations. I thought that was
bringing God's holy people together into one body,
and so I also joined the association. No one was
allowed to join the association except those that belonged to some denomination. It was not long until
God began to show me that it was not God's will for
us to belong to a sect. My Bible said, "Be not unequally yoked together with unbelievers"; but there
we were yoked up with those who were unbelievers in
holiness. About this time God began to show me the
ungodliness of secret societies. The Methodist Episcopal sect opened their door wide enough to let in
Free Masons and Odd Fellows by the wholesale, and it
was not long until the Evangelicals opened their door
for them. I heard one of their preachers say, "If we
do not take in secret-society men, they will all join
the Methodists." The United Brethren stood against
this evil the longest, but they finally came to the same
conclusion, and opened their door also to secrecy. It
was not long then until nine out of ten of their
preachers belonged to secret societies. I think then
is when God went out and the sects died a spiritual
death, and to-day they are filled with an Antichrist
spirit.

After joining the Holiness Association we were

banded together into bands. We had about thirty members at Jerry City, Ohio, that professed sanctification, and I was acknowledged as their leader. I felt my inability, but I searched the scriptures and asked God for help. I would read where Christ said, "I am the door: by me if any man enter in, he shall be saved"; also the words of Acts 2:47—"And the Lord added to the church daily such as should be saved." But the mists of Babylon had not all cleared away yet, and I could not see clearly; yet God led me in a mysterious way. A brother handed me a Gospel Trumpet, desiring me to read an article headed "The One Church," and he asked me after I had read it what I thought of it. I said I would not dare to say a word against it; for that was just what I was looking for. I had expressed myself not long before this in a United Brethren meeting that I did not expect to meet a United Brethren, nor a Methodist, nor an Evangelical in heaven. I said all these names would be left out of heaven. So you see how God was leading me in reference to the one church, and showing me the evils of sectism. He also showed me that I could not give of my means to support such unholy institutions. The word of God taught me, in 2 Cor. 6:14-18, to come out from among them, and be separate, and touch not the unclean thing, and the Lord would be a Father unto me, and I would be his daughter. Then again I read: "Be ye not unequally yoked together with unbelievers." Here I was yoked up with saints and sinners, and my name in a sect, also banded up with the Holiness Association, bound under rules how I should conduct the meetings. I saw that I had no need for such rules as these, as the Holy Spirit was my leader; and so they were thrown to the flames, and we let God lead us, and he was with us in mighty power. By his Holy Spirit and his blessed Word he finally brought me out of all sectism, including the Holiness Association. Then I was perfectly free, and I am yet to-day as free as the birds that fly in the air. Whom the Son makes free is free indeed. Praise God for heavenly freedom in Christ Jesus!

Well, I would like to tell something more about our meetings, and how God led us out. We held our meetings four times a week, and God was truly leading in a mysterious way. I saw a light and would tell the people that there was a light coming, but what it was I could not tell, but I knew it was of God, and if we would reject it we would go into darkness. I saw by the word of God that sectism was spiritual Babylon, and that the ministers who were the shepherds were feeding themselves and not the flock. Ezek. 34; Jer. 51; Rev. 18:2-4. I was always ready and willing, as fast as I could understand, to accept what is Bible. At this time (January, 1882) we had a meeting in Bro. Miller's house at Jerry City, Ohio, which shall never be forgotten. It lasted until three o'clock in the morning; truly God was in our midst in wonderful power. Rev. 19; Jer. 51; and Ezek. 34 were read. That meeting brought me to where I was like Moses when he came to the Red sea. That morning before I closed the meeting I said, "I can lead you no further." The Lord said to me, "Stand still and see the salvation of the Lord." We commenced praying for God to send some one who would be able to lead us further. In a few weeks the Lord answered our prayers by sending dear Bro. D. S. Warner. He by the Spirit and word of God proved to us what Babylon was, and how God's people had been led into this spiritual Babylon, and had been kept until the time came when he would call them out. He proved it by the Word, and the Spirit bore witness to my spirit that he was preaching Bible.

Bro. A. J. Kilpatrick was also sent among us, who set before us the one church, by scriptures too numerous to mention here. He proved to us that Jesus Christ is the door and that when we are converted we come through Jesus Christ into the church before the preacher can have time to open the door of his church and take us in. The meeting had commenced on Monday night, and on Thursday evening as I stepped into the meeting-house the Spirit of God said to me, "Will you do it?" I said, "What, Lord?" And the same question was repeated. I answered again, "What, Lord?" After I had taken my seat the same strange question was repeated again. Then I answered, "Yes, Lord; anything thou wilt have me to do." I did not know at the time what it was the Lord wanted me to do. But as soon as the sermon was over the Lord had me on my feet, in front of the pulpit with both hands raised. I began to exclaim, "It is come! It is come!" "Will you walk in the light, or will you go into darkness?" I also said, "As many as are willing to declare your freedom in Christ Jesus, make it manifest by rising to your feet." Twenty arose. Praise God! That meeting will never be forgotten, neither in this world, nor in the world to

come. Souls were sealed for heaven in that meeting,
and others rejected the light and went into darkness.
Well, God so completely saved me from sectism that I
never for a single moment had a desire to go back. I
was asked how I would let my light shine if I never
went back. I, said I would let it shine by staying
away. I was one among the first to accept this light
on *the one church* clear from sectism.

I first met Bro. Warner in 1877, while he was preaching sanctification to the Winebrennerians, of which
sect he was a member at that time.   As near as I can
remember he commenced preaching the one church
in the evening light in the year 1880   God had his
hand upon this work.   The devil tried to destroy it,
but God protected it   I remember of hearing a Methodist preacher at Jerry City pray for God to scatter
this work to the four winds of the earth. I said that
was the best prayer he ever prayed, and truly since
then it has spread throughout the earth

In 1884 God sent forth the first evangelistic company in this reformation, and he chose me as a mother
in the company. I was old enough to be the mother
of the whole company. There were five of us in all.
D. S. Warner, Barney E. Warren, Frankie Miller,
Nannie Kigar, and myself. This company traveled
together a little over four years, with perfect harmony.
We were all of one heart and one mind, and we saw
eye to eye. They were dearer to me than my own kin
in the flesh, and to-day there is an attachment that
can never be broken   The many precious seasons we
enjoyed together in the Lord were unspeakable and
full of glory. Praise God! We met with much oppo-

sition. The devil did everything possible to overthrow
the work, as he did in the days of Nehemiah. For
"when Sanballat heard that we builded the walls, he
was wroth, and took great indignation, and mocked
the Jews. And he spake before his brethren and
the army of Samaria, and said, What do these feeble
Jews? will they fortify themselves? will they sacrifice? will they make an end in a day? will they
revive the stones out of the heaps of the rubbish
which are burned? Now Tobiah the Ammonite was
by him, and he said, Even that which they build, if a
fox go up, he shall even break down their stone wall."
—Neh. 4:1-3. The work has been going on for twenty
years, and a fox has not broken the wall yet. The
Lord has fought every battle. We traveled over and
visited different parts of ten states, and Canada, held
many meetings, and in every meeting preached the
whole truth—justification, sanctification, one church,
and divine healing of the body. We saw many precious souls saved and brought into this blessed light.
While in our travels we saw the sick healed by the
power of God, devils cast out, the blind eyes opened,
and rain sent or withheld in answer to prayer. God
protected us through mobs and storms, and gave
us complete victory over wicked men and devils,
and in answer to prayer he supplied all our needs.
We never in all our travels took up a collection.
Through our labors God established his church in
Ohio, Indiana, Michigan, Illinois, Iowa, Kansas,
Nebraska, Colorado, and Canada. Dear Bro. Warner
was wonderfully helped in preaching the gospel. He
was very frail in body, yet God always stood by him in

delivering the word. He often would preach from two to three hours. Bro. Warner was a holy man of God; his life was without spot or blame.

I am a living witness to-day for Christ. In 1881 he saved me from tea and coffee. And I have not taken a drop of medicine since 1878. The Lord has healed me at different times and he keeps this body free from pain. To him be all the glory and praise. Amen.

A. B. PALMER.

I was converted in February, 1857, and joined the Methodist Episcopal sect the same year. In 1877 the Lord reclaimed me from a backslidden condition. At that time, at a camp-meeting, I saw for the first time the light on sanctification as a second work of grace which would destroy the inbred sin. A few days after the Lord reclaimed me I made a consecration for entire sanctification, and, to my great delight and satisfaction, received it. Before the Lord sanctified me I believed the Methodist Episcopal denomination was the best there was; and I labored faithfully to promulgate her doctrines; but as soon as I was sanctified I found to my surprise that the sectarian *spirit* was all taken away; yet I remained *in* the sect for want of understanding. I verily believed that human sect organization was necessary. You see I was educated that way.

In January, 1882 Sister Lottie Blackwood told me one day that sectarianism was not right, that she had found a better way, and that some ministers were preaching around Bangor against it, and that many had left the sects and embraced the "evening light." I did not raise any opposition to her, because of the esteem and respect I had for her, but inwardly I felt very sad to think she would leave the good old Methodists and go with a class of people that had no respect for system attained through human organization; therefore I resolved to study the Bible to qualify me to convince her of the error. I did study the Word, faithfully, but to my surprise and delight I found she was right. So, before I ever heard a sermon preached on the church question, I was thoroughly convinced that the word of God stood out in bold condemnation of human church organization. -

In my ministerial relations with the Methodists I many times was so hampered by human machinery that I felt the spiritual life almost crushed out of me. I will relate one instance (among the many). I think it was in 1873 or 1874. I had spent the latter part of my sinful life in Oshtemo, Kalamazoo county, Michigan. A few months before my conversion I went into Cass county to work. There is where I was converted. In after years I returned to Oshtemo to live. After being there a few weeks I was appointed class-leader, steward, and Sunday-school superintendent, and was licensed as local preacher. My old associates and acquaintances seemed to rejoice that such a thorough reformation had taken place in me; and urged me very much to go into a neighborhood about three miles from the village to organize a Sunday-school and to preach to them. I did so, and much good was done. I continued in that work until quarterly meeting was held at the village. At the quarterly conference I absented myself from the house until the conference could investigate my character with a view of renewing my license to preach. After investigation I was informed that the brethren could bring nothing against my character, but found fault with my going down into the other neighborhood to work, as it drew away from the congregation and interfered with the support of the circuit preacher. The presiding elder (Peck) asked me what I was going to do about it. I told him (after thinking a while) that I did not see as I could do any different from what I had been doing, as there was such an earnest desire for me to do so, by the people of the neighborhood. He (Peck) asked, "Supposing we take your license away?" I stated that I had a license that no presiding elder in Michigan could touch, and by the grace of God I should use it. Now you know the duty of that conference was not to renew my license; but mercy, you know, is the pardoning power and favor shown to guilty men. My character was passed, my license as a local preacher renewed, advice given that I should be subject to the preacher in charge, etc., etc. I do not know why they should have been so lenient towards me, a rebel; for such I was, but one thing I do know, I was assessed $15 00 a year for the support of the preacher in charge, and I paid it too. I have known individuals to be expelled from the church for a less crime than I had committed, and they did not pay a cent for the support of the preacher This and other similar proceedings caused me to think a great deal, but I knew of no remedy until, as I have stated above, I commenced studying the Word to prove that sectarianism was right. And now I have great cause for rejoicing for the glorious light that shines all through the word of God. It grows brighter and brighter all the time. Hallelujah!

What wonderful comparisons!—In sectism we have to haw and gee as the driver saith. In the church of God we are willingly obedient to the Holy Spirit. In sectism we are unequally yoked together with unbelievers. In the church we are yoked with each other in Christ, or have the yoke of Christ upon us, and pull together harmoniously. In sectism we may be prisoners, captured by Satan. "Whosoever committeth sin is the servant of sin." In Christ we are prisoners, captured by the Holy Ghost. "But now being made free from sin, and become servants to God, we have our fruit unto holiness, and the end everlasting life." In sectism we are subject to rules framed by man. In the church we are subject to rules framed by God the Father. Praise the Lord! there is no end to the beautiful contrasts between God's way and man's way.

Now I wish to say that since taking a stand against all divisions, strifes, and confusions the blessed Lord has wonderfully blessed and prospered me both spiritually and temporally; also blessed my labors of love to his glory in the bettering of the conditions of mankind and the building up of the church of God. I praise his holy name for salvation from sin, both committed and inherited: first from sins committed, by a free and full justification; second, from sin inherited, by a free and full sanctification. The good Lord keeps me saved and in good health.

Yours in holy love,
A. B. Palmer.

Bangor, Mich., Feb. 23, 1900.

SEBASTIAN MICHELS.

In writing my experience for seventeen years it will be quite necessary to leave out some very important parts for the sake of brevity. So by the help of God I will endeavor to be as pointed as possible.

For years my heart yearned after God.   I sought to find him.   When going to the places of worship to find God I found him absent, and the god of this world had taken his place.   My heart was discouraged; finally my very soul cried unto God for help, and to know where his people were.   God with his great loving heart of pity came to my rescue, revealed to me the church of the morning and how it was in captivity, how his people had gone astray; also showed me how he would gather his people together.   Oh, how my heart bounded within me when I saw the beautiful church—how God set the members in the church, and how we were all members one of another and by one Spirit were all baptized into the one body, which is the church!   Praise his name!   I then yielded my heart to him, forsook all my sins, began family worship, set my house in order for God, and left off all my evil habits. My very soul longed to be a Bible Christian.   When I met the conditions of his word he freely pardoned me, gave me the glorious evidence in my heart that I was his child.   A week later I became convicted for entire sanctification.   I yielded my entire life and all my will to him.   He then called me to the ministry.

I soon began my work at home from house to house. Sinners began seeking God, and soon a glorious revival was held in the neighborhood.   As soon as we returned to Zion with songs and everlasting joy on our

heads God revealed that he was all in all to us, and
that he was our physician—that he not only forgave
all our sins but also healed our diseases. As the joy
of the Lord increased, persecution began; but thanks
be to God, he always gave us the victory. For ten
years my wife and I labored in the gospel work, laboring with our hands during the day and preaching the
gospel evenings and on Sundays. God blessed our
labor. We did not withhold time nor means to spread
the gospel. As I was very limited in my education,
scarcely able to read the Bible without the assistance
of my wife, it was necessary for me to live very close
to God so he could talk to my soul and thus enable
me to deliver his messages by his power.

After ten years I became very much interested in
the work in general, and as I had a family of six children and my wife was obliged to stay at home in order
that our children might have the privilege of attending
school, I bowed in earnest prayer before God to know
his will in the matter. That night he gave me a beautiful vision of a children's home and just how to
arrange matters in order to bring about the children's
home. As I was away from home engaged in the gospel
work at the time, my entire being became impressed
with the thought of a children's home and school.
The matter rested on my mind for days; the object of
the home loomed before me, and that was that a home
might be prepared for the children of ministers who
were engaged in the gospel work. I returned to my farm
home, and explained the beautiful vision to my wife.
After a few moments' pause she said, "That would be a
great undertaking; who would be able to build up such

a home without means?" I had not considered the means, knowing God talked to me and that he was able to supply the means for all his undertakings. My wife being a true companion to me, when she could not see a way out she would quietly submit the matter to me and with all her life and strength join me in the labor for God, and thus become a true helpmate.

All arrangements were made for the move; our farm rented; our personal property sold, all except three horses and a wagon and some implements which we would need on the new farm called "the campground," located one mile north of Grand Junction, Michigan. This farm was unimproved, lay as it were in a wilderness of brush and logs. There were about ten acres of standing timber, very large trees. In the midst of this timber was a large building erected for the purpose of holding public services. Cottages were built around this large building, leaving a space of about one hundred feet between the row of cottages and the large building. Near the northeast corner of the large building we had the year before built a boarding-hall, wherein Bro. and Sister Bixler were living when the Lord moved us to take possession of that place and build it up. There was an association of nine brethren to whom this property was deeded. After God made known to me his will, before moving on the ground I made known to the brethren of the association how the Lord led me in the matter. All agreed that I was the chosen one.

Having in my possession about three hundred fifty dollars received from the sale of personal property, we

immediately began the work. It was the latter part of February. In March we began a large addition to the boarding-hall, which enabled us to take in about thirty children. A schoolhouse was needed. The capital on hand was only about seven dollars. One night during the assembly-meeting of the church of God, God awakened me with a beautiful scene of a two-roomed schoolhouse all arranged. I submitted my plans to the brethren. No change was suggested; no one offered any proposition, as there was no capital on hand. I did not confer with flesh and blood in the matter, having become thoroughly acquainted with the Great Master Builder of this universe. Knowing he was able to furnish the capital, on the last day of the meeting heretofore mentioned I stood up before a large congregation and stated to the people that in four weeks of good weather the plan God had given me would be executed, and that I did not stand before them to see how much they would give, but did earnestly solicit their prayers. A few very earnest brethren who stood by me in the clearing up of the farm and the building up of the home always were ready for any improvement the Lord directed. Had I the space, I would gladly give the names of the dear brethren who assisted me in the work, and also give some very striking instances of God's wonderful leadings and dealings with us in his work.

Our family soon increased until we numbered from seventy to seventy-five. Oftentimes our flour was all baked into bread; one meal more would exhaust all in the house. A family of fifty children and no one to look to, as we never appealed to the association one single time for the space of three years, but always to the One who employed us in his great work; many times alone on our knees, alone before God, holding the promises before him, which we knew could not fail; and in due time we were always supplied. To him be all the glory! Many times we received letters from some one, saying, "God leads me to send you help at once; obedience is better than sacrifice." They may not always have known just how it was, but obedience on their part proved a blessing to us and enabled us to pour out our heart of gratitude and praise to God for supplying our daily needs. God not only supplied our needs, but amidst the toil and care of the home life with so large a family he made the work very precious.

To go back to our ministerial labor, it was a frontier gospel work to hold up Jesus alone, the Head of the church, the Savior of the body. This caused much persecution. Oftentimes after preaching the word of God with authority from him who called us, we were very thankful for the privilege of a barn to lodge in. Many times we were egged, stoned, and in many other ways were persecuted, and for years with the apostle Paul could say, "Hereunto were we called." Several times we were gladly received into homes until the word of God went forth, when those who received us would slip out and leave us in the schoolhouse in the country without any one to care for us. But thanks be to God who always caused us to triumph and always opened the way for us! These trials were all for our good, to fit us for the future. Never a trial too hard; never one too many; they were all necessary. So we with all our heart thank God for them all.

In the third summer of our labor at the Children's Home God most wonderfully and miraculously moved upon me. About midsummer very strangely I would come up to a very large pile of brick. It seemed real for a moment or two then passed away, and then my mind would ponder on what it meant. This was repeatedly brought before me until I went to God in prayer to know what it meant. Later in the summer or early in the fall of 1895 a beautiful plan of a large brick building came before me with a voice accompanying it: "Build according to the plan." This building was to be for the aged and infirm. In order to bring this about I must have the liberty of conscience and Spirit in the matter; and as others did not have the knowledge of the leadings of God's Spirit with me I could not come under the dictation of men and have the liberty of the Spirit. I loved the dear brethren dearly, but as they could not understand how these things were brought about, they as an associated body of men appointed me from year to year as superintendent of the work that God called me to. This point came before us at our annual meeting: Suppose I labor all the useful days of my life in this capacity as superintendent of this work, and at any time by the voice of this association I would be set aside and another would take my place and I would step out without a dollar. This was the first discouraging feature in my work. I could trust God, but I could not trust man.

So in order for me to continue the work God had called me to, I resigned my position in the Children's Home and at once began the Old People's Home, which has prospered beyond my expectation. For nearly four years we have proved God faithful to his word in this enterprise. He is making ways for us where we see no way, and we are encouraged day by day to obey him in all things.

We have now a family of from forty-six to forty-eight—thirty-four aged and infirm, and some very feeble and about to step off from the stage of action to be with Jesus. We are consecrated with all we have and are for the service of God. Having met the requirements of the laws of the state we are an incorporated body for the perpetuation of the Old People's Charitable Home. I as the proprietor of this Home hold an unchangeable position during my life. God alone assigned the position to me and he alone can make the change. Your brother saved by the power of God,

Sebastian Michels.

South Haven, Michigan.

J. N. HOWARD.

In the name of Christ, who hath redeemed my soul from sin—both committed and inherited—for the glory of God, and for the good of all into whose hands this may chance to fall, hoping and earnestly praying that it may prove a benefit to both saint and sinner, I write this brief autobiography.

I was born in Harlan county, Kentucky, on the 8th day of June, 1859. I am of German and English decent. My life for the most part has been spent in Greene, Shelby, Auglaize, and Paulding counties, Ohio. With due respect to my parents, I am sorry to say they were not Christians, and for this reason I was deprived of a Christian example from that source. As early in life as between nine and ten years of age I was convicted of my sins, and in a series of meetings held by the Methodists in Shelby county, Ohio; (father having moved north during the Civil war) in the winter of 1868 or 1869 I went to the altar several nights but did not obtain pardon; consequently I plunged deeper into sin, and so continued until I was sixteen years of age, and then I yielded to God, sought and obtained pardon, was born of God, in the spring of 1875, and about two months later I joined the United Brethren sect.

Not long after my conversion I received a definite call from God to preach the gospel, which, had I understood, was virtually a call to holiness. (1 Thess. 4:7 and Isa. 52:11.) Several years passed in which I had abundance of opportunities to know that the "old man," "body of sin," was not destroyed in regeneration. I also often longed to be delivered from it, but did not know it was my privilege to have it destroyed, being told by those who ought to have known better, that we must fight it till death. But thank God the time came when I learned better.

About seven years after my conversion I heard a sermon on Bible holiness, or sanctification, by Bro. A. J. Kilpatrick. Strange to say, this was the first time I had ever heard Bible holiness preached; it was in 1882. Through the preaching of the Word and by the Holy Spirit God let me see that my life since conversion had not all been pleasing to him, and that unless I repented of that wherein I had displeased him, I would not be ready to meet him in judgment.

So, upon my face on the earth before God with bitter repentance, I settled it once and for all with him, and got the witness of his Spirit that all was forgiven; and I also saw that God's word taught not only that to be a Bible Christian we must live without sinning, but that it was God's will that we be subsequently sanctified. But I did not at that time get an understanding of what to do in order to get sanctified. During the following year it was my privilege to hear a few more sermons on holiness, and the dear Lord so enlightened me that I not only saw what to do, but that it was my duty as well as privilege to consecrate and be sanctified.

The last week of December, 1883, I consecrated according to Rom. 12:1, 2, and the very God of peace did sanctify me wholly (1 Thess. 5:23), destroyed the body of sin (Rom. 6:6), and I then and there was enabled to put off the "old man" and to put on the "new man." I was filled with joy unspeakable and full of glory. The old foe was gone. Oh, hallelujah! Another wonderful thing God did for me, he gave me the Holy Ghost as he gave them (apostles) at the beginning, and also showed me the true church and delivered me from sectism. Glory to his name! He then renewed my call to preach the gospel, and I could then see that one reason why I had never been able to go before was, that I lacked the qualifications—"power from on high," the Holy Spirit. A little over seventeen years ago God sanctified me, and some little over eighteen years he has kept me free from sinning against him.

I am by his grace every day experiencing 2 Thess.

3:3—"But the Lord is faithful, who shall stablish you, and keep you from evil." Now ever since the gospel light in this evening time of the world has shone into my heart, I have seen and clearly understood that the "church of God" is not the sect institutions, and that no one nor all of the sect organizations is the church of God. Oh, how I do praise God for the old apostolic church and way.

I have devoted the greater part of my sanctified life to gospel and evangelistic labor. Have seen hundreds of precious souls saved in Jesus, first justified and afterwards sanctified; have also seen the power of God manifested in casting out devils and healing the sick, opening blind eyes and unstopping deaf ears and loosing the dumb tongue. Christ is our family physician. I have often been healed by his almighty power (once from lung disease), and my wife has been healed of deafness and of cancer. All glory to his name! Many have been the tribulations, conflicts, trials, and oppositions we have had to encounter; but in all of these we are more than conquerors through Jesus, and with Paul can say none of these things move us. We have suffered many things from sinful professors, even to the threatening of our lives for Christ's sake; have been in perils among false brethren, and have been falsely accused; but God's grace has been sufficient, and has brought us off victorious in every conflict. I mean to fight it through on this line—all others will prove too short to reach heaven. In short I testify to the glory of God that wicked men, women, or devils assault my soul but in vain; "for greater is he that is in us than he that is in the world," and my trust is in

him. So be of good courage and he shall strengthen
your hearts, all ye that hope in the Lord. Thank
God the darkness is past, and the true light now
shineth.

My evangelistic usefulness and labors have been
much hindered for reasons known to God, but I am
content to labor every day and preach at night if this
be Father's will. But woe is me if I preach not the
gospel. Permit me to say that at the time I was sanctified and delivered out of sectism I did not know that
there was any one else on the earth that had this glorious light, but the few of us in this locality (Payne,
Ohio). But we had obtained the holy fire and spirit
of reformation in our souls, and we could not keep
silent. We began to canvass the country for God.
Holiness revival meetings were held in every locality
where we could find an open door in private houses,
and schoolhouses. Meeting-houses were generally
locked against us (with a few exceptions), as were also
the schoolhouses in some instances. In those days
Bro. A. J. Kilpatrick, whom I esteem in holy love,
did the principal part of the preaching, and God wonderfully blessed his labors, and as a result churches were
raised up in several localities in northwestern Ohio.
In the meantime some one of the saints chanced to get
hold of a small paper published and edited by Bro.
D. S. Warner, and this led to sending for him to
come and hold a meeting in our locality, and it was
by him that we learned that God had many more out on
this same line, besides the few societies in our locality.
We soon learned that God had raised his hand to bring
again Zion, as spoken of in Isa 52:8, and had already be-

gun to send his angels (messengers) to gather together
his elect (Matt. 24:31), and that we were already in the
time spoken of by the prophets in Isa. 58:8 and Zech.
14:7. Hallelujah! I saw the church, bride of Christ,
the Lamb's wife, as spoken of by Solomon (See Cant.
8:5.) coming out of the wilderness of sectism, Babylon
confusion, leaning on the arm of her beloved (Cant.
4:10), and God gave me to see and understand that he
was in this reformation, and that he would carry it forward to the end, and no opposition however great
could ever prevail against or stop it. And in the past
seventeen years instead of dying out or coming to
naught, as many who were opposed to it predicted and
hoped, God has by his Holy Spirit and through his
holy ministers carried the work forward, until this last
and midnight cry has reached almost over the entire
continent, and to many parts of the old world. Also
much good literature is being sent out into all parts of
the world along this line. I have been a reader of
The Gospel Trumpet for about sixteen years. I think it
is the best religious paper published. I expect God
to carry the work forward until he makes Jerusalem a
praise in the earth, and until every true Christian
shall be gathered out of sectism into the one body, and
all the gathered "see eye to eye" and are perfectly
joined together in one mind and judgment, perfected
in one. Amen. May it please God to hasten it in his
own time and way. To all, and especially to those it
has been my privilege to meet in my labors, I am
glad to report perfect victory in my soul, and that I
am fully saved in Jesus: first saved from my sins—
washed from them—(Rev. 1:5 and Eph. 1:7); second,

or subsequently, sanctified by a second work of grace
—cleansed by the blood—(Heb. 13:12, 20, 21; 1 Pet.
1:2; 1 Jno. 1:7).   I have the dear Holy Spirit dwell-
ing in my soul.   I am your blood-washed brother and
humble servant of Christ,   J. N. Howard.

SAMUEL L. SPECK.

Samuel L. Speck, one among the first and most
active ministers of this reformation, was born in Cornwall, Ontario, June 15, 1862. He is of French descent.
His father died when he was but ten years of age,
leaving his mother with ten children and in a poor
financial condition, which required Samuel to leave
school to help maintain the family.   Therefore he
obtained a very limited education, not reaching higher
in his studies than the second reader.   He became
newsboy until the age of fourteen, when he was employed by one Mr. D. Ross to attend his billiard
saloon, and also as a chore-boy in a general store,
where he remained until he was seventeen years old.
Then he was employed as clerk in a wholesale whisky
store.

This last employment proved more of a curse to
young Samuel than a blessing.   While here he became
a lover of ardent spirits, and during the latter part of
his stay here he was constantly under the influence of
strong drink.   His mother, eldest brother, and sister
reproved him for the life of shame he was bringing
upon himself, and the disgrace already brought upon
the family at home and abroad.   But rather than
yield to their wishes, he left home, Feb. 21, 1881, and
went west into the state of Michigan.   While in

Michigan he engaged in work in the timber, where he continued until May, when he went to Chicago. There he remained during the summer. While in Chicago he again fell into bad company, and became a gambler, both for pleasure and for money. Fleeing again, in the fall of 1881, from his bad companions, he returned to Michigan, where he again engaged in the timber.

In the fall of 1882 one J. C. Fisher, with his wife, came into the neighborhood where he was at work, and commenced to preach the full gospel. Under the influence of the gospel he came under conviction, and Oct. 28, 1882, gave his heart to God, and God for Christ's sake forgave him of all his past sins and took him into his family as his child. The following month he presented his body a living sacrifice to God, and God wholly sanctified him, cleansing him from the carnal nature and giving him a pure heart. In 1883 he felt the hand of God upon him to preach the gospel. In December of the same year he obeyed the divine injunction, and in company with Bros. S. Michels and A. B. Palmer he held his first revival meeting at Grand Junction, Mich., which resulted in the salvation of seventeen souls. His next meeting was five miles northeast of that place. In this meeting he witnessed the salvation of thirty more. Also in another meeting after this, about three miles northwest of Grand Junction, a few more souls were added to the church, which greatly encouraged the young evangelist. He held three meetings that winter, laboring during the day with his hands. He received as compensation for his preaching the above-mentioned souls and one dollar in money.

In June, 1884, his ordination to the ministry was recognized by the laying on of hands.   He then traveled some in company with Bro. D. S. Warner, but mostly in company with J. C. Fisher, until Fisher fell.   During his evangelistic travels he has witnessed the salvation of many precious souls, the healing of many sick, and opening of the eyes of the blind. He was present in the Bangor, Michigan, camp-meeting when Emma Miller, of Battle Creek, Michigan, was healed of blindness.

The first revival meeting that he held alone, so far as ministerial help was concerned, was in 1887, at Beaver Dam, Indiana.   In this meeting about thirty-five souls were saved.   This he says was the most powerful meeting he ever witnessed in his travels.   At this place he made the acquaintance of Miss Amanda Bear, with whom he was afterwards united in marriage, Nov. 10, 1889.   His home and family are still in that neighborhood.   But Samuel is away most of the time engaged in ministerial work.

He is very successful as a revivalist.   Many souls are being saved annually through his preaching.   During the summer season he travels with a tent, in company with others, preaching in cities and large towns.   His natural way of preaching and his humble and sociable way of getting along with the world cause him to be highly respected by all wherever he goes.   Since his call to the ministry he has preached the gospel in eleven states of the Union, and also in the Dominion of Canada.

LENA L. SHOFFNER.

I was born Feb. 26, 1868, near the small village of Nishnabotna, in Atchison county, Missouri. From this place we moved to Carthage in Jasper county, where the greater part of my life has been spent. I had a very pious training from my parents. They forbade my going to worldly amusements, such as theaters, balls, and card and wine parties. Neither would they allow me to read novels or continued stories of any kind.

Being thrown out into the world to make my own living I came under an opposite influence from that of my home; because the professors of religion indulged in all these things, and assured me there was no harm in them. My heart being filled with pride and love of the world, it was not a hard matter for me to break over the rules and admonitions of my parents, and I soon fell in with the tide of the world. Deception soon filled my heart, insomuch that I practiced all these things and kept it from my parents. Oh, the remorse of conscience, and rebellion that soon filled my heart! I had almost absented myself from places of worship. At the age of fifteen I was brought under conviction while upon a bed of sickness. There I promised God that I would turn from the paths of pleasure and follow him. This was a promise made only to be broken; I had not the power to carry it out. Upon recovery I again sought the paths of pleasure, desiring to drown my convictions and ease my conscience. Oh, the goodness of God in sparing my unprofitable life! Many times when I would be dancing and in the greatest of my glee the Spirit of God

would come in thundering tones telling me that I
ought to be saved.

As I was returning from my work one cold winter
night, a gentleman and two ladies were standing on
the street corner singing a beautiful hymn, "Oh, Why
Should I be Lost?" I paused a moment and listened,
and conviction came, so forcible that I trembled. The
announcement was made of a meeting in a little white
meeting-house on the corner just opposite the place
where I was working. I resolved on my way home
that I would attend those services. The following
evening in company with others I listened to a sermon
from these words: "What think ye of Christ?" All
who desired prayer were invited to remain for the after
meeting. I remained, and prayer was offered for myself and others. I did not receive any experience, and
the next day I was greatly tempted to give it all up,
which I did, and remained away from the meeting two
weeks. I attended other places of worship during the
time, as there were various other meetings in progress
at the same time. I had many invitations to join, but
owing to my former teaching I knew I must be born
again. During this time conviction increased until I
could not enjoy my sleep or food, and at length I resolved to go back to the former meeting. I attended
the service Sunday morning, and in company with a
friend went to the mercy-seat when the call was given,
with no intention of getting saved. While some one
was praying the Lord asked me to settle this question.
I replied that I was afraid I could not hold out. He
seemed to force me to a decision, giving me to understand that if I decided for Satan, he would make it

stronger. I decided for God. Being ignorant of the plan of salvation and many things it contained, as I bowed before God forgetting my circumstances and surroundings and seeing only my guilt and shame, I called upon him for deliverance. It was then that God forgave me all. My name was written in heaven and I was his child. This was in February, 1886.

I spent four years in rather an up-and-down experience. In the year 1890 I discerned the body of Christ, in a meeting held by D. S. Warner and company. I took my stand and embraced the experience of full salvation. I could for the first time in my life say that I was saved from all sin and sanctified wholly, by a second work of grace. The town where I lived being large, it afforded me a good field of labor. I knew before I came into this experience that God had laid his hand upon me to preach the gospel, and I felt I was not qualified, as I did not clearly discern my place in the body. In the year 1892 the Lord made it clear that he had chosen me as an evangelist, and gave me the words found in Acts 13:2—"Separate me Barnabas and Saul for the work." I bade adieu to my dear ones in the month of January, expecting to be gone ten days. I was gone just two years, then paid them a visit of ten days.

The Lord having laid upon my heart the work in England, I made a tour of meetings from Arkansas City, Kansas to Grand Junction, Michigan and on through eastern Pennsylvania. On Nov. 4, 1893 at 3:00 p. m. I took passage on the Umbria for Liverpool, England. I never felt more composed and in the order of God than at this time. Such a hallowed

influence filled my soul, as the Lord had given me repeatedly "Go, doubting nothing; for I have sent
thee." I arrived in Liverpool Nov. 12 and found the
dear ones waiting for me. I was taken to the saints'
home, enjoyed a lunch, and immediately went into the
chapel, where the Lord again assured me that I was in
his order by pouring showers of blessings upon my
soul while delivering his Word. This was my first
time to meet dear Bro. and Sister Rupert and many
other of God's dear children. I was made to feel the
depths of Eph. 2:19—"Now therefore ye are no more
strangers and foreigners, but fellow citizens with the
saints, and of the household of God." I encountered
many hard trials while in England, but God delivered
me out of them all. I spent nine months in Liverpool
and three months in London, and visited other places,
spending a short time at Birkenhead, where God used
me in helping Bro. and Sister Rupert on the "Gospel
Van." A great many souls obtained salvation during these meetings. We attended a camp-meeting near
this place, where the Lord made known that he wished
me to return again to this country. I could not
understand it then, but I understand it now.

August 22, 1895 I set sail from Glasgow, Scotland
for New York city, on board the City of Rome. I
arrived in New York Aug. 31. I attended a camp-
meeting in Pennsylvania, after which in company with
Sister Hunter and others I went to Maryland, where
the Lord saved many souls and raised up a church.
Although I enjoyed much of God's presence, and his
blessing was upon my work in every way, yet I felt
deeply moved to seek a closer walk with God, which I

accordingly did.   From that time until this I can say
that my Christian experience has been on the increase.
At the present time I am enjoying a rest in faith,
which gives me under all circumstances a calm sweet
peace.   The way I obtained this was by reaching a
point of submissiveness where it was no longer I but
Christ in all things.

I have found the Lord very precious in healing the
afflicted, saving the lost, sanctifying believers, calling
his people out of sectism to stand in the one body
only, and supplying my every need.   During my travels of the past eight years many times I have had a
company of three beside myself, and I am glad to testify that God always supplied my every need. Oh, how
different from the hireling ministry of to-day!   While
they insist upon having a stipulated salary, and their
congregation is constantly embarrassed by the plate or
basket for a collection, I can say such never occurred
in any of my meetings.   There were times that I did
not even have a postage stamp, nevertheless I wrote my
letters and by the time the letters were ready the
stamps or money for the same had arrived.   Different
times I have made ready for a journey, sending my
trunk to the depot with only five or ten cents in
purse, but before time to purchase the ticket, God
through letters or individuals would send me the
amount.   He faileth not.

Your sister in defense of the gospel,

Lena L. Shoffner.

MARY COLE.

"A Bit of My Experience."

I was born Aug. 23, 1854 in the state of Iowa, near Decatur. When I was a year old my parents moved to Illinois, where they remained two years, and then moved to Missouri, near Windsor, where I was raised and where I spent all the weary years of my invalid life. It was at this place that the Lord saved, sanctified, and healed me. I was converted in my eighteenth year, and four weeks later was wholly sanctified. I had joined the Methodist Episcopal sect the fall before, but knew I was not saved, nor did the minister who took me in ask me if I was. My salvation was brought about by my brother, who was saved, becoming burdened for my soul and earnestly praying and holding on to God until the Lord convicted and converted me. It was through the same instrumentality that I was sanctified. All this occurred at my home; so I give Babylon no honor for any of it. A little over five years after I was saved I received my first call to preach the gospel, but was not sent of God until five years later. Nine years after I was saved, the same brother was healed in answer to prayer, and God also used him in my healing. I had been an invalid from my childhood. Truly misery stole me at my birth. I began having hard fits when I was but little more than a year old, but had very few from that time until I was six years of age. After that they became more frequent. They were caused by my mother overheating herself before I was born; therefore it seemed there would be no deliverance for me—but what is impossible with man is possible with God. I also had

dyspepsia and indigestion from near the same age.
When I was about fourteen I was troubled with female
weakness, my spine was affected, and altogether I was
rendered useless for this life. I often bemoaned my
condition and wished myself dead. Many a time I
would sit beside my mother crying, and say, "Why
can't I die? Why didn't I die when I was a child? I
am a trial to myself and to all around me." I also
had a stammering tongue, which helped to make me
more miserable. I lay sick for months, and at different
times was almost helpless, both before and after I was
saved. Doctors gave me up, and said it would be
easier to make a world than to restore me to health.
After I was healed I had a chance to tell them that the
Lord alone could make a world, and the Lord alone
could restore me to health.

God convicted me for healing just the same as he
did for salvation, and showed me that if I did not accept it and believe God's word for the same, I would
soon doubt it all and die an infidel, and not only be lost
myself, but be the means of thousands of others being
lost. So I began to pray for healing, and God showed
me I did not have enough faith then. I trusted him
for an increase of faith, and he gave it to me. Then I
took him at his Word and claimed this promise: "Again
I say unto you, That if two of you shall agree on earth
as touching anything that they shall ask, it shall be
done for them of my Father which is in heaven." And
my mother and I on bended knees alone in prayer
plead the promise, knowing that we were agreed, and
God sent the answer. I was well for the first time in
my life. Oh, praise his dear name! My soul bounded

with joy. It seemed too good to be true—a poor invalid now well, all through the merits of Jesus. Some said that it was all excitement, and as soon as that was over I would be as sick as ever, but the devil's prophecy proved untrue. It has been over nineteen years since I was healed, and I am well of all those different afflictions, and have been healed of many others which I have had since I was first healed, and have never since applied to an earthly physician. Jesus, the Great Physician, has been my only and perfect healer of soul and body. To him alone do I ascribe all the glory and honor and praise for it all. Before the Lord healed me I had never been able to wash or do any hard work, and had lain sick for months at different times. I was sick both before and after I was saved, but since I was healed I have done many a washing, and held meetings alone for weeks at a time.

One year and a half after I was healed the Lord sent me out into his harvest-field and gave me a dispensation of his Word, and made me to feel, "Woe is me if I preach not the gospel." Bless his holy name! he put the preach in me and preached through me himself; so it was not I, but Christ. "By the grace of God I am what I am." When the Lord first called me I made the excuses that I had no education, no talent, no money, and was of a stammering tongue. To these excuses the Lord made three answers. He told me he would be my wisdom, my prophet, priest, and king. "Yea, the Almighty shall be thy defense, and thou shalt have plenty of silver." "Who made man's mouth?" He showed me he would be to me all I needed for soul and body. Many times when I would

be up preaching and did not have words to explain my
thoughts, the Lord would bring the proper words to
my mind and show me by the Spirit to use them.
After the service was over I would go to the dictionary
to see if I had used them correctly, and would find that
I had. In this way he became education to me. I had
been such an invalid that I was able to go to school
but for a very short time.

I preached for the sect preachers for three or four
years when I first went out, because I had not yet discerned the one body, but as soon as I did discern it
I was spoiled for Babylon. Truly I was crucified to the
world and the world to me; so I did not receive many
more calls from the Babylon preachers. But the Lord
led me out into a large room and set before me an
open door, and no man could shut it. The Lord
showed me I should not take up collections for my
support, nor allow any one else to do it for me, but
trust him fully for all things. I have had all I
needed, traveling expenses included. He has truly
verified the promise "My God shall supply all your
needs according to his riches in glory by Christ
Jesus." I have had enough, and that is plenty.
While I was in Babylon, I did not dare to preach the
whole truth. They said if I preached holiness I would
tear down their churches, which was sufficient proof
that their so-called churches were not the church of
God; for his church is established in the mountain of
his holiness, and the whole limits round about shall be
most holy. Jesus says, "Upon this rock I will build
my church; and the gates of hell shall not prevail
against it." I want to say that since I have discerned

the one body I have had full privilege to preach the whole truth with the power of God sent down from heaven, and the results have been satisfactory, which was not the case in Babylon.

I am perfectly satisfied with the body of Christ and with my place in it. I have no desire whatever to return to the mists and fogs of Babylon. I am sure this is the fulfillment of the prophecy that at evening time it shall be light. The secret of my success and usefulness in the cause of God lies in this, that God has given me an experience of salvation according to his precious Word. By meeting proper conditions I was both justified by faith and sanctified by faith as a second, instantaneous cleansing, the 'Holy Ghost coming in as the Comforter. By keeping the conditions met I continually retain the same experience, and as a result I am growing in grace and in the knowledge of the truth as it is in him. My path is growing brighter. All who read this, pray for me.

Mary Cole.

GEORGE L. COLE.

I was born near Windsor, Missouri Feb. 10, 1867. I was converted within one week of my tenth birthday, at my parents' fireside, during a season of prayer, as all at home except myself were saved before that time. I soon joined the Methodist Episcopal sect, supposing it was the church of God, and that I was doing right by joining it. However, I could have obtained the light on the one body of Christ at that time with a very little instruction on one or two points. But for want of proper help it was about eleven years from the date of my conversion until I saw the church of God, or discerned the body of Christ.' I was familiar with the doctrine of sanctification from childhood, and after my conversion desired the experience but did not obtain it. For five years I lived a life devoted to God. Of course I battled against a high temper and other carnal elements common to all who are not wholly sanctified. At the age of fifteen I fell back into sin, and from that time tried worldly pleasures, to the wrecking of my moral and physical being. About six weeks before I reached the age of twenty-one I was reclaimed from my wretched backslidden state, and soon I found the glorious experience of sanctification—something I never had experienced before. Thank God, the old temper was taken out! No wonder Paul said God saves us by the washing of regeneration and the renewing of the Holy Ghost. Thank God for the "renewing." I was about twelve years old when Jeremiah (my oldest brother) and my sister Mary, who had been invalids for years, were gloriously healed of chronic diseases. From that time I had the light on divine healing, and never doubted it for a moment.

From the date of my sanctification the Holy Spirit in a wonderful manner began to teach and unfold the scriptures to my understanding, and the following fall the holy people held a tabernacle meeting near Windsor, and twenty or more stepped into the light. A little meeting-house owned by an Adventist was repaired and put to use for God, and soon a dispensation of the gospel was laid on my heart, and for more than a year the Lord's hand was upon me to feed the little flock, and many showers of grace came down upon us all, with refreshings from the presence of the Lord. In the spring of 1890 I closed out my farming business, as I was reared on a farm. Mother went to live with a married son, and I joined my sister Mary in the work. She and Sister Lodema Kaser were near Humboldt, Kansas at that time. That summer I attended the saints' camp-meeting at Bangor, Michigan; also at Beaver Dam, Indiana. I did but little preaching as an evangelist until the fall of 1890. Our company usually ranged from three to six, and traveled extensively, stopping about two weeks in a place and holding meetings in tents, groves, meeting-houses, halls, school-houses, and private houses, on the streets, in court-houses, and wherever the way was open for the pure gospel. Our work was most extensive in Kansas. However, we have also held meetings in Nebraska, Missouri, Oklahoma, Illinois, Iowa, Indiana, Michigan, Ohio, Kansas, West Virginia, Arizona, and California. We spent nearly a year and a half in the state last named. We have labored in old fields, among the churches, also in new fields where the evening light had never been heard of before; have preached in old, settled countries, and in pioneer districts; have labored in cities, villages, and rural districts. Two summers were spent in the west with a large company of workers and a tabernacle, conducting a line of camp-meetings ranging from fifty to three hundred miles apart, ten days of meeting being held out of every two weeks during the camping season. We have seen many souls won to Christ, and believers sanctified, the churches edified, and many sick healed—some were marvelous cases. A man in Oklahoma who had been blind in

one eye for thirty-four years was instantly restored to sight. A lady in Kansas almost deaf from catarrh was perfectly restored. A brother in northern Kansas almost deaf was instantly restored. A child in California at death's door, failing to break out with measles, was healed, broke out in a few hours, and was soon strong again. An opium fiend in California, of more than thirty years' standing (it was said), having used about an average of twenty grains of morphine per day, and at times as high as sixty grains in twenty-four hours, having spent over a thousand dollars to get cured and failing, was at death's door with dropsy caused by morphine-using, the flesh having been covered with purple spots for years, the case having been considered hopeless. In answer to prayer the victim was enabled to stop the use suddenly, and was able to walk and enjoy life in less than two weeks, with no tonic but the power of God. In northern Kansas a woman hopelessly insane and near death's door, being reduced in flesh from 195 to 110 pounds could not walk alone, and had been six months under the care of a doctor She was perfectly healed by the power of God, and in six weeks was doing her own work and caring for her family. Typhoid and other fevers were removed by the faith of Jesus Christ, the same yesterday, to-day, and forever.

I do not wish to be misunderstood. I usually had the co-operation of my sister Mary, and other faithful workers. But I attribute this good work to God, who hath done the work through his humble servants, and I claim no honor for myself, nor yet for the others— only Christ and the faith of him. Amen.

The Chicago Work. I came to Chicago two years ago in company with Mary. After the assembly-meeting we remained to help push forward the work, of which Bro. Gorham Tufts was then in charge, he who had been with the work from its beginning. The Open Door Mission of 59 Plymouth Place was then in operation as a five-cent lodging-house. The penniless were fed free mornings, and services were held every night in the hall on the first floor. Also there was a general gathering of the saints in Masonic Temple every Sunday afternoon. We took up cottage-meeting work, preaching at Chicago, Roseland, South Englewood, and in the Mission and Temple meetings, and at other places. At that time there was no home for workers in the city. In May, 1898 in answer to prayer a large, beautiful home at 1612 Prairie Avenue was opened. However, Mary and I left in July, and did not return until November, after which we remained in the city until June, 1899. After the camp-meeting at Moundsville, W. Va. we held meetings in Joliet, Aurora, and Kankakee, returning to Chicago in October, when we found that through the late heresy (opposing the cleansing work of sanctification) and the apostasy of Keeling, Hahn, and others, the work was much crippled. But the Holy Spirit came in power and inspiration and the work began to be set in order. The interest in the general meeting wonderfully increased on certain lines, also the attendance. Soon the Lord opened a new home for workers at 7300 Stewart Avenue, and in six weeks more a large mission hall at 314 West Madison Street (renting at $50 per month) was furnished and in order. Then came the assembly-meeting of ten days, Jan. 4-14. Victory has prevailed up to date. Many souls are being saved, backsliders are returning, believers are being sanctified, and the work is pushing into new fields. The prospects for the work in Chicago and elsewhere are brighter now than at any time in the past. It is truly marvelous how God has answered prayer, and furnished the home and mission, and supplied all our needs; but we give him all the glory. The rents of the different places are now $90.00 per month, besides other expenses—fuel, light, food, clothing, car-fare, and incidental expenses. But with God's blessing we mean to push out. Lovingly yours all for Christ,

George L. Cole.

Chicago, Ill., Feb. 10, 1900.

E. E. BYRUM.

Enoch E. Byrum was born in Randolph county, Indiana, Oct. 13, 1861. His father was a farmer, and he was therefore brought up on a farm, as most other farm boys are, with nothing of any particular note transpiring during his rural life. He received what is considered a fair common-school education. He was considered a remarkably good boy. When he was fifteen years of age his father died. His parents were very devoted Christians and he thus having been brought up under religious influence was led to realize the sinful condition of his heart, and was converted a few weeks before his father's death. His father's death, however, was sublime. He spent hours before his departure in praising the Lord, even unto his last breath. After his father's death it fell his lot to take charge of the home farm and responsibilities of the family at home.

After his conversion he remained on the farm for several years. Frequently during this time he felt a desire in his heart to be useful in the service of the Lord, but, feeling his inabilities on this line, had almost given up hope of ever doing any active service in the gospel work. The time came when the Lord seemed to lay his hand upon him and give him a special calling for his work. This call came to him most vividly, as he was plowing in the field. Many times before had he felt the leadings of the Holy Spirit unto more active work for God, but now it came as a direct call. He could not throw it off. He would kneel in the furrow and ask the Lord to let him off, and say, "Anybody else, Lord, but me. I am unfit for the work of the Lord. I am not able to compose anything to write, I can not preach, can not talk publicly nor do public work, and have no talent in private work"; in fact he felt that he could scarcely claim a right to one talent. He says he would plow to the end of the field and kneel in a fence-corner, or stop along the way behind a stump, or almost any place where he could call upon the Lord. This continued day after day, but still he felt he could not well yield to the call. He knew nothing that the Lord would have any one do but preach. Having been brought up on the farm, he was quite ignorant of what could be done in the Master's vineyard. The thought would come that if he consecrated to preach, the next thing would be to go to Africa, and above all things it seemed that was out of the question with him, because that would require, as he supposed, learning a foreign language. With this came an almost irresistible desire to go to school. At that time he could scarcely tell why.

Finally, weak, and bashful as he was he ventured to promise God that he would obey him, and he made this covenant with the Lord: that if he opened up the way for him to go to school, whenever he called him into his vineyard, let it be whatever it would, he would go. The consecration was complete, as much so as if to be put in action the next day. The burden was removed. Although he could not see a way open for years to come for him to attend school, yet almost in a miraculous way there was an opening, and within two weeks he was away from home attending school. As he now looks back upon his school-days from that time, he can see the hand of the Lord through it all. He was pushed forward in many lines despite his backwardness and his averseness to publicity. During his school-days he continued to let his light shine as a child of God, knowing that he was his child.

For several years after his conversion he felt there was something more to be obtained in a Christian experience, but did not know just what it was; having never been taught anything concerning a deeper work of grace, and that it is our privilege to be healed of our sicknesses in this life. He had been afflicted for five years before entering school, and after a few months in school he ventured to ask the Lord to heal him of his afflictions. He had then heard that there were people living who believed in divine healing, and he found some passages of scripture that taught the same. In answer to prayer the Lord healed him. He then began to search the word of God more closely, and felt more and more the need of a deeper work of grace. During his last year in school five of the students formed a private Bible class. Neither of them understood the doctrine of holiness, but as thy began to read from week to week and pray the Lord to open their understanding to his word, it was but a short time until they were all convicted for holiness of heart. Although this was at Otterbein University, a religious institution of the United Brethren denomination, they found no spiritual food there, in fact almost all of them opposed holiness. In a few months their little Bible class spent most of the time talking on this subject and praying for the experience.

About the first of January, 1887, Byrum had reached the point where he could so yield himself to God as to receive the experience of entire sanctification. Many times before had he knelt before the Lord and tried to yield himself to him, thinking that he would accept his consecration or offering, but God required it complete; and when he came to the point where he really did yield all to him according to his Word and call upon him for a cleansing, the work was done. He had been expecting to receive it in a way that would cause him to leap and shout, as he imagined they did on the day of Pentecost, but when he came to the point that he was willing to obey the Lord in all things and meet the conditions of his Word and receive the experience in God's way, the Spirit did his office work, and the work was done. Instead of leaping and shouting, it was a time of calmness and serenity. It was just as positive as was his conversion. It was not merely a blessing, but the Blesser. The Holy Spirit had taken up his abode in his soul as an abiding Comforter. It was in a spiritual sense entering the land of Canaan to the soul. From that time the word of God began to open up to him like a new book. He had been a Bible reader for years, but now began to find he had understood but very little of what had been read. The promises began to be more of a reality as he learned to appropriate them to his life.

On June 9, 1887, at the close of the school year, he attended a camp-meeting at Grand Junction, Michigan. This meeting was not only undenominational, but anti-sectarian, and the first of the kind he had ever attended. Here Bro. Byrum met a people who believed in fulfilling the word of God, who believed that we have reached the time the prophet Zechariah foretold, when he said, "At evening time it shall be light." Prior to this time he had read a few copies of The Gospel Trumpet, published then at Grand Junction, Michigan, about seven miles from where the camp-meeting was held. He had never met D. S. Warner, who was then editor. But as Bro. Warner was on the lookout for some one to take the place of J. C. Fisher, who then had become unfit for his position, Bro. Byrum, being commended by some others, was asked to take the position as publisher and business manager in the Gospel Trumpet Office, as some one was required to take that place immediately after the meeting. At first thought it seemed preposterous for him to think of undertaking to fill such a position, as he had never done any work in a publishing house. Immediately the Lord brought before his mind the consecration he had made while plowing in the field a few years before, when he said, "Lord, if you open up the way for me to go to school, whenever you call me into the work, let it be whatever it will, I will go." He tried to find one excuse after another, but the Lord gave him to understand that it meant obedience, and he would take care of his inabilities if his will was fulfilled through him in all things. After fully considering the matter, and being informed that to take the position meant a life of faith, giving his time without a salary, trusting God not only for his living, but also for others and the work under his charge, Bro. Byrum entered upon his labors June 21, 1887. Shortly before this he had sold his possessions, and now the time came to make use of the same in the work of the Lord, and he soon learned what it was to have not only his means but his entire life consecrated to the will of God. It proved to be a place wherein many tests of faith were ahead of him. It no doubt was well that he did not fully realize the responsibilities before him, but as one after another was reached God gave the needed faith and needed grace and help in every time of need. D. S. Warner, the editor of The Gospel Trumpet, left in a few days after his arrival, to hold revival meetings throughout the western states and did not return until the middle of the next April. By the time of his return there had been many experiences of faith, many close places financially and otherwise. There were many battles to fight for God on various lines, but Bro. Byrum could truly praise God for the victories won.

A few months after beginning this work, as the requests for prayer, and for advice and help on many other lines, came in from every direction, he realized it was necessary for him to have some of the special gifts of the Spirit mentioned in the twelfth chapter of 1 Corinthians. He therefore called upon the Lord for the gift of faith, which was granted to him, and later as he was led out on the line of divine healing the Lord saw fit to bestow a special gift on that line, which was developed as he exercised the same. The first manifestation to any great extent of the power of healing after this was in the case of a thirteen-year-old boy who had been sick with fever, and was instantly healed by the laying on of hands of Bro. Byrum and another brother. A week later a woman was instantly healed of erysipelas; and from time to time persons were healed of various diseases. Since that time he has witnessed the healing of thousands of people of almost all kinds of disease.

In the summer of 1895 a number of persons felt the Lord impressing them to take a more active stand and exercise of faith on the line of divine healing. During the camp-meeting at Grand Junction, Michigan, that year were a number of remarkable cases of healing. Among the number was a young man who had been kicked by a horse, his shoulder dislocated, and his ribs broken. He lay at the point of death until the next afternoon. Thousands of people were in attendance on that day expecting to see the man die. In answer to prayer, and by the anointing with oil and the laying on of hands the man was almost instantly healed, insomuch that in a few minutes' time he arose, dressed himself, and walked the floor praising God, and three times in succession testified to the vast assembly of people of what the Lord had done for him. There were also other marvelous cases.

Following the Grand Junction meeting Bro. Byrum attended camp-meetings in Washington, Oregon, California, and Oklahoma, and there were many marvelous cases of healing of paralysis and other diseases, blind eyes opened, deaf ears unstopped, and the name of the Lord glorified both in the salvation of souls and the healing of many people. God is still manifesting his power in a marvelous way. During the past few years letters are coming from all parts of the world for special prayer for the healing of diseases and for the salvation of souls. Hundreds of telegrams from all parts of the United States and Canada are received, asking him to pray for the healing of the sick or the casting out of demons. Even cablegrams are sent requesting prayer.

A few years ago he felt impressed to send a handkerchief to a sister in Binghamton, New York. She had been lying at the point of death for some time, and upon receipt of the handkerchief and application to her body, as mentioned in Acts 19:12, she was instantly healed. Soon others began to send handkerchiefs to be prayed over in like manner, and there have been many marvelous cases of healing in this way. Among the number was a native of India whose body was drawn up with rheumatism and who was suffering excruciating pains. He had one of the brethren in that far-off land send for a handkerchief for the healing of his body. Two months later the handkerchief reached him and was applied, and the Lord sent his healing power insomuch that he was made well.

It would be impossible for me to relate the hundreds and thousands of remarkable answers to prayer which he has personally witnessed among God's believing children in the church. It is his belief, that were ministers to preach the gospel in all its purity, and lift up the standard of truth as Jesus Christ meant it should be lifted up, there would be as great an awakening among the people as there was in the early days of the apostolic times. We believe the promises of God are to be enjoyed by believers of his Word, and not by doubters. May God enable us all not only to believe his Word, but to put it in practice, and thereby enjoy the great riches of his kingdom.

WM. G. SCHELL.

I was born June 30, 1869 in Darke county, Ohio. My parents were both religiously inclined, and taught me the ways of God to the best of their knowledge in my early youth. From childhood the Spirit of God wrought upon my heart, and I oftentimes felt those inward yearnings for the peace of God that are felt by those who are truly awakened by God's Holy Spirit. At the age of nine I was so wrought upon by the Spirit of God, in a Methodist revival, that I went to the mercy-seat and endeavored to give my heart to God, but having such poor instruction from those who ought to have been qualified to teach me, I failed to receive a change of heart, and soon the conviction of God's Spirit seemed to depart from me, and then I became very wicked. At the age of fourteen, in another Methodist revival, the Spirit of God found me and I sought and obtained the pardon of my sins, and pledged eternal trueness to God and his word. At that time I united with the Methodist denomination, with whom I held membership until August, 1886, when I was for the first time blessed with the privilege of attending a holiness meeting.

I had often heard rumors of unseemly actions of the sanctified people in their meetings, and my curiosity was aroused to attend one of those meetings. Consequently, out of curiosity, when the holiness people came near enough to my home I went to hear them preach. The meeting was being held by Brothers A. J. Kilpatrick and J. N. Howard, of Payne, Ohio. On the way to the first service the Spirit of God began to speak to my heart about holiness, and although I had never been taught in regard to it, I began to feel that there was a reality in it, and promised God that I would listen to those holiness teachers with an unprejudiced heart. When I entered the congregation Bro. Kilpatrick was in the pulpit. There seemed to be such a holy awe about those men and such a sweet influence of God's Spirit flowed out from the words they were uttering to my heart as I had never experienced before. In a few minutes I was made to see clearly that they had an experience of salvation beyond anything I had ever attained unto, and my heart within me seemed to melt like wax. When the services were dismissed I introduced myself to the strange ministers and remarked: "I am a Methodist, but you brethren enjoy something that we do not." "God bless you, my dear brother, it is for you," was the reply, with a hearty shake of the hand, such as only the pure in heart can give.   23

I had heard ideas advanced that I had never heard before. The inherited sin in the heart, which remains after we are regenerated, was pictured out in the sermon in exact accordance with my experience, and the minister showed by God's word that the anger, jealous feelings, and man-fear caused by this inherited nature were purged out of our hearts when we are sanctified. "O God," said my heart within me, "that is just what I want!" I went home, but I was so convicted for a pure heart that I could scarcely sleep. The next morning (Sunday) I went to hear those holiness preachers again. This time I heard a sermon on the pure church of God. Oh, how the scriptures illuminated my mind as they were expounded by this man of God. I had never seen the pure church before, but I was so thoroughly convinced that the only church recognized in the New Testament was the universal body of those who are truly saved, that I resolved I would no longer have my name recorded on any book, except that one which would contain the names of all the blessed in that great day. When the services closed I went forward and clasped the hand of one of the ministers, exclaiming: "Thank God there is one Methodist less." This I said not because I felt any prejudice arising in my heart against the Methodist people, but because I felt that for me a membership in the church of the living God only was needed. In the afternoon and in the evening of the same day I listened again to the setting forth of God's word on the subject of holiness, and at the close of the evening service I went to the mercy-seat, consecrated my all to God, and was sanctified wholly. The following Lord's day I severed my connection with the Methodist sect. Persecutions then arose on every hand, until it seemed that I scarcely had a friend among all my acqaintances. For some months, feeling myself so abandoned by my friends, I was almost entirely isolated from society, except when I attended the holiness meetings, while numberless rumors were being spread far and near about me.

During these months, God showed me that the time had come for me to fill a long-felt call into the ministry. I therefore gave out an appointment and endeavored to preach the pure gospel unto the people. God greatly blessed my labors, and souls began to seek God. Soon I was called to adjacent neighborhoods, and finally from state to state, preaching the glorious doctrine of holiness under which my soul had become so illuminated. The Gospel Trumpet, at the time I was led into the light, was a semimonthly paper containing four pages, and was being published at Williamston, Michigan. About that time the Trumpet Office was moved to Grand Junction. The Trumpet was then edited and published by D. S. Warner and J. C. Fisher.

In the autumn of 1886 some strange visions appeared to some of the holiness people. Bert Spalding, who was then foreman of the Trumpet Office had a vision which was published in the Trumpet, as follows: He seemed to be going to the office to begin his daily labors one morning, when he observed that the Trumpet Office was on fire. Soon the entire building was wrapped in the dreadful flames, and it was evident that the entire printing office was lost. "How is this,

Lord?" he exclaimed, "Did you not tell me the Trumpet Office was yours, and that you would take care of it?" "Look up," came the answer, and when he looked up he saw the Trumpets arising out of the flames and flying in every direction until the whole earth was filled with them. When he awoke from this vision he felt assured that God was revealing to him a dreadful trial that was about to come upon the holiness work. The following spring J. C. Fisher, the publisher of the Trumpet, forsook his wife and eloped with a grass-widow. This brought an awful persecution upon the church, and it seemed for a time that the work would be destroyed. Many weak souls fell under the dreadful trial. For about three months the brethren labored to restore this man unto God, but all in vain. We then remembered Bro. Spaulding's vision, and knew the signification of that part of it which related to the burning of the Trumpet Office.

With this awful stench upon the cause the church assembled in a general camp-meeting at Bangor, Michigan, in June, 1887. But this meeting was not accompanied by the usual power of God. These general meetings in previous years had been so accompanied by the power of the Holy Spirit that souls were brought to Christ in many marvelous ways. I might relate a remarkable incident that was related to me by the man who had the experience. He came upon the camp-ground intoxicated, leading an ox which was blind in one eye, stating to some that he was going to have J. C. Fisher lay hands on the ox and heal him, and to others that he was going to offer him upon the altar in the saints' camp-meeting. He was armed with

a revolver to shoot the first man who would interfere.
A brother, who discovered what he was about to do,
loosened the drunken man's rope from the ox and led
him off the ground.   When the drunken man discovered his defeat, with his mouth filled with profanity and
threatenings against the life of whomsoever had interfered with his work, he started to leave the grounds.
He had gone but a few hundred yards from the
camp-ground when his limbs gave way and refused to
carry him further.   He lay prostrate upon the ground
for some time, while the Spirit of God was working
upon his heart.   He said he had not power to arise
and walk further until he promised God that if he
would cause strength to return to his limbs, he would
return to the camp and give his heart to God.   Immediately he received strength to walk and, according to
his promise, went directly to the camp and gave
his heart to God.   Many similar, remarkable manifestations of God's power were witnessed in those meetings.   The sick were healed, blind eyes were opened,
deaf ears were unstopped, as in the time of Christ.
But this power seemed greatly hindered when the
church assembled in June, 1887.   God revealed by
visions, unto his people that the good work could not
go on except that wicked preacher (Fisher) was renounced by the church.   I will relate a remarkable
vision given to a sister at that meeting.   She saw a
cemetery, in the midst of which rose a stone building,
clean and white as snow.   She cast her eyes toward it,
when she saw a little golden railroad track from this
white building unto heaven.   Soon she saw a little
golden train come up out of this white building,

and start up the track, moving rapidly. Suddenly it stopped, the engineer and fireman poked their heads out of the cab windows and looked forward as though they saw something on the track. At this moment the sister looked in the direction they were looking and saw a large black wedge lying upon one of the rails. Near the wedge were four black stakes, driven between the ties. It was evident that an enemy was trying to wreck the little train. God then spoke to the sister, saying: "This train can go no further until that wedge and those stakes are removed." Soon after this the church openly renounced J. C. Fisher and those who were clinging to him, and the work moved on again with power as before. It was not until June, 1888, that I was permitted to attend the first of these general camp-meetings. At this meeting I witnessed the manifestation of God's power in many ways. The altar was crowded with seekers in every service. The sick were healed, devils were cast out, and the miraculous power of God was manifested in many ways. Bro. D. S. Warner and company had just returned from a tour in the western states, and we all listened with interest to the relation of their successes and persecutions on that trip. At St. James, Missouri, they met some people who were influenced by a supernatural power known as the "jerks." They would hop about on one foot, twist their bodies into almost every conceivable shape, and act very unseemly; they also claimed to have those among them who possessed the apostolic gift of tongues and the interpretation of tongues. Bro. Warner took a stand against the spirit by which they were actuated and ascribed their manifestations to the spirit of the devil, and forbade the devil, in the name of the Lord, to proceed any further with his work. Their manifestations soon came to naught, and nearly every one of them was delivered from that influence that had caused them to act so strangely. Many of them were found to be possessed with devils, and had to have them cast out before they were able to get salvation. This defeat of the devil caused him to stir up the baser sort against the brethren, and before their series of meetings closed a mob came upon the camp-ground, at a late hour of the night, and demanded that the ground at once be cleared of all the saints, which orders, under the circumstances, had to be obeyed. The ministers were sought for by the mob, but by the aid of the brethren and the protection of Almighty God, they escaped. A great many churches had been raised up under the labors of Bro. Warner and his colaborers during their western tour. Also during this trip Brothers Warner and Warren were preparing the manuscript for the second song-book that was published by the saints, the "Anthems from the Throne." Their first song-book, "Songs of Victory" had been compiled by J. C. Fisher, and since he had now fallen it was thought best to prepare a new book. One of the leading preachers who attended this camp-meeting, C. Z. Lindley, soon afterwards turned away from the faith and began to publish a paper against the teachings of The Gospel Trumpet.

From this camp-meeting I went into the state of Ohio, and for several years I traveled in the states of Ohio, Indiana, and Pennsylvania. In 1889 I was not permitted to attend the general camp-meeting at Bangor, Michigan, but I was present in 1890. This was the last camp-meeting held at Bangor. The next year the general camp-meeting was moved to Grand Junction. In the autumn of 1890 I made my first trip to Pennsylvania. In the spring of 1891 I held several meetings in different parts of western Ohio. About twelve miles south of Kenton I held a series of meetings for about two weeks, in a schoolhouse. Near the beginning of this series of meetings, while I was asking a manifestation from those who 'desired 'the prayers of God's people that they might be saved, a young man raised his hand in derision. I felt that the Spirit of God was greatly grieved, and told the congregation that the young man was mocking God, and asked the Christian people present to kneel with me while I prayed for him. My soul seemed' greatly burdened for his eternal welfare. I felt that God was offended by what he had done. About three days after this the young man took violently sick, and about the time my series of meetings closed, he died.

In June of this same year I made a second trip to Pennsylvania. In the autumn of this year, Bro. D. S. Warner and others assisted me in several camp and grove meetings in western Ohio. During our meeting near New Hampshire, in Auglaize county, I witnessed a remarkable manifestation of God's power as follows: During one of the night services a company of worldly young men was heard coming through the woods towards the camp. They rent the air with their fiendish yells; as they came closer and closer the speaker (D. S. Warner) was more and more annoyed,

and suddenly he paused and sighed: then in a loud voice
he said, "In the name of Jesus Christ I rebuke all the
devils in this woods." Instantly the hallooing ceased,
and the boys all came up to the grounds, and quietly
took seats among the listeners, nor was there any further interruption that night. About the first of September, 1891, in company with my wife, Bro. D. S.
Warner, and others, I made a third trip to Pennsylvania, where I labored about three months, and then returned to my home at West Liberty, Ohio.

Up to this time my life had been one of extreme
poverty since I had embraced the glorious evening
light. Myself and family even suffered from insufficient clothing, but we never suffered for bread. Our
faith was weak, but we knew we were walking in the
light of God's truth and we decided we would go
through on the line of faith regardless of the consequences. My wife and I had long prayed to God for a
home of our own, that we might be freed from the in-
convenience of moving about and paying rent. In
March, 1892, we decided that we would build a house.
We had $10.00 for which my wife had sold the chick-
ens she had raised the year before. We moved to
Clark county, Ohio, and purchased a lot from a farmer,
for which we obligated ourselves to pay $30.00. I paid
the $10.00 on the lot to bind the bargain, and began to
build the house. I had no money to pay my bills, and
did not know where it was to come from; but I had
prayed enough over this matter to know I was moving
in God's order. I applied to a building and loan association in Springfield, Ohio, for a loan on my house,
which they promised to grant, but later refused. I

took the matter in earnest prayer to God, and the
Spirit of the Lord said to me: "You shall have the
money, but you must first be tried." I tried several
times to borrow the money and failed. By this time
the carpenters were building my house and I had not
a cent to pay my bills, but I went on with confidence,
knowing that the Lord was leading. By the time my
bills began to come due a brother came to me and
handed me $60.00, saying: "Brother Schell, I believe
you have been asking God for the money with which
to pay your bills; here is $60.00 which you can use, and
you may pay me back in sixty days." I took the
money believing that it was of the Lord to do so, but
did not know where the money would come from to
pay it back sixty days hence. Later I called upon
another building and loan association in New Carlisle,
Ohio, and asked for a loan of $250.00 upon my house.
They sent a committee to examine the property, after
which they decided that they could not risk more than
$200.00 upon it. I borrowed this amount from them,
but it lacked about $100.00 of paying my bills. I
paid the dues on the $200.00 for six months, but was
unable to obtain money to pay the remainder of my
bills. I did not at that time have sufficient faith to
trust God to give me that much money; so I asked
him to make that loan association let me have another
$100.00, which I asked them for, and they granted my
request without hesitancy.

In the winter of 1892-93, assisted by Bro. B. E.
Warren and others, I held a very fruitful revival meeting at Lawrenceville, Ohio. I had been invited by
some of the citizens of that town to come and preach

in their schoolhouse. I sent an appointment, and went and preached to them over Lord's day, with the intention of continuing the meeting the coming week. Just before the services Sunday evening, the trustees of the schoolhouse informed me that for certain reasons they thought best not to continue the meetings any longer in the schoolhouse, and requested me to make a statement at the close of my service of their request, and said they thought the trustees of the Reformed church-house would invite me to continue the meeting in their house of worship. I made the statement according to their request, but not one of the trustees, although they were all present, made any move toward inviting me into their house of worship; so I closed the meeting with the statement that I was now free from the blood of the souls of the people in that town, unless a building of some kind would be opened for me to preach in, and that if any one present was able to assist God's work by offering me a room of some kind to preach in and did not do it, God would hold him responsible for all the souls who would have been saved had the meeting continued. That night I went home with a family of saints who lived two miles west of the town. I felt greatly burdened for the souls of the people and could not prevent the feeling that it would be wrong for us to leave that place without continuing the meeting longer. Before we retired that night we agreed to pray God to so burden the trustees of the house of worship that they could not sleep. The next morning, before I arose, a knock was heard at my bedroom door. The sister who had entered the agreement with me the night before had rushed to my room to tell me that one of the trustees of the house of worship had come to inform me that we could continue our meeting in their meeting-house. I hastened to meet the man, who told me he felt very sorry for having treated us with such indifference the night before, and said he was so troubled all night that he could not sleep. "Now," said he, "I arose very early this morning and have been to see all the trustees, and they are all willing, except one, for you to use the church, on condition that you continue to preach the word of God as you have since coming into our midst." I assured him that I would. "Then," said he, "you may go ahead with your meetings and we will send out the word that you will preach for us to-night and will have a large congregation for you." We continued that meeting for four weeks, and a great number of souls were saved, and many were healed of bodily afflictions. The word went out through the secular papers that the sick were being healed in our meetings. In different parts of the country there were sick who read these reports in the papers and wrote me in regard to their healing. I instructed them in the doctrine of divine healing the best I could, and some of them were healed.

Among those who wrote to me at that time, was Mrs. M. N. Wing, who was in a hospital in Columbus, Ohio, in a hopeless condition. She had many afflictions and had also a withered hand. I sent her The Gospel Trumpet and a book on divine healing and instructed her in the way of the Lord by letter; the entire church in the community where I lived united with me in prayer for her healing; also, I instructed the afflicted party to write to the Trumpet Office for prayers, and in a very short time I received a letter from her, which read as follows: "Bro. Schell, the Lord has wonderfully healed my body and made my withered hand as whole as the other in one night." I have never been permitted to meet this sister, but those who have seen her say the flesh of her restored hand, like that of Naaman, resembled the flesh of a little child.

During the winter of 1893-94, in company with B. E. Warren, I labored in Pennsylvania. We held some very fruitful meetings, and as calls from new places came in so fast, we felt led to separate so that we could hold two meetings at the same time, and thus reach more people. I went to Tionesta, where I preached for about two weeks. Near the close of this meeting I was called about four miles from town to pray for a sick child that had been given up to die, by several physicians. Before answering this call I went in earnest prayer to God to know if it was his will for me to go, and the Spirit said to me: "Go with them, doubting nothing; for I have sent them." I knew by this that the Lord was going to heal the child. I went with them, anointed the child, laid my hands upon it, and prayed fervently for its healing. The power of God came down upon the child and it was instantly healed. I went back to town and continued my meeting as before. Soon I received a call to come to the neighborhood where the child was healed and hold a series of meetings in their schoolhouse. The parents of the child that was healed had reported the miracle to the neighbors, and the entire neighborhood was convinced that God had wrought a mighty work among them, and they were ready to turn unto the Lord. I opened up a series of meetings in their schoolhouse at three o'clock Friday afternoon. I never had commenced such a meeting. The people came together to hear the words of God, but I was so burdened with real soul-travail that I could hardly preach to them. I talked to them for a short time and then gave an invitation for sinners to come forward and seek salvation. There were two old-fashioned recitation benches in the schoolhouse, and I set them both out for a mercy-seat. They both together reached almost across the schoolhouse. I began to sing a hymn and the whole congregation arose and came forward to seek Christ. The altar was filled from end to end two or three deep. I spent some time praying with them, and then dismissed the service. That night both altar benches were filled as before. I continued the meeting on Saturday night and Sunday and Sunday night, with the altar filled with seekers in every service. Monday I baptized them and preached to them again on Monday evening, and on Tuesday bade farewell to the happy church that had been raised up in a few days to carry the glad tidings to the perishing souls in other parts.

In July, 1895, assisted by Bro. J. N. Howard and others, I held a tabernacle meeting at Muncie, Indiana. Some of the sisters who were visiting the people who lived near to where our tabernacle was pitched, found an afflicted sister who had just been brought home from a hospital where she had been pronounced incurable by physicians. The sisters instructed her in the doctrine of divine healing, and she was soon led to

believe that the Lord was able to heal her body.   She
sent for us to come and anoint her, which we did, and
the Lord instantly healed her.   She arose and went to
our meetings that same day, and some of the people
when they saw what a mighty work the Lord had done
for her, turned to the Lord.   During this meeting,
Bro. Howard and I slept in our tent.   One night three
sinners who lived twenty miles from where we were
preaching asked us if they might not stay in the tent
with us over night.   We told them they could, and we
all retired.   I felt a peculiar burden that evening, which
prevented my sleep.   A little gust of wind would strike
the tabernacle occasionally and we feared that it might
be blown down.   We had two large gas lights burning in the tabernacle, which would burn it up should
the wind blow it down.   A short time after we
retired, the Spirit of God said to me: "You must arise
and take this tabernacle down immediately or it will
be blown down by the wind."   I sprang from my bed
and announced what the Lord had told me.   The entire company arose hastily and helped make ready to
lower the tabernacle.   We had just got the gas turned
out and had laid hold of the ropes to lower the tent
when the gale struck us, blowing our tent flat upon
us, breaking one of our large center-poles and tearing
the tent in several places, but fortunately no one was
hurt.

In December, 1895, I assisted G. W. Howard in a
revival meeting in Castine, Ohio.   This was the sad-
dest series of meetings I ever helped to hold.   The
Lord helped us in preaching the word and it seemed
to be taking good effect upon the hearts of the people,

but I felt such a burden as it seemed I had never felt before. On Wednesday evening, Dec. 11 my heart was so overwhelmed with sorrow that I could not preach the word. I communicated to the church a knowledge of my feelings, and suggested that we spend the time of that service largely in fervent prayer, which we did, and while there earnestly calling upon the Lord, I felt the seal of God upon my heart to enable me to endure the coming blow. On Thursday morning notwithstanding the sadness of my heart, I endeavored to preach on the subject of advancement. About eleven o'clock, when I had perhaps about half completed my sermon, the chapel door slowly opened, and the form of the telegraph operator appeared in the door with a small envelope in his hand. My first thought was: "He has a sad message for me." He paused just inside the door (as though he bore an important message but feared it out of order to communicate it to me while in the pulpit) then advancing part way up the aisle, dropped the envelope in the hand of Bro. G. W. Howard, at the same time telling him something in a whisper. Bro. Howard immediately turned his eyes upon me, which fully confirmed my belief that the message was for me, and I paused to receive it. Oh, what sadness filled my heart as I reached forth my hand to receive the envelope! As I was tearing it open, Bro. H. suggested that the congregation engage in singing No. 1 in "Echoes from Glory" while I was reading the message.

> "Far away among the angels,
> In the sweet celestial bowers
> Start the songs whose echoes gladden
> As they reach this world of ours,"

Little did I think as they began to sing those beautiful words that the echoes that were then reaching our ears from the glory world, were of the songs the angels were just then singing to welcome our dear sainted brother Warner to his eternal rest in Christ. I read the message first to myself. My heart was so overwhelmed with sorrow that I could not read it aloud at first. When I had gained sufficient command of myself, I said: "Brethren, I can not finish this lesson now." After another short pause, I read the message aloud—

"Brother D. S. Warner died this morning. Be buried Sunday. Come, preach funeral."

O God, what a blow to our hearts! We fell upon our knees and called upon the Lord to help us bear the burden of our sorrow. The next day I took train for Grand Junction, and oh, how sad I felt as I looked upon the pale, though sweet face I had so often greeted with a kiss of charity. "O God," thought I, "how can we spare this bold witness to the truth?" Again I thought, "Who could chide the just providence of God who has taken this lifelong sufferer for Christ to the rest he truly deserves?" His remains were laid away until the resurrection day in the humble little graveyard of the saints, near the Children's Home, one mile north of Grand Junction, on Sunday, Dec. 15, 1895.

In the spring of 1896 I sold my house in Ohio and moved to Grand Junction. On my way to Grand Junction, I helped to hold a remarkable revival meeting, four miles west of Antwerp, Ohio. We preached for many days unto the people, without any visible

24

effect upon them; so we closed the meeting with scarcely a convert to Christ. As soon as we had closed the meeting a dreadful burden of some kind fell upon my heart. I prayed much that night to know what it meant. The next day I prayed all day. I went into the barn, climbed into the mow, threw myself upon the hay, and there prayed and wrestled beneath my burden, but could not find out what it meant. In the evening the brother with whom we were staying came to me and told me that a young man from the neighborhood had come to talk with us. He said he thought the man wanted to be saved. I arose and went with him to the house, and asked the young man if he had come to get saved. He said he had; so we knelt with him before the Lord and in a few minutes he was born into the kingdom. We then asked the wife of the brother with whom we were staying if she also did not want to be saved. (She was a backslider.) She said she did. We then knelt with her, and soon she also was born of the Spirit. We then decided that we would go to the house of one of the nearest neighbors, and pray with them. (The husband and wife were both backsliders.) When we told them that we had come to pray for their salvation, they decided to give their hearts unto the Lord, and after a few minutes' prayer they both testified that they had obtained peace with God. By this time another neighbor, who was also a backslider, was passing by. We went out and invited him to come into the house and give his heart to God. He decided he would, and in a few minutes he was also born into the kingdom. We then went together from house to house until we had canvassed the neighborhood and in nearly every house we found some one who was willing to be saved. About a dozen souls were, in this manner, brought into the kingdom. The burden had by this time left me, and we went on to Grand Junction.

In the autumn of 1896 I traveled through the state of Missouri. I was at this time in very poor health. I had suffered for more than ten years from indigestion, and by this time I had become so very badly afflicted that it became evident that I must receive healing from the Lord or I must die. My food would not digest sufficiently to keep up my bodily strength. At Thayer, Missouri, I made a statement of my condition before the saints, who were assembled in the camp-meeting at that place, and requested them to pray earnestly for my healing. I also wrote to the church at Carthage, to unite their prayers with ours, for my healing. The Lord answered these prayers by appearing to me in a most wonderful manner, and giving me the witness that I was perfectly healed. I felt his power going through my entire body, purging out the last iota of disease. At that time my weight was 154 lbs.; one week after I was healed it was 166 lbs. Soon I had reached 174 lbs., and I kept on increasing until I weighed more than 200 lbs. I have never since fell below that weight.

During the winter of 1896-7 I accompanied Bro. E. E. Byrum on a tour through the southern states. We enjoyed many precious seasons with the churches. At Tullahoma, Tennessee, we held a few days' meeting, which resulted in the salvation of a few souls. The wicked elements of the unsaved were greatly stirred against us, and one night just after the services were closed, a rock was thrown from the rear end of the house of worship, which barely missed my head, and struck the wall just behind me, making an indentation fully one-half inch deep, but the Lord did not allow a hair of our heads to perish. Soon after the close of this meeting we attended a ten days' assembly of the saints at Hartsells, Alabama. This was one of the most precious and spiritual meetings I have ever attended. We held a number of meetings at five o'clock in the morning, which were attended by some of God's children living as far away as three miles. Wave after wave of the power of the Holy Spirit descended upon the church as the little ones endeavored to sink deeper and deeper into God's holy will. Sometimes sinners would attend those early morning meetings. At one of these meetings the saints united in a fervent prayer for God to lay his hand in convicting power upon every sinner present. In answer to this prayer the Spirit wrought so effectively upon the sinners that some of them immediately came to the altar and got saved, and the rest, every one of them, fled from the meeting. At the close of this meeting, Bro. Otto Bolds accompanied us to Renfroe, Mississippi, where we enjoyed another precious assembling of the saints. At this meeting we saw a great many sinners brought to Christ, and many believers sanctified, also a great many sick were healed. A little girl about three years old, belonging to one of the ministers present, became very sick during this meeting, with something like cholera infantum. A few hours after she was taken sick, we were sent for to come and

pray for her.   She was lying in an unconscious state
with her eyes closed, as it seemed, in death.   We all
knelt and prayed to God to spare the child, then all
the ministers present laid their hands upon her and
rebuked the affliction in the name of Jesus, and almost
instantly upon the removal of our hands from her
body, the child opened her eyes, and arising, sat up,
inquired for her wraps, and asked to be taken to meeting.   She was then taken to the house of worship,
where the father related the marvelous work the Lord
had wrought upon the child, and many hearing thereof
gave glory to God.   At the close of this meeting, we
separated.   Bro. Byrum went into the state of Georgia and I in company with other ministers, proceeded
southward as far as Hammond, Louisiana, from
whence I returned home.

During the winter of 1896-7 I labored under a debt
of $350.00, incurred by building a house in Grand
Junction, the summer before.   I prayed earnestly to
God for means to pay this debt, and during the general camp-meeting at Grand Junction in June, 1897 I
was called into a tent to converse with a brother and
sister, who gave me money enough to pay all my debts.
In the autumn of this same year I attended a very precious camp-meeting at Hartsells, Alabama; from there
I went to Wichita, Kansas, to attend the first general
western camp-meeting.

In the autumn of 1897 I made a western tour, holding meetings at Colfax, Washington; Woodburn and
Scio, Oregon; Oakland, Fresno, Los Angeles, and
San Diego, California; and Phœnix, Arizona.   While
in Oakland, I passed through a test of faith and gained

a victory that I shall never forget. I was 3,000 miles
from home, had my family to support, and my clothing
was very poor, especially my overcoat and pants. Just
before I left home I had borrowed $25.00 to assist
in the support of my family, which I had agreed to pay
upon my return. Now I had but $10.00 in my pocket.
I went to God in earnest prayer, and asked him to
supply all my needs. I believed he would do it, and
rested sweetly in the full assurance that my needs
would be supplied. In a short time after this I received money enough to purchase a ticket to Chicago,
which I purchased via the Southern Pacific Railway,
so that I might be permitted to visit some of the
churches in southern California and Arizona during
the thirty days' limit that was on my ticket. My first
stop-off was at Fresno, California, where we saw souls
saved and the sick healed in our meetings. From
Fresno I went to Los Angeles. There were but few
of the saints living in Los Angeles, but the Lord
blessed our united efforts to rescue souls in the little
hall which they had rented. The brethren had advertised the meetings in the papers, and a soldier from
the Home near Los Angeles saw the advertisement,
and came to the meeting. He was fascinated by the
truth and came to the altar to seek holiness. At the
close of the last service, at this place, this soldier when
saying good-by to me dropped a $20.00 gold piece into
my hand. From Los Angeles I went to San Diego,
where I had a very precious meeting with the saints
for a few days; souls were saved, and the children of
God seemed to be greatly edified under the preaching
of the Word. At this meeting God moved the people

to share their means with me.   One sister gave me
$23.00.   At the close of this meeting I started to
Phœnix, Arizona, via Los Angeles.   I had made arrangements to stop over at Los Angeles and hold two
more services with the saints there.   The soldier previously mentioned brought another soldier with him to
these meetings, unto whom he had been endeavoring
to teach the true way.   The first evening this other
soldier came to the altar to consecrate himself unto
the Lord.   At the close of the service he handed me
a $50.00 bill, with the words, "Take this and use it to
the glory of God."   After holding a short series of
meetings in Phœnix, I proceeded to Chicago to enjoy
a most blessed assembly of the saints.

When I arrived in Chicago, I received a letter from
a sister at Wymore, Nebraska, which had been written
soon after I had prayed so earnestly for means in Oakland.   It had been forwarded from place to place and
had finally overtaken me in Chicago.   It read about
as follows: "Brother Schell, I had a dream about you.
I do not go much on dreams, but I believe there is
something in this one because I dreamed it twice.   I
dreamed that I saw you and that your clothing was
very poor, especially your overcoat and pants.   I have
no money at this date, but please let me know if you
are really in need."   In my reply I told the sister that
her dream was doubtless of the Lord, because my
clothes were getting somewhat shabby, but told her
the Lord had been supplying me with some means and
I was going to get a new suit of clothes soon.   She
immediately sent me another letter with $5.00 in it to
help purchase my clothes.

During the winter of 1897-8 some of the saints began to feel the necessity of moving the Trumpet Office from Grand Junction, as the work was getting too large for that village. During the following spring through a train of circumstances, which we believe to have been the hand of God, it was decided to move the Trumpet Office to Moundsville, West Virginia, and the move was made in July, 1898. A special train consisting of nine freight cars, two passenger cars, and a baggage car, moved the machinery and the Trumpet Family to Moundsville.

During the summer of 1898, a burden came upon the hearts of many of the ministers of a crisis of some kind that was to come upon the church. At the Emlenton camp-meeting Bro. A. B. Palmer arose and told the saints that God had showed him there was a dreadful crisis of some kind ahead, and warned all to be prepared for it. Soon after this a delusive spirit became manifest in several of the ministers, that was causing them to oppose the doctrine of sanctification. It continued to spread until more than a dozen of the ministers took a decided stand against the second cleansing, and spread havoc through a number of churches, especially in the west. They were faithfully admonished concerning their error, but stubbornly resisted every admonition. The work suffered greatly under the influence of these men until they were renounced through the Trumpet, and the church took a decided stand against them at the general camp-meeting at Moundsville, in 1899. Since that time the light has spread rapidly throughout the world, and God has shown his approval upon his people as in former years.

With this I close my autobiography, leaving the future to add such things as the good hand of our God may determine, and ask the prayers of all the saints that God may make my life in the future, more spiritual and more useful to God, than in the past.

Yours for the whole gospel,

Wm. G. Schell.

Moundsville, W. Va. Mar. 21, 1900.

CHARLES AND MINNIE ORR.

For the purpose of impressing the heart and mind of the reader with the realities of God, and the blessings of his salvation I here tell of his wonderful dealings and great goodness to me. This evening in a beautiful reminiscence I live again through all my past life. I recall to memory the many acts of providential care. I see here and there the pitfalls and snares of sin carefully planned and laid by Satan to destroy my soul, but the hand of wisdom ordered the occurrence of events which turned me from their way. As I now behold the care and loving-kindness of God to me, deep gratitude fills my heart and a rich glory fills my soul, drawing me very near to him. The warmest affections of my heart are aroused, making all things in the kingdom of heaven especially dear to me. I know that God has done the very best for me all along my journey of life. I humbly confess that "God is love," and that it is by his grace and mercy that I am in life and health, and that his peace and glory enriching my soul makes my life an Eden. In telling of the blessings and goodness of God to me in the following pages I shall not overdraw—that would be impossible.

My words are inadequate to picture to your mind in a true light the Fatherly care and mercy and loving-kindness of God.

My boyhood days were spent upon a large and beautiful farm. There was much in my surroundings calculated to turn the heart and mind to noble and pure things. In those youthful days I found more pleasure and had a deeper love for the elevating and sublime things of nature than many older heads, and even those of my parents, were aware. The flowers in the beauty of their bloom and the birds in the sweetness of their songs even in those childhood days spoke to me of God, and influenced me to virtuous ways. There were also some things in my surroundings well calculated to turn my feet in the ways of sensuality. The power of evil is employed to destroy the better and nobler faculties of the human heart.

I was the youngest, save one, of a large family. Except my mother, none of our family made any profession of Christianity. Judging from what I have now learned of the nature of Christianity, I can see but little evidence of a Christian experience in the life of my mother, but I love to hope for the best. She was kind and affectionate, and taught me the right and the wrong, but more from the standpoint of morality than of Christianity. When about eight years old I committed the first transgression for which I experienced a sense of guilt and shame. I felt I had incurred some one's displeasure. I thought it must be my mother's; so I went to her and to ease my smitten conscience I made excuses to her for my crime, and even added falsehood, which only increased the sense of guilt in my heart. Had I been taught of God at this time, in all probability I would not have been led into the ways of sin in which I have since walked. As it was, the voice of conscience spoke loudly to my soul and warned me of the dangers of vice, but sin swayed its scepter over me and despite the reprovings of conscience I was led on in the ordinary way of the young. When about ten years old one sunny afternoon in company with two of my sisters a remarkable incident occurred, which awakened me to the fact that there is a Supreme Power and Being.

Life went on, the years went by. There were seasons when I would experience great aspirations for high and noble things. I admired the pure and virtuous. I would look upon a holy and unspotted character as the most beautiful thing upon the earth. Many a time in those youthful days I have absented myself from company to give my heart opportunity for meditation. I would picture before me a life of honor and usefulness. I would fancy myself as being a great benefactor of my fellow man, and doing great services in the kingdom of God. No doubt many of those meditations originated from self and pride, but not all.

Again, there would come seasons of discouragement and despondency. Hopes and aspirations would take wings and fly away. I would listen to the voice of the tempter, and to still the voice of conscience would throw myself into the current of sensuality and be swept onward in the ways of vice. At this point of my life I have given my experiene in another work about as follows. "One night on my way home from the ballroom where inebriacy and sensuality ran high, a pleading came to the better part of my nature, endeavoring to move me to a higher, purer life. Strange were the sensations that came upon me. I looked along down through the future and saw misery, wretchedness, and woe in this life, and an eternity with lost souls in the torturing flames of hell if I continued in such a course. I saw also a life of usefulness, bright and happy days, a pure and holy character, and a blessed immortality in the paradise of God, if I would but surrender to the gentle persuadings of the angelic voice within my heart. Alas, Satan baffled the angel of mercy by enabling me to console and ease my conscience in the hope that God would hear and answer the prayers of my kind mother, spare my life; and after a few more years of sensual indulgence I would then turn to God and live to his praise. But this gentle monitor was not thus to be put aside; it came again and again, until my conscience was smitten by the mighty hand, and I was made to tremble before the dark, uncertain future. As I would awake in the morning, an unseen hand would point out to me my sins, a fear would come over me, and I, startled, would look around as if ready to flee from some hideous monster of the dark. The day would be spent in planning for the evening; for to spend it in the privacy of my chamber was more than I could endure. The place of revelry was sought to drown the voice of conscience. I would throw myself into the festivities with all the force of my being and appear the gayest of the gay. But when the sound of revelry was hushed, when the cup of sin had been drained, and I had reached the silence of my chamber, there with all the world shut out and naught to stand between me and the whisperings of my soul, I would be again brought face to face with eternal things. As I would look across the dark valley of death to the fertile fields of glory, a pain would pierce my heart at the thought of forever being denied the privilege of entering there. My sins would lie heavy upon my heart and seem to crush me down into the dark abyss of woe. To lie upon my bed was to toss to and fro in uneasiness, fearing to close my eyes in slumber lest I should never awake. Thus days came and went and grew to months and years.''

During these years from the age of twenty to twenty-five I would oftentimes be deeply convicted of sin. There seemed to be no man to care for my soul. In all these years no one ever spoke to me individually of God and his salvation. God, however, taught me of himself. In these seasons when the Holy Spirit was striving with my heart I frequently made attempts at prayer. Though unsaved, God gave some unmistakably answers to my prayers, and thus saved me from infidelity. At one time when I was about to engage in an important affair of life, I felt my need of God and his direction. I sought the Lord in humble earnest prayer, and he very preciously manifested himself to me. At another time when passing by a dense forest I felt a great drawing of my soul to God. I went in prayer, and was assured in my heart that my prayer came up as a memorial before him. I was very ignorant. I knew not how to believe upon God that I might gain a constant victory over sin, consequently I would be frequently overcome, and never professed to be saved.   One night when taking a horseback ride of some seven miles God so wonderfully answered my prayer and taught me of himself as to make it impossible for Satan ever to have me doubt that there was a God.   I left one village at nine o'clock at night to go to another seven miles distant.   After riding a little more than a mile my horse suddenly became lame.   In pity for the animal I dismounted, and placing the bridle rein over the saddle started the horse on before me.   After walking nearly two miles, I suppose, I noticed my horse had greatly improved.   I then thought I would ride, but failed in my attempt to catch the horse.   I repeatedly attempted to come up with him, but when I would approach quite near he would trot off from me.   After several unsuccessful attempts to catch him, I seemed to be spoken to in these words: "If you should ask God to help you catch the horse, he would help you."   Upon this impressive suggestion I lifted my heart for a moment to God imploring his aid in catching the horse.   Real confidence came into my heart, and I felt as I started out to gain possession of the animal that I was a "worker together with God" in the matter.   As I came up with the horse, instead of his trotting off as before he stopped and stood quietly while I mounted.   I went on my way in deep thought, knowing that God is real and that he does lend a helping hand to man in the affairs of life.   Glory to his name!

In the early spring of 1887 my soul became filled with deep longings for the salvation of God.   I became especially desirous of preparing for the mansion my Savior had prepared for me.   I began attending a pro-

tracted meeting which was in progress in the village in
which I lived. One evening when I returned from
school, as I was engaged in teaching at that time, I
told my wife I intended to join church that night. So
great was my ignorance in those days that I thought it
necessary to join some denomination in order to gain
heaven. I united with the religious society at that
place and was baptized. I was disappointed. I found
about the same affections in my heart for the world as
were there before. I also retained the same hasty,
impatient disposition. As I looked beyond the regions
of death, all was as dark and uncertain as before. I
wondered if I had not taken the way that leads to
heaven, and yet I had no certain evidence that I was
in that way. I inquired of some of the old members
of this society how it was with them. "If God should
call for you to-night, do you know you would go to
heaven?" They would answer me in about these
words: "We can never know that in this world; we
do the best we can here, and hope all will be well over
there." Satan tried to console me with this, but I
was not to be thus consoled. Often I became troubled
about my soul. I was seeking something positive,
some certain evidence that I was ready to meet God.
An incident occurred at this time that greatly awakened
me. One night shortly after retiring I was aroused by
the cry of "Fire, fire!" upon the street. I hurriedly
arose, and on looking out the whole heavenly expanse
appeared to be one leaping, surging flame of fire. My
first thought was: "The world is on fire, and the end
of time has come." The fear, despair, and horror that
possessed me is indescribable. Oh, could but the

rocks and mountains fall upon me and forever hide me! What appeared to me to be a flame of fire overhead was only the reflection of light upon the overhanging clouds from a burning mill on the opposite side of the hill. The next day, time went on as before, but why should I experience such alarm at the thought of eternity's dawning? I who professed to be a Christian, who professed and strove to love and serve God—why should I so fear the coming of my Redeemer? This experience was not soon forgotten. There was a faithful monitor ever whispering to my soul these words: "Make your calling and election sure."

My Conversion. During the summer of 1889 I became more deeply convicted of sin than ever before. It is impossible for me to tell you of my feelings at this time in such a way that you could get any correct conception of them. Day after day the load of sin grew heavier. At times despair seemed to be written all over earth and heaven. I kept praying as best I could. There was no one to whom I could go for help and instruction but the Lord alone. Every time I asked man for instruction I became confused. On Sunday evening, Oct. 26, I became more in earnest than ever before in my life, but went to my bed without having obtained any assurance of my acceptance with God. On Monday morning as I started to go to my school I asked my wife to pray for me. I had about one and one-half miles to walk. The morning was clear and calm and cool. I was seemingly unconscious to all around me. My soul was wrestling with God. As I walked on praying, suddenly a sweet sensation thrilled my entire being, a soft mellow light shone

round me.   The hitherto stillness of the morning was
disturbed by the faintest and sweetest strains of mel-
ody I ever heard.   It was the voice of gladness in my
soul.   The whole earth was full of light and music.
The sun just rising shone with an unsurpassed splendor.   A glorious resurrection was effected in my soul.
I was brought forth from the tomb and made the in-
habitant of a new world.   It appeared that I was suddenly transported to some happy land where the
beauty and magnificence of nature were increased a
thousandfold.   The blue and purple tinted autumn
leaves embroidered with frost glistened in the sunlight
like the robe of an ephod of blue embroidered with
pomegranates of blue, of purple, and of scarlet, with
bells of gold between them.   See Ex. 28:31-33.   The
air contained a fragrant odor; the sky looked peaceful
and pure.   Everything in nature, together with my
happy heart, seemed intent on praising God.   Life and
peace from God flowed through my soul like a tranquil
stream, and I wished I could spend an eternity in this
elysian spot.   That day in school was one of peace and
rest.   The meeting with my wife in the evening seemed
like the meeting of happy spirits on celestial shores.
In the days of our deep conviction and sorrow of heart
we were wont to fancy to ourselves the happiness of
angels and heaven.   We had now come into an experience of happiness that surpassed our strongest imagina-
tions of the happiness of angels.

> My soul was filled with sweetest rest:
> All heaven seemed lodged within my breast.

My wife was converted in her home about one week
prior to my conversion.   She had been making a pro-

fession of Christianity for several years, and I for nearly three years. Our connection was with a very formal people. They did not believe in the instantaneous regeneration of man by the Spirit. As we began to tell them of the wonderful change God had wrought in our hearts, they looked upon us with a suspicious eye and welcomed us no longer to their meetings. Many were the attempts of man and Satan to persuade us to disbelieve the mighty work of God in our soul, but to no avail. We knew what God had done for us. That uneasiness that once filled my breast at the thought of death was gone. I could now welcome death as a child its peaceful slumber. Everything before me was bright and hopeful. I knew that should death come to me, heaven would be my eternal home. All doubts and fears were gone, and I was blessed and happy as mortal could wish to be. Sometime after my conversion an incident occurred that caused me again to think the end of time had come. One evening after retiring and falling into a peaceful sleep, a strong gust of wind blew the lower sash of my bedroom window in. It came with a crash upon the uncarpeted floor. Instantly the thought came to my half-awakened mind, "The world is passing away with a great noise," and I called aloud to my wife, "Praise the Lord, my dear! I believe the Savior is coming.". It proved not to be his coming, but, oh, what a joy came into my soul as I now compared the feelings of my heart at the thought of Christ's coming with those of my former experience. Dear reader, I knew I was in possession of eternal life.

My Experience with Tobacco. I believe it to be to

the glory of God to tell of my experience with tobacco. My father was a tobacco-grower; consequently, when a boy I labored considerably in a tobacco-field. At about the age of nine I learned to chew. I did not become a constant user until about the age of fifteen. At this age I found myself so in bondage to tobacco that I could not leave off its use for a single half day. By the time I was twenty years old this habit had succeeded in greatly impairing my health. Great damage was done to my nervous system. My heart became seriously affected. I became aware that I must either conquer this habit or die. I was afraid of death, and through fear I succeeded in quitting the use of tobacco for three years. My health during this time greatly improved. My nervous system grew strong. I had not succeeded, however, in delivering myself from the desire for tobacco; consequently, after the fear of death had been removed by improved health, I returned to its use. Only a short time indulging in this habit was necessary to bring me completely under its control. It became my master. Of all the sins that lay so heavy upon my conscience none was so weighty as that of tobacco-using. It was the blackest sin of my life. It stood like a mountain between me and God. I was condemned for that one sin more than for all my other sins. In my conviction I would throw away all the tobacco that I had, only soon to be searching for it or buying more. During the summer just prior to my conversion, when conviction lay heaviest upon me, many were the times I resolved to abandon its use, but tobacco was king, and I bowed a burdened slave at its idolatrous shrine. Whenever a

thunder-storm would gather during these summer
months, and the lightning vividly flash, I would become alarmed and would promise God if he would
protect my life and let me live, I would quit using
tobacco. The storm would pass by, the sun shine out,
and I trembling would yield to the appetite for tobacco.
Thus it went on until the Sunday evening before my
conversion. I that night threw away my tobacco with
a deeper resolve than ever that by the help of God I
would never use it again. On awakening the next
morning, among my earliest thoughts was that of
tobacco. The appetite was very strong, but I resisted
and started to my school without any, and imploring
victory from God. My conversion was so blessed and
God's glory so filled my soul that I am quite sure it
was as much as a week before I thought of tobacco,
and when I did I no more desired it than if I never
had used it. The power of the blood so cleansed my
system from this nicotine poison that tobacco was as
repugnant to me as to an innocent child, and I believe
if I had taken a chew or smoke it would have produced the same awful effect as the boy's first chew.
Ten years have gone by, and I have never been tempted
the slightest to return to its use. Glory to the name
of Jesus!

Hungering and Thirsting for Purity. For nearly
two weeks after my conversion heaven's peace and
glory in my soul were uninterrupted. I thought my
happiness was complete, and that my joys would never
end. But one day while I was doing some work which
became very aggravating I was strongly tempted to
evil. I felt a wrong disposition in my very nature,

and was surprised and alarmed. However, calling upon God for grace, I proceeded with the work, when the second time it became aggravating, and I was more strongly tempted than before. I trembled, but trusting in God as best I could with my fainting heart, I began to do the work over, when the third time it went wrong, and I was overcome. I spoke an evil word, but I had no sooner done so than I fell upon my knees and called upon God for forgiveness. I there received the blessed assurance that I was forgiven, but in this experience I became aware of an evil in my nature that was going to make it very difficult to live and serve God as I desired.

From that hour my soul began to call upon God for deliverance from that inward foe. About this time I providentially received a copy of a holiness paper called *The Gospel Trumpet*. The testimonies that I read in this paper from those who were wholly sanctified only increased the hungering in my soul for that blessed experience. Days were spent in fasting and prayer before God for a clean heart, but we had no man to teach us; yet God led us on from one ray of light and knowledge to another. I remember one night after the family had gone to bed and to sleep such a longing seized my soul for perfected holiness that I left my home for a distant wood-lot, and there on my knees in the darkness of the woods implored God for the experience of sanctification, but because of my ignorance, I returned without the blessing. One Sunday morning my wife and I decided we would neither eat nor sleep until God sanctified us. We began to read the Bible, and then to pray for a while, and then to read again, and then to pray, until in the afternoon a local preacher who claimed the experience of holiness came and poured "cold water" on us, and we becoming discouraged gave up the attempt.

The time of Christmas was now near. Space will not permit telling all the many things that God taught us previous to this time. He had shown us the evil of secret societies, from which we had withdrawn. He taught us the evil of worldly pleasure, and how those who love him can find no enjoyment there. He taught us the evil of a foolish and frivolous conversation, and how his children must be grave and sober. God taught us these things, and many more, independently of his word; because we were very ignorant of his word. It was at this Christmas time that God taught us our first lesson in divine healing. It is true he wonderfully healed my wife of lung trouble at the time of her conversion, but it was unasked for; consequently we did not call it divine healing in direct answer to prayer. On Christmas eve when all the village was astir and people were gathering from a distance to engage in the festivities, we decided to show our appreciation of the gift of the Son of God by remaining at home and reading and praying. Late in the afternoon wife was taken with an intense pain in the head and ear. The time for our reading and prayer service drew near, and the aching only increased. We wondered why this could be. Since all the people were spending the evening in pleasure and wantonness and we had withdrawn from such revelry to spend the evening in praising God, we were puzzled as to why we should be thus disturbed. God spoke gently to us, saying, "I want to teach you of the good things I have in store for those that love me; ask of me, and I will heal her." We at once fell upon our knees and asked God to take away the pain, when instantly it was removed and the glory of the Lord shone round about us, no doubt not unlike the glory that shone round about the shepherds so many years ago. The Spirit's voice in our soul shouted, "Glory to God in the highest and on earth peace, good will toward men." Until late in the evening we offered up the incense of prayer and praise unto the holy child Jesus.

The days went by, and deeper grew the longing of my soul for all the fullness of God. As I would read weekly in the Trumpet of the glorious meetings in different places, I became very desirous of having a holy minister come to our place and teach us the way of God more perfectly. My experience in this matter reminds me very much of the experience of Cornelius as related in the tenth chapter of the Acts of the Apostles. God talked with Cornelius, the one who desired and needed instruction, and at the same time talked with Peter, the one chosen to give Cornelius the needed help. I wrote to the office of the Gospel Trumpet Publishing Co., asking them if they could give me the address of some holy man whom we in all probability could get to come to our place and hold a meeting. At the same time that God put it into my heart to make such a request he put it into the heart of a minister of God (the author of this work), whose home was in eastern Indiana, to write to the Trumpet office asking the brethren if they knew of any one in southern Indiana (the place of our home) that desired

meeting. These two letters came in the same mail to
the office; accordingly my letter was sent to the minister and the minister's letter was sent to me. A meeting was arranged for and about the 10th of February it
was begun.   Should I live to be old, I shall not forget
that meeting.   These brethren were the first holy
people, to my knowledge, I had ever met.   I felt
strange in their presence.   There was something peculiar about them that made them appear unnatural
to the creature of earth.   The first night of the meeting my wife and I went forward to the altar for sanctification.   Only a little instruction was necessary to
enable me to grasp the promise of God, and the Holy
Spirit and fire came into my soul in such power and
glory that it seemed to transport me far above.   My
conversion was glorious, but my sanctification was
more glorious. I was conscious in my heart of a cleansing.   I actually felt pure.   Just as a stained cloth
being washed comes forth clean and spotless and
white, just so I could see my soul purged, cleansed,
and made whiter than snow.   Through the night,
though my sleep was profound and deep, I was conscious of a purity and glory in my soul.   During this
meeting I was shown many beautiful and glorious
things by the Spirit and word of God.   There was
disclosed to my spiritual vision the holy character of
God as imaged in the heart and life of a Christian.
Oh, how sublime to my soul was the holy life which
God set before me, and in which he said I must live.
I was shown the one true church of God all radiant
in her holiness.   I saw the gulf separating the church
from the world.   I saw the exalted plane where walk

the redeemed, where there is not a sin, but all is holy even as God is holy. The life of God was assimilated into mine, and mine was hid in him. This world had no place in my affections or my thoughts.

Soon after this meeting God began to lead me out into his work. For a while I did not publicly acknowledge that God had called me to the ministry, but I was quite active for the Lord in my home neighborhood, holding meetings in private houses and schoolhouses. God gave us souls for our labor. Some three months after we received the experience of sanctification the Lord sent me about forty miles from home to tell a people among whom we had formerly dwelt of the greatness and goodness of the Lord, and of his mercy and power to save. This may not seem of much consequence to those who have long been in the ministry, nor to those who never had such a calling, but to me it was a mammoth undertaking. I saw my own helplessness and inability, and trembled. God revealed himself to me and said, "Be strong and of good courage; for I am with thee." The night before I was to go on this my first attempt in evangelistic work, I dreamed that I stood on the bank of a river. A fishing pole and line were given, and almost immediately upon casting the hook into the water I drew forth a large and beautiful fish. The next day while on my journey this dream was brought to my memory, and I knew it was not without signification. At the meeting a young man, whose heart the Lord opened, received the word of God with gladness. He sought God earnestly and was converted; and later he came to our home and received the experience of sanctification.

The Lord soon called him to the ministry and used him in the salvation of many souls. From this few days' meeting the work of God has spread until now the congregations in a few counties in this section of the state reach the number of a score.

A few months afterwards while at this same place for meeting, the Lord very clearly showed me that I should dispose of our little cottage and go forth in his work trusting in him. I conferred not with flesh and blood, but with the Lord alone. I was called to be a minister not by men but by the Lord. He commissioned me to go into all the world and preach the gospel to every creature. My wife received a special call to join me in the Master's work. God had given us an apo- tolic experience. We were filled with the Holy Ghost and faith and power. God demanded of us to "sell all we had" and go forth with no other source of income than faith in God. Since the Lord had given us an apostolic experience and an apostolic commission, we decided to continue the work on the apostolic line; therefore we purposed to "make the gospel of Christ without charge, that we abuse not our power in the gospel." Freely we had received, and we decided to give freely. We purposed that the "poor should have the gospel preached unto them." A hireling ministry is very disapprovingly spoken of by the Lord Jesus in Jno. 10:12, 13; therefore we decided to follow Jesus and preach his gospel without money and without price, that we might be approved of him. In every time of need we came to him who promised to "supply all our needs by Christ Jesus according to his riches in glory." Our work in the vineyard of the Lord became a work of faith from the beginning. By faith we ate our daily bread; by faith we wore our raiment, and by faith we preached the gospel. When money for food or clothing or traveling expenses was needed, we took the matter unto him who said, "Oh, fear the Lord, ye his saints: for there is no want to them that fear him. The young lions do lack, and suffer hunger: but they that seek the Lord shall not want any good thing"; and who also said, "If God so clothe the grass of the field, . . . shall he not much more clothe you?" The disagreeable custom of taking up collections, so universal in the sectarian ministry, we wholly abandoned. In all the years of our evangelistic and pastoral work we have not taken up a collection. As we have before said, our only source of income was faith in God.

Some may not understand in what manner God provided for us. He has in time past supplied his servants with the necessaries of life in different ways. He sent down manna from heaven for the children of Israel. He prevented their clothing from wearing out. The ravens were sent with bread and flesh in the morning, and bread and flesh in the evening to feed Elijah by the brook Cherith. The widow's meal wasted not nor her oil, as she fed the man of God. At another time in the life of Elijah he, weary and hungry, laid himself down under a juniper tree, requesting God that he might die, and while he slept he was touched by an angel, who said, "Arise and eat," and he looked, and behold there was a cake baked on the coals, and a cruse of water at his head, and he ate and drank and slept and was awakened and told to eat, which he did,

and went in the strength of that meat forty days and
forty nights. Jesus fed the multitude from a few
loaves and a few fishes, and whenever we have had need
of food, clothing, money, or other things, God has supplied them in his own way.

God Has Supplied Our Needs. I believe it would be
to his glory to relate a few of the many instances in
which God has supplied our needs. We had not long
been in the gospel work until the little we received
cash from the sale of our home was exhausted and it
became necessary that we ask God for food or money
to buy it. Shortly afterward we received a letter from a
man in Pennsylvania, which contained five dollars.
This was used, and again we were in need, and again
we prayed. We received a letter containing five dollars
from the same man. When this was used and we
again found it necessary to ask God for our daily
bread, we received a third letter containing five dollars, from the same gentleman. This was repeated five
times. Five letters we received from this gentleman,
each containing five dollars. I never heard from this
man before I received his first letter. I have never
heard from him since I received the last one of these
five. I have made some inquiry concerning him, but
never met any one that knew him. I pray God even
to this day to reward him. At another time when we
had been earnestly praying for a few dollars a brother
living about twenty-five miles from us felt deeply impressed to send us five dollars. He obeyed the impression, and we gave thanks to him and God. We would
go into a place to hold meetings, and God would move
upon the hearts of the saved and the unsaved to give

us money and clothing just as we needed. Thus our food and raiment were procured, and traveling expenses defrayed. We thus from place to place traveled over the states of Indiana, Ohio, Illinois, Michigan, Iowa, and Missouri preaching the gospel, never taking a collection nor begging money in any way. Our God supplied our needs; bless his name! One evening we came by train into a small town in eastern Iowa. We were strangers in the town. Our money was all spent in car-fare, and knowing no one, we did not know what to do only to trust in God as we were wont to do. A kind man invited us into his home. God moved upon the hearts of the authorities of the Methodist meeting-house to offer us their house for meetings. We began in Jesus' name. Satan often endeavored to make us faint-hearted by telling us we would never get money enough to get out of town; but we proved him a liar. Before two weeks we saw the salvation of a few souls and had money enough to bring us to Chicago, the place God wanted us for the next meeting.

In our work for the Lord we have not been all the time engaged in evangelistic work, but a portion of the time we have been located and in pastoral and other duties and labors in the interest of Christianity. Our life in pastoral labors was a life of faith, just as when in the evangelistic work. We received no salary, nor begged bread, but prayed to God always. One Friday evening we fed the last of the corn to our horse. It was in extremely cold weather. Saturday morning the horse was given nothing but a little fodder, which was all we had to give. This affected us more than if we had had no bread for our breakfast.

We felt much humbled in heart before God, and petitioned him for corn. About three o'clock of the same day an unconverted man living about three miles in the country drove to our door and unloaded three bushels of corn. Only those who have had a similar experience can know of the joy and glory and thanksgiving that filled our hearts. One summer we desired a pig, that we might grow it for meat the coming winter. One morning on going out at the front door a box was seen in the path that led to the front gate. On examination this box was found to contain a fine, healthy pig bearing this placard: "Feed me, and I will grow and make a large hog." To this day we do not know who left the box there—only we know it was the favor of God to his children. At one time wife desired a spool of thread. Some one had given her some gingham to make our little daughter a dress, but she had only two pennies with which to buy, while it required four pennies. The Lord was earnestly petitioned for the needed two pennies. Our little boy and girl a few moments after, while playing near the front walk, were each given a penny by a gentleman passing by. They brought the pennies to me, and thus God heard and answered prayer. One morning wife desired to do her washing but had no soap, and no money to buy with. She went on her knees before God and earnestly prayed for soap, and while yet upon her knees a lady came and presented her with a bar of soap.

We could go on relating instance after instance similar to the foregoing, until a large volume would be written. It may appear to some that this would be an unpleasant life. In this you are very much mistaken. It might be if one's faith was all the time very weak, but when we know that God will not fail, we have the sweetest rest, and such a life is full of hope and glory. A life of daily trust draws us very near to God, and makes his service full of delight. We remember at one time during our life of daily asking God to supply temporal needs, a note which I held for one hundred dollars fell due. We received the money, and for a time we had no need to ask God for our bread. I well remember the night when I spent the last of this money. After making a few purchases at a store, with money all gone, I came out upon the street with a deep sense of gratitude and joy filling my soul. I was glad the money was gone, and I must now fall back to my life of daily asking God for what I needed, and with all my heart I appreciated it.

We are at present engaged in pastoral labors near the village of Federalsburg, Maryland. We have been living here almost two years. We receive no salary, nor beg for money, but daily pray to God to supply our needs, and he does. One day not long since in a time of need I found a dollar bill in my vest pocket. I do not know from whence it came. Wife also found a dollar in a cup on the mantel. Not long ago I felt a gentleman stuffing something into my vest pocket, and upon examination it proved to be a five-dollar note. Thus we are given money and provisions, unsolicited, by saint and sinner, and we go on in the work of the Master, taking no thought for the morrow, but trusting God to supply all our needs. Sometimes our faith is put to quite a test, which only makes the life of faith more enjoyable. When our faith is sorely tested and we are compelled to importune the Lord for things needed, we appreciate the blessing when we receive it. For some time I have been needing a suit of clothes. I have asked God very many times for them. They seemed slow about coming, but last evening God gave them to me—praise his name! It was in a marvelous way. Some man had ordered our home merchant to have him a suit of clothes made in the city, but when they came they did not fit him. Then they were left on the merchant's hands, and he reduced them to about their cost price, and we were then enabled to get them. Last evening at supper wife remarked that she would like to have buckwheat cakes for breakfast, but they were not very good without butter, and she had no butter, and so it was suggested that we pray God to send us some butter, and some time between that and bedtime a lady came to our door and presented wife with two beautiful rolls of yellow butter. These things may appear very insignificant to some, and mere happen-sos; but to us they are more. I recognize the hand of God in these things. Bless his name! We could go on relating incident after incident of God's answering our prayers for food and raiment.

Divine Healing. We shall conclude our testimony by giving you some of our experience in divine healing. At the time of my conversion, God wonderfully healed me of dyspepsia, and wife of a serious lung trouble. However, the first instance of divine healing in direct answer to our prayers I have already related. Some time after this my wife was taken suddenly sick

26

in the night. I was absent from home, but the next day was sent for. For one week she suffered greatly. The blood would stop circulating and gather around the heart. Each night she would have to walk the floor to keep alive. On Saturday morning, after having walked the greater part of the night, she said, "I can go no longer, and may as well lie down and die." I told her I believed it was God's will to heal her, and that I would send for an elder, who lived some twenty-five miles distant. He arrived at our place about night, and after reading some of the word of God, he anointed her with oil and laid on hands and prayed according to Jas. 5:14, 15, and the Lord healed her. She went to bed and rested all night, and the next day went to meeting.

In the autumn of 1893 our little one-year-old boy was taken sick and brought very low. One evening when it appeared that he could not live I went into a secluded place to talk with God. There I knew that the child was wholly given to God, and that he would do what was best. Some ladies of our village were in to see him in the evening, and said he could not possibly live until morning. About seven o'clock this same evening a man of God came to our home, and he anointed the little one. About nine o'clock wife and I being in much need of sleep and rest lay down, without seeing any change. We left a lady who was a disbeliever in divine healing sitting up with the child. When we awoke the lady told us that the baby was healed. She said at about eleven o'clock she could see life and health as it were coming into his countenance. In the morning he was laughing and playing as usual,

Shortly after this our eldest child fell out of bed one night and received some injury about the collar-bone. I gathered her up and laid her upon my bed and tried to find the extent of her injury. We found this impossible; for to touch her shoulder was to add to the violence of her screams. Speaking to my wife, I said, "Our only help is in God; let us pray." We knelt by the bed and began to pray; her crying increased, and we increased the fervency of our prayers. Suddenly she ceased crying and, looking up into my face (She was five years old.), she said, "Papa, I am healed." As she spoke these words, a sweetness fell from the glory world and filled our souls with rapture. A mellow light of rich glory filled the room, and for about an half-hour we could only walk the floor and praise God.

We could occupy many more pages telling of wonderful instances of divine healing in our family. Ten years have gone by since we were saved, and within that time we have not given a penny for medicine; neither have we given teas of any kind, but when we are sick we do just what God has told us to do, and he heals us. Headaches, earaches, toothaches, and all aches and pains and fevers and broken bones are taken to God in prayer. Our little boy had a leg broken, and God healed him without even so much as a doctor setting the bones. Last autumn three of our children were taken sick: one on Thursday, a second on Friday, and the third on Saturday. An aged brother living near us has a son who is a practicing physician of considerable repute in the city of New York. The next week after our children were taken sick this son came to visit his father. When I learned of this physician being in our community, I prayed that if it was to the glory of God that this doctor should see our children and tell us the nature of the sickness, he would put it into the heart of the father to visit us with his son. That same evening they came, and after a short conversation the doctor said, "I see you have some sick children." We asked him if he would like to look at them. He carefully examined two of them, and said they were clear cases of typhoid fever. He did not examine the third, but said in all probability he had the same fever. He said if we wished to trust in God, he did not feel like insisting on us giving medicine. He said he admired a life of faith. He thought it beautiful to have such faith in God that we could appropriate his virtue to the healing of our bodies. He said he had a great many friends in the city who were firm believers in divine healing; oftentimes when they were sick, he said, they would send for him and he would tell them what was the trouble, then they would pray, and he knew of some being instantly healed, but he said, "I have never known a case of typhoid fever healed; that dreaded disease must run its course, and if those children are out of bed under four to six weeks, I want you to let me know." In less than one week the one he pronounced the most dangerous was out in the kitchen to dinner with us, and in much less time than he said they were all out, and not one dose of medicine or tea of any kind was given. Praise our God! Scarcely a week goes by without us having occasion to come to God for physical aid, and he always heals us. Just this morning we anointed our little boy, who was troubled with worms, and prayed for him, and now he is well.

To-day we are saved to the uttermost and filled with the love and glory of God   Not a sin upon earth has any dominion over us; we are free—hallelujah!   We live by the word of God.   We believe it all, and enjoy it.   We as a family live economically—do not use alcohol, tobacco, tea, coffee, or medicines; no pearls or jewels or gold; no braids and ruffles and laces; no plumed hats: but dress common and clean and comfortable, and eat common and healthful articles of food. We preach from three to nine times a week, but receive no salary, nor take up any collections.   We have all we need, and are just as happy and contented as we could wish to be, and all because God is our salvation.

In conclusion I would say that the author of this work requested us to allow him to use our photographs. We have consented to this, not to make a show of self —God forbid—but hoping they would make our testimony more impressive and real to the readers. God bless you all.   Yours in Christian love,

Charles Orr.

Federalsburg, Maryland.

THE AUTOBIOGRAPHY OF THE AUTHOR.

"Many, O Lord my God, are thy wonderful works which thou hast done, and thy thoughts which are to usward: they can not be reckoned up in order unto thee: and if I would declare and speak of them, they are more than can be numbered."—Ps. 45:5.   To glorify my ·Lord and Master I will give the readers a brief account of my life, and some of the ways it has pleased the Lord to lead me. In reference to my Christian experience I shall relate only such facts as will be a help to lead others to the great Savior and Comforter. I was born in Randolph county, Indiana, May 19, 1850, and when seven years of age moved to Jay county with my parents, where my father is still living, mother having died six years ago. I received a preliminary education in the country schools, and afterward attended the Ridgeville College of Indiana several terms, without completing a course of study, but by which I was enabled to teach several terms of school. My father's name is Jesse G., and he was born in Wayne county, Indiana. His father, James Wickersham, was born near Harrisburg, Pennsylvania, in 1780. Grandfather lived to the good old age of 93. He was a descendant of one Thomas Wickersham, who came across the ocean from England with William Penn to make the first settlement of Pennsylvania. Huldah, my mother, was born in Tennessee June 5, 1829. When she was four years old she was brought by her parents to Randolph county, Indiana. Her father, Lansford Fields, was born in Tennessee in 1802; died in Indiana in 1868. In the year 1872 I was united in marriage to Miss Clara Bella Walters, of Jay county, Indiana, who has always been a faithful wife and mother. She accepted Christ in 1886, receiving full salvation in this evening light, and has been a stay and help to me since that time, to encourage and strengthen in the hour of temptation and adversity.

My religious inclinations were felt and manifested very early in life. At the age of ten or eleven I began to feel the wooings of the Spirit of God; pobably developed by the early efforts of mother urging, and hiring me to read the New Testament; and also teaching to me the love of Jesus to save sinners. I had a desire to be a Christian, and at the age of sixteen I began to seek the Lord, and went to a public altar under the preaching of Jacob Stover, a United Brethren in Christ minister. I did not realize the desire of my heart at the public altar, but on my way home while in secret devotion to God, I accepted by faith the blood of Christ to my heart, and felt the burden of my sins taken away. I went home that night rejoicing that I had found Jesus my Savior. I became a member of the United Brethren Church, and lived up to the standard held up by that denomination. In 1870 I was licensed to exhort, and in 1875 received credentials as a preacher of the gospel in that sect. During my life in the sect I had many ups and downs. I was always devotional, and always went to the Lord with my troubles and trials, and always found him a "present help in every time of need." Often before entering into any engagement or business of life I would first ask God's approval and success. I thank God to-day that I started early in life to be a Christian; having a disposition, desires, passions, and appetites, that would have led me into sin so deep that I would have been eternally lost, if I had not turned to God when young. I had a natural appetite for tobacco and strong drink. Though I did become a slave for a while to the former, yet the devil by the help of my natural appetite was never able to get me to surrender to the latter. I was never under the influence of whisky or wine in my life.

About the first of January, 1886 the congregation at our place of worship (Prospect Chapel) had just closed a protracted meeting. During this meeting and for some time before we had been praying for more light, and some of us were praying for God to send some holy man to teach us in all the doctrine of the New Testament. But we were not expecting our prayers to be answered in the way that they were, and so some were not able to receive it, but rejected the truth when it came. About the last of January the Lord answered our prayers by sending into our midst a company of holiness preachers and workers (D. S. Warner and others). Their heavenly songs, and the manner in which they presented the gospel soon convinced us that they were the children of God. They set before us the one church, the unity of believers, and also the corruption of sect Babylon. Wife and I with eleven others accepted the truth, consecrated for sanctification, received the desire of our hearts, and from that time began to declare ourselves free. Those who rejected the truth began to oppose and fight us, by contending for their sins and their creed, and by shutting the door against us. They would not permit us to meet in the chapel, even pushing me down the aisle and out of doors, telling me to go out and stay out. We that had taken a stand for the truth gave up the house, though we had built it, with the exception of a few dollars, but we were willing to suffer the loss of all things for the sake of Christ. From that time we held our meetings in private houses and a schoolhouse, where the Lord wonderfully met with us to bless and save souls in every meeting. Love was the great band that bound us together in the unity of the Spirit. The shouts and praises of God were heard daily. God manifested himself in a miraculous way in opening our understanding to the scriptures, in preaching the gospel, and in healing the sick. In fact the country was stirred for miles around.

Within two years we were able to build a new house of worship better than the one we had been compelled to give up, costing probably about $1,000. From this time persecution increased, and many disturbances arose on account of the opposing spirit. The house was stoned, windows and doors crushed in, and congregations egged, and insulted by profane, vulgar, and obscene language. One evening as wife and I were on our road home from the place of worship we were assaulted by a masked man with a weapon, who knocked me down and then ran. Our lives and property were threatened, our house of worship threatened with fire; but the Lord delivered us out of the hands of our enemies, and to-day we can serve him with fear, in holiness and righteousness. Praise the Lord forever! From that place the truth spread to other neighborhoods, and congregations were established. A yearly camp-meeting was also established about this time, near Deerfield, Indiana, on the farm of Bro. Samuel Grow, where it was successfully carried on for six years, although the persecuting element caused no little trouble.

About the first of February, 1891, I started to southern Indiana, in company with B. F. Roe, as an evangelist. We visited Freedom, Odon, Tampico, and a few other places on this trip of eight weeks. Free-

dom, the first place we visited, was a very dark place
of a few hundred inhabitants.   Drunkards openly
raged in her streets and homes.   Scoffers were bold
and daring, even assaulting us on the streets by calling
us bad names, but we bore all things for Jesus' sake;
having perfect love in our souls, and praying for those
who despitefully used us and cast our names out as
evil.   The first place at which we put up was with a
man whose wife was saved, but he was a drunkard.
He was very kind to us when we went there, but in a
few days he became intoxicated, and being urged on
by the opposers to the truth, he turned against us,
came to the house where we were preaching, opened
the door and called for his wife, and cursed me, telling me never to come inside his house any more.
Then he went back home and kicked my baggage out
of doors.   His daughter came over to inform us.   I
was yet preaching; so I advised Bro. Roe to go and get
my things.   But he met with the same fate, receiving
two kicks from him as he fled from the yard.   And
such was my introductory evangelistic trip.   At the
other two places mentioned we were more successful
and did not meet with such barbarous opposition, but
the Lord blessed in preaching and the salvation of
souls.   It was at this time, while at Tampico, that we
first met Bro. and Sister Orr.

Previous to this I had made some short trips to
points near home, in company with the church.   The
meeting at Saratoga, especially, I would like to notice
before going further.   That meeting was held at the
home of grandmother Lollar; part of the time in her
house, but when the weather would permit, it was held

in her barn, being very largely attended. This sister was a member of the United Brethren sect, but had become disgusted with the unholiness practiced in that denomination, and desired to hear the gospel preached in its purity. So it was that she kindly invited us to come over and hold a meeting at her house, which was truly blessed of the Lord. Many souls received light, and consecrated themselves to the Lord. Some even came to the altar, desiring salvation, and confessed that they had been fighters of this way, and that they were ashamed that they had treated us so. The shouts and praises that went up caused quite a commotion in the neighborhood. The baser sort were stirred against us and caused considerable disturbance. One man arose in one of the meetings and said we ought to be booted out of the neighborhood. Such has been the reception in many places where we have gone, having nothing to present to the people but the gospel of Christ. We see that the gospel has the same effect to-day when preached by the Holy Ghost as it did in the days of the apostles, or in any other reformation when the whole truth was set forth.

Since my start in the evangelistic work I have not devoted my whole time as an evangelist, but have devoted part of the time in that way, and part as a pastor of the congregation at New Pittsburg, Indiana, living upon a farm with my wife and eight children, near that place. The Lord has wonderfully blessed us as a family, during the last fourteen years. During that time we have taken the Lord for our family physician. We have always found him a good physician. He healeth all our diseases. Praise his holy name forever!

In the winter of 1898 we felt impressed to move to
Moundsville, West Virginia, feeling that the Lord had
something for us to do there, thinking also that it
would be a good place to get the children more under
the influence of the gospel, at which place we are still
living.   . Henry C. Wickersham.

CHAPTER XXXIII.

TRAVELS IN INDIA.

G. Tufts, Jr., a zealous young minister of the gospel of Christ, who had been engaged for some time in
the mission work in Chicago, notably at a place called
the Open Door Mission, felt that the Lord would have
him go to India during the great famine of that
country in 1897 to see that the offerings sent in for
the suffering people of that country were properly
distributed, and also to carry the news of full salvation, and distribute holy literature among them. He
made this trip, and is now on his second trip to that
dark land.   The following are extracts from his
travels in India, as reported by himself in The Gospel
Trumpet of 1897.

HIS REPORTS.

I left New York, July 10, 1897, after visiting the
slums of that city in company with Bro. Blewitt. I
was surprised to find the missions in New York so
small, and they were exceedingly dead spiritually. I
never knew how to appreciate the Open Door Mission

in Chicago until I saw what the slum mission work is in New York. From what I have seen and can find out the saints have really the largest mission of the kind in the world. I saw nothing so large even in London. I also visited Dr. Simpson's place on Friday afternoon. They have a divine-healing meeting at that time, and I do believe there are many dear children of God who will be brought out of there into the true light.

We had fine sailing the first three days, when we struck a great storm gale, and then for three days we had it exceedingly rough; waves rolled at least twenty-five feet high, and I was very sick. I distributed tracts and books that went to Ireland, Wales, Sweden, and England; also preached on the boat. I met Dr. H. Grattan Guinness, one of England's great spiritual teachers. He has a large missionary training-school. He is in England what Moody is in America. He denounced me and the tracts in the very strongest terms, and asked me, for God's sake, not to go to India; saying it was the devil instead of God sending me. I gently took out my Bible and began to read some scriptures to him on divine healing, and asked him what I would do with them; and that distinguished gentleman had the audacity to close my Bible while it was in my own hands, and said these words: "Along the coasts of Ireland are great rocks out in the harbor, and many vessels have run against them and become completely wrecked. So now they have great danger signals on them to warn others against like fate. So the promises you spoke of in the Bible are great rocks that many bright young men and women in their Christian

experience have run against and made complete ship-wreck of their lives, and many others, too, and the many graves that are filled with the bodies of missionaries in foreign fields are a danger-signal against them." Poor man! He then left me.

I arrived at Liverpool on Sunday afternoon at 1:30. No one met me; so I went over to Birkenhead, and found the mission home, and was warmly welcomed by the saints. They were all surprised to see me. We went that evening up to Chester, about fifteen miles away, where we met Bro. and Sister Rupert. Oh, how they did praise God as they saw me! They really were so glad to see somebody from America that they did not know how to act. I preached for one and one-half hours that night from the "Gospel Van" to about seven hundred of the most intelligent listeners I have ever faced. They stood all the time I was preaching, and would scarcely go away even after I got through. I left England July 23 on the steamer Rome. Found it very rough in the bay of Biscay. I was seasick for thirty-six hours. The boat stopped for five hours at Gibraltar; so I had a nice little visit. Gibraltar is a little walled city of about 22,000 inhabitants. It is a trading center for the people who live in northern Africa, and I saw many nationalities there. The African men are all dressed in long black gowns peculiarly made. The city is built on the side of a great mountainous rock on the seacoast. On one side the rock is perpendicular; on the other side the city is standing. Among the different religious bodies I found Catholics principally, also Methodists, and the Salvation Army.

We landed ten hours to take on coal, at Malta. This place was very interesting to me; for I had been studying the book of Acts, and especially with reference to Paul's missionary journey, and it was on this island that Paul was saved from shipwreck, and stayed three months and seven days, and where many sick were healed. Acts 28. I visited St. John's Cathedral. It is the grandest building I ever was in. It even surpasses St. Paul's cathedral of London; however, it is not quite so large. Underneath the floor are tombs of noted Catholics, and each tomb is inlaid with the finest Mosaic work. The walls are all made of the finest marble, and inlaid with fine Bible pictures, made in Mosaic work; the pictures are made of different kinds of stone, until it is as beautiful as an oil painting. Michael Angelo and other noted painters have many fine paintings in this building. A most impressive picture of the beheading of St. John, made by Michael Angelo, is in one of the many chapels of this building. Also the landing of Paul in Malta is very beautiful. The gates of the north chapel are very high, and weigh, I believe, two tons; and these are made of solid silver. Most of the lamps are solid silver. Malta is a place of 37,000 inhabitants. It is said that for every one hundred people they have a church, and it is even more. It is entirely Roman Catholic. I never saw so many priests. All wear heavy black or brown robes, and broad-brimmed soft hats. As I walked the streets I saw at least three hundred of them. The women mostly wear a black covering over the head and face. I went into several of these Catholic meeting-houses, and as I saw the poor people kneeling there in seeming devotion, oh, how my heart went out to God to send somebody to this dark place to tell them of the real true Christ, who saves and heals!

I also saw the rock that Moses struck with his rod and water came forth to give drink to the children of Israel. I passed Mt. Sinai and the place where the children of Israel crossed the Red Sea dry shod. It was exceedingly warm going through the Red Sea. On the Indian ocean we were caught in the monsoon storms, which made it very rough. One night the waves washed over the decks of our boat and filled the cabins with eighteen inches of water, but throughout all I shall never forget the sweet peace that filled my soul and the perfect confidence I had that our God would pilot us safely through. Praise his name!

I am here at last in this dark country, after five weeks' traveling, and the God who kept me on land has kept me on the rough sea. Praise our God! As I placed my feet upon the shores of India, how the Spirit did witness to my soul that I was just where he wanted me! After visiting and seeing what I have of India, of the terrible darkness and awful sin, which I can not describe, and the hardness of their hearts, and idolatry, I am constrained to believe that as God dealt with the Jews (Amos, fourth chapter), so is he sending his awful judgments upon India. India to-day is suffering from famine, earthquakes, wars, plagues, locusts, and leprosy. The famine that I have seen is something indescribable, although I have not yet been in the worst part. I shall leave to-morrow for the central provinces, where I shall see it in its worst form. India

had earthquakes every day from June 12 until the last
day, except the 24th and 25th. The people are sure
they are living right over a volcano. The earthquakes
are doing much damage in some parts. The whole
frontier of India, from what I can learn, is in a terrible
war, and thousands are lying upon the bloody battle-
field dying. The plague and cholera have been, and
are to-day, carrying off their thousands wherever they
reach, although in Bombay and other places where
they were the worst, they are dying out. The locust
was never known to be so bad as this year, and is
spreading all over India. To-day there are over one
million lepers in India.

Thus India is oppressed on every hand, and yet she
hardens her heart and will not acknowledge God's
awful warnings. O my dear brethren, my heart bleeds
to-day, and the tears roll fast down my face as I see
the awful darkness and superstition. On the streets I
see precious immortal souls, for whom Jesus shed his
precious blood, kneeling around a tree to worship it,
and to the idols along the public road. Also I see
them taking the food they need to sustain their own
poor bodies and feeding it to the crows, which fly on
the streets like the sparrows in America, thinking they
are feeding the departed spirits of loved ones. Last
week was a special holy day, and the dear poor ignorant
natives spent their hard-earned pennies and bought
cocoanuts and threw them into the river, thinking they
were pleasing the gods. In speaking with some of the
Brahmans who could speak English, about our Christ,
they said this to me: "What shall we believe, and whom?
You Christians have more beliefs and castes than we

27

have.   One of you teaches one thing, and another
something just to the contrary." O my brethren,
pray that God will raise up some Holy Ghost gospel
workers to come to India and tell these people the
truth.   The missionaries as well as the heathen are
confounded, and it is all a typical picture of ancient
Babylon.   However, I have met some dear honest
missionaries who are here suffering for the gospel's
sake, walking in all the light they have.   As I visit
the relief camps, poorhouses, and hospitals, where
cholera, and plague, and leprosy abound, the Lord
Jehovah takes care of me.   As I go, I sing with the
poet,

> "I shall fear no evil,
> Trusting in his grace."

My first visit to see the famine sufferers was at the
farm of Pundita Ramabai, where she has almost 200
high-caste Hindu child-widows, famine sufferers.
She has taken these children out of hospitals, poor-
houses, and relief camps, and found many lying along
the road almost at death's door from starvation.   I
found Ramabai a blessed saint of God, whom the Lord
has chosen especially, and the Holy Spirit has been her
teacher and leader.   She was once a high-caste Hindu
widow, bowing down to idols and worshiping stone.
But very marvelously a few years ago she was led to
see the true God, and gave up her idolatrous worship.
After reading the Bible she became convinced that
there was something more needed than an intellectual
belief, and she became convicted of sin; and after
wrestling with the Lord she received a new heart and
was born again.   Praise God!   Soon after she felt the

great need of a clean heart, the taking out of the carnal nature, and sought very earnestly for deliverance
and the infilling of the Holy Ghost, which she obtained as positively and definitely as she did a change
of heart.   She was at once led to see healing for her
body in the scriptures, and has been most marvelously
healed. Now she trusts the Lord for the healing of
all her famine girls. In a little tract (before me now)
she states that the thing that always puzzled her more
than anything else was denominations—sects.   She
states that after she became a Christian she could not
join a sect, and never has, saying, "It is sufficient for
me to be a Christian."

She now has a large farm, and takes care of all these
girls, and will soon have a hundred more. She lives
a life of simple faith, takes up no collections, nor asks
a penny of anybody. Yet God stands true to his word
and supplies. Her persecutions have been great. She
first began to take care of these poor little sufferers at
her home in the city, but was driven out by the people
and the government. So she took them out on this
barren desert farm, which God put into her hands.
There were no buildings on it; so she built a few
temporary sheds, consisting of a sort of straw matting
put up on four poles for a roof, and hardly enough to
cover the sides. Thus she lived with her girls, feeding
and teaching them all through the excessive heat of
an Indian summer.   Brethren, as I saw these and
many other things which I can not speak of now, I
thought many of us in America did not know what
sacrificing for Christ means. May God bless Ramabai,
and may you add her to your prayer list; and if God

puts it into your hearts, send her an offering to help raise these children for the Lord's work. Ramabai has since put up several buildings on this farm, and a meeting-house that will hold seven hundred people comfortably. There are a large number of villagers around her who have never heard the name of Jesus, and she is praying earnestly for some straight gospel worker. She says she sees by faith her meeting-house filled with people, with some Holy Ghost preacher to teach them. She at present is all alone. Who will go and help this dear saint out here in this dark part of the world?

There is no class of human-beings on the face of the earth who so much need your sympathy, prayers, and help, as the poor high-caste Hindu widow. She is married in the cradle, often before she is three weeks old, and if her husband dies after she is married, she is at once treated in a most shameful and cruel manner. The parents of the husband usually consider that the death of their boy was caused by this girl being some terrible sinner or murderer when she was on earth before. And until recently, many times she was burned on the funeral pile with her husband, as this was considered the only means of her salvation. The British government has stopped this awful custom, but now there is nothing that is too mean, or cruel, or hard to be said or practiced on this poor unfortunate creature. After the husband's death her head is shaved every fourteen days. It is considered worse than death for a Hindu girl to lose her hair. The very coarsest garments are given her to wear—of red or yellow color. She must never wear any ornaments, of which the women of this country are passionately fond. She is never educated or allowed to go into society, never allowed to speak to any one except her brother or uncle. She must eat only one meal in twenty-four hours; besides she must keep all the fasts and sacred days, which are many. During these times she is not to eat or drink anything. She must not take part in family feasts or jubilees with others. She must never show herself to people on auspicious occasions. People think themselves unlucky if they behold a widow's face before seeing any other object in the morning. A man will postpone his journey if his path happens to be crossed by a widow at the time of his departure. A widow is called "Rand," by which name she is generally known, and it is the same as that borne by a harlot. She is always called by bad names by relatives and neighbors, and addressed in most abusive language at every opportunity. There is scarcely a day of her life on which she is not cursed by these people as the cause of their beloved friend's death. She is many times at the least provocation whipped and beaten unmercifully, and many, many, many times tied in the branches of a thorn-tree with her bare body exposed to the thorns, and red pepper burned under her nose, and she must inhale the smoke. She has no one to sympathize with her. Her own parents, with whom she lives in case her husband has no relatives or they are too poor to care for her, of course in a way sympathize with her; but custom and religious faith have a stronger hold on them than parental love. This is only a brief sketch of some of the things I have found out among these poor, patient, suffering creatures.

I shall never forget a few days ago I was at a station where a large number of famine sufferers were being fed, and off to one side were about 350 children ranging from two and a half to ten years of age. Through an interpreter I asked those of them who were married to arise, and nearly all arose. I was told that most of the girls were widows. So, dear ones, you can at once see the need of a kind Christian home in which to rescue these poor innocent creatures from a life of suffering and ignorance and idolatry.

From Poona I went to Akola, where I was warmly received by some children of God who are living up to all the light they have, and God is blessing their labors. With them I visited the relief camps, where men, women, and children were breaking rock for a few pennies per day. I also visited the poorhouses, which are not as good as the worst cow-shed I ever saw, and the people—men, women, and children—lie right down on the bare damp ground without a thing over or under them. They were just feeding at one place. The food was the awfulest smelling stuff. It would actually turn one's stomach to see it. And these poor people sat down in the mud, and the rain was pouring down, and there they sat eating with great greediness this awful filthy stuff. I could not keep from crying like a child, when I beheld their suffering condition. I never imagined it half so bad.

One pitiful sight I saw while at the home of a missionary was a poor old Hindu father, who was a living skeleton, with a little child one year old in his arms and two poor, thin little boys, eight and ten years of age, by his side. All were almost at death's door

from starvation, and the poor old father, with tears
rolling down his face, begged the missionaries to take
his two eldest boys and keep them, for they would
starve in a day or so if he kept them any longer. The
mother had starved to death a few days before. The
missionaries consented to take the children.   The old
father, clasping the baby closer in his poor bony arms,
said he would try to do what he could to keep the
youngest; for it would kill him to give them all up.
He turned to the boys as he was about to leave and
said, "Boys, serve the missionaries' Jesus, for your
father's god is no good, and will not help us; but
Jesus takes care of the missionaries, and will take care
of you." And off the poor old man went without
looking back, lest his heart should fail him and he
would take his boys back again. Many mothers in the
same way give their children to the missionaries to
keep them from starving. But the most heartrending
scene of all was at one place where a brother and sister had worked hard feeding thousands of famine
sufferers, and were worn out from hard work and no
help, although they had plenty of grain, and money to
buy with. They told me the evening I was there
that was the last evening they could feed the people
unless they had somebody to help them. At this place
the famine was the worst I have seen. People were
dying by the dozen every day, and as I left the next
morning I had to step over the bodies of poor, sick,
starving skeletons who had dragged themselves several
miles to come for food, and had fallen from exhaus-
tion in front of the gate. Oh! how I felt when I
thought of the hundreds of young people at home who

are strong, soul and body, and who are waiting to
know where to go or what to do.   Oh, how I wish you
could hear to-day the awful groans of India's starving
millions!   Again and again shall I sing when I return,

"Quickly leave thy cottage door,
  Spread the truth from shore to shore;
  For the blessed Savior shed his blood for all."

  Before the missionaries feed the people, who come
by thousands, they always preach to them, and it is
astonishing how attentively they listen.   They all with
one accord acknowledge that it is on account of their
sins that this awful judgment is sent upon them.   And
now what India needs is not so much more money,
but a large force of real, true, straight gospel workers
filled with the Holy Ghost.   The dear Lord has enabled me to preach once or twice in most every place
where I go, and to give out tracts.   At Akola and several
other places I talked through an interpreter to a large
audience of natives.   Even without the language,
brethren, I have calls enough to keep me here a long
time preaching night and day.

  Last night I met the dear native brethren who have
been reading The Gospel Trumpet.   They had been
waiting patiently for me ever since they heard I had
started for India.   I had a hard time to find them,
having missed them at the depot; but when I did find
them, they were all in an upper room with their Bibles
and Gospel Trumpets beside them, praying that God
would bring me safely to them.   They were the hap-
piest people I ever saw to see me, as I was the first
from America, whom they had longed to see.   Oh,
how they love The Gospel Trumpet and the dear breth-

ren in America, and speak your names and seem to be as well acquainted with you as I am. The Holy Ghost has most marvelously been leading these dear people. Most that I have seen are very young men, and much in earnest.

I traveled nearly four weeks night and day in trains, and in bullock-carts, and on foot from large cities to small villages, from Bombay to Calcutta, visiting poor-houses, hospitals, and famine-relief stations, where I saw such suffering as I never can describe, and do full justice. I have never seen anything in print that exaggerates the condition of the suffering in India. However, I am happy to say the famine is about to an end, as the rains there have brought about fair crops and some work whereby the natives are enabled to earn food enough to sustain life.

Aside from the terrible condition I found in physical and temporal suffering was the awful spiritual condition of those who profess to be missionaries and teachers of the precious Word, which caused me to leave India with a heavy burden and prayer that God would send somebody to India to live Christ before the dear natives, if nothing else. During my travels in India I was thrown among missionaries of every denomination, and got a good insight of their life and work. While I rejoice to say I found a few dear children of God living up to all the light they have, and toiling boldly night and day bearing the hardships and privations that fall to their lot, and with one object before them—the salvation of precious souls—yet I am constrained to say that the majority of missionaries of India are as stiff-necked, lazy, hypocritical lot of

people as I ever met, using freely whisky, wine, and
tobacco; and they offered to me as an excuse, when I
questioned them about it, that the climate demanded
it. Many of the missionaries live in the finest of style,
having large and beautiful residences, and with a large
number of salaried servants, who are treated worse than
slaves. One man and his wife, where I stopped over
night, and who are quite prominent missionaries, em-
ploy nine native servants simply to wait upon them.
They indulge in the greatest extravagance and hold
themselves so high that the poor natives are afraid of
them, as though they were some great lords. I visited
one evening a large number of missionaries, and it was
the most disgusting crowd I had ever been in since I
have been a Christian. The gentlemen were all dressed
in full evening dress, while the ladies wore extremely
low-necked and short-sleeved dresses and were decked
with jewels; and from the giddy, foolish talking and
jesting I would have thought I was in some fashionable ballroom, had I not been told I was with prominent missionaries. I could not stay there for weeping
at the awful example of the so-called Christians before
the poor heathen. Besides the awful sect confusion,
the natives see the lives of these hypocrites and false
shepherds, and consequently, as their lives are the
only Bible they read, they are disgusted with Christianity. O dear ones, it is with sadness that I write to
you the awful spiritual condition of India. But pray
that God may send some Holy Ghost missionaries who
are dead to the world, and who will be willing to lay
down their lives for the poor natives, and who will live
Christ before them.

In Calcutta after considerable time and trouble I found about twenty dear precious saints, all natives, and most of them young men from eighteen to twenty-two years of age, attending college. They had been looking forward to my coming with great anxiety and joy, and I shall never forget the glorious rejoicing and sweet fellowship as we met. After traveling so many thousand miles it really seemed I had got home. Oh, how they appreciate *The Gospel Trumpet*, because through the reading of its pages, and comparing it with the word of God, they have been led into the truth. I held a few meetings with them, and, oh, how they drank in the truth! I also held an ordinance-meeting with them before I left. All of these dear young men have once been idol-worshipers and lived in great darkness, and in order to accept Christ have had to suffer cruel persecutions and extreme hardships, such as I can not describe now. But the Lord has wonderfully blessed their souls, and has led them in a wondrous way, and to-day they stand ready to give up their lives for the truth. They all accompanied me to the train, and the last words said to me were: "Send us a Spirit-filled man from America, who will be like a hammer in the hands of God." Calcutta is the largest college student center in the world. There are over ten thousand native students there, and most all speak English. One brother has rented a room in Calcutta, where will be the headquarters for the Gospel Trumpet Publishing Company in India, and where our publications and tracts may be obtained.

My soul is stirred for the needs of India, and to help

our dear brethren at Calcutta. I praise God for the privilege of meeting them. As I leave India I praise the Lord that the money sent to the famine sufferers was put into the hands of those who are out of sectism, and who are doing straight work for God, and it went to the places where they needed it most, which would not have been the case had we sent it by mail without knowing to whom we were sending it, and so helped to build up sectism. It is to be seriously regretted that much of the money sent from America to the famine sufferers was put into the hands of injudicious persons and many dishonest men. I can prove all my statements. I consider my trip a most profitable one, and I can see in many ways why the Lord sent me to that dark, suffering country.

I left India on Sept. 3. On my way home I visited Jerusalem. I found in Jerusalem division and strife and hatred and warring against one another. After I visited Jerusalem and saw the terrible division among the so-called Christians, worse than anything I saw in India, I came to the conclusion that what the heathen land needs is not more preachers, but more people who will live the real gospel of Christ before them. As I talked to the Mohammedans and Hindus, they told me that if somebody would come and live the gospel, they would listen to it. Many more told me they would not be guilty of doing the things that the missionaries were doing. On my way home, on the steamship Lucania, the Lord gave one precious soul for my hire. I arrived at home in Chicago Oct. 26, 1897.

CHAPTER XXXIV.

THE GOSPEL TRUMPET.

THE GOSPEL TRUMPET is an eight-page weekly holiness journal of which E. E. Byrum is the editor-in-chief. It is published by the Gospel Trumpet Publishing Company. This paper in doctrine is definite, radical, and anti-sectarian, setting forth full salvation, divine healing of the body, and the unity of all Christians as taught in the New Testament.

In order to get at the origin of this paper we will commence with the year 1879. D. S. Warner at this time had become editor of a small paper called The Herald of Gospel Freedom, published semimonthly by the Board of Publication of the Northern Indiana Eldership of the Church of God, located at Rome City, Indiana. We see in the editorial column of that paper its doctrine and object stated as follows. Its Motto: Earnestly contend for the faith which was once delivered to the saints. Its Object: The glory of God and the salvation of men from all sin; the promotion of holiness of heart and life, the promulgation and defense of all the truth as it is in Christ Jesus, and the union of all true believers in the Spirit of God and upon the inspired Word. Its Standard: Separation from the world, and entire devotion to the service and will of God. Its Peculiarities: No creed but the Bible; no bond of union but the love of God; no test of fellowship but Christian character; the baptism of the Holy Spirit essential to full salvation; the baptism, or immersion, of believers in water, and the washing of saints' feet essential to perfect obedience; separation from all human organizations that are not authorized in the word of God.

In 1880 the editor was placed in full control of the paper, and being impressed that its name ought to be changed, he laid the matter before the Lord, asking what it should be called. "Gospel Trumpet" came ringing in his soul. This was the name he received from heaven, and this name is no doubt destined to become familiar with God's children throughout the length and breadth of the earth. The first paper that was sent by the name Gospel Trumpet went forth, as near as can be ascertained, in January, 1881; although in the latter part of 1880 he had declared himself free from sectism, and had received from the Lord the name of the new paper which should be the great herald that should send forth the truth into all the world in this last reformation.

About this time the office was removed to Indianapolis, Indiana; and in a short time, from there to Cardington, Ohio; and then in 1883 the paper was published in Bucyrus, Ohio. At this place the editor passed through some fiery trials. It was at this place the devil made a desperate effort to capture the office, and also succeeded in turning Bro. Warner's wife against him. The following quotation is a part of a letter from Bro. John N. Slagle of Bucyrus, Ohio.

"I have taken The Gospel Trumpet ever since it has been published. Bro. Warner while at Bucyrus visited me often. I was greatly attached to him. I went to Wood county, Ohio several times to meetings where he was, also in Medina county, where he baptized me. He always had 'Praise the Lord!' on his tongue. The assembly-meeting at Annapolis, Ohio was largely attended by his enemies, to destroy the publishing work and the truth that he was preaching, but he was unwavering. A woman from Medina county said the Lord wanted her to give one thousand dollars to the Trumpet Office, but Bro. Warner refused to take it. Stockwell, Warner's partner, said he would take it, so he did, and paid off the Trumpet's debts. Then Stockwell, Rice, and others came over to Bucyrus, held a meeting, and with the assistance of Bro. Warner's wife they tried to wrest the office from his hands. He almost consented to give it up, but the Lord prevented him. You will get a history of these things by reading in his 'Poems of Grace and Truth,' pages 77, 78, 79. The John spoken of in this poem was myself. In 1884 the office was removed to Williamston, Michigan, but Bro. Warner's wife would not go with him. He did everything in his power to reconcile her to him, but without avail."

During the first few years of the publication of The Gospel Trumpet the outfit was a very small affair. Sometimes the paper was printed on a job press, sometimes on a larger one. Occasionally through extreme poverty and opposition and persecution it would seem that it was almost wiped out of existence, but, as the old adage says, "Truth crushed to earth will rise again"; so it was with The Gospel Trumpet, which probably after a few month's silence would find its way to the readers and be read with great rejoicing and praises to God; while its opposers would receive it with contempt and disgust and be made to rail out against the truth. Sometimes the editor alone was the only one to write the articles, set the type, do the printing and mailing, and these under the most adverse circumstances; but while it was coming up through great tribulations God had the same in remembrance, and the messages from time to time went forth declaring the word of the Lord and his power to save to the uttermost in pardoning sinners who came in humble repentance, and sanctifying believers, and God began to increase his work and gather together from various parts of the earth his faithful ones,

In the year 1880 the editor, D. S. Warner, issued a
book consisting of about 400 pages entitled "Bible
Proofs of the Second Work of Grace." A few thousand of these books were published, and in a few years
the entire edition was exhausted. In later years he
wrote a volume of poems. Shortly before his death in
1895 he completed a small volume entitled "Salvation:
Present, Perfect, Now or Never," which was published
shortly after his death; also he had almost completed
a volume on "The Cleansing of the Sanctuary," of a
few hundred pages, which has not at this date been
printed.

While engaged in the work at Bucyrus, Ohio he was
in correspondence with J. C. and Allie R. Fisher, of
Williamston, Michigan, who afterwards met with him
and entered upon the work of publishing The Gospel
Trumpet at Williamston about the year 1884, and the
work was continued at that place until June, 1886,
when it was moved to Grand Junction, Michigan,
there having been a camp-meeting that summer at
Bangor, near Grand Junction, where a number of people were saved and desired to have the office moved to
that locality. Arrangements were made and the entire
outfit of office material, machinery, and household
goods was stowed away in one freight car.

While at Williamston Bro. S. Michels of South
Haven, Michigan became directly connected with the
publishing work, and his name was placed upon the publishing staff, although his calling was principally as an
evangelist and pioneer worker. He held that position
until superseded by N. H. Byrum in 1895. J. C.
Fisher having been the principal publisher from the

time the office was moved to Williamston and after it
was moved to Grand Junction, continued to hold his
position as such until June, 1887, when it became
necessary to have some one to supersede him. On
account of the position Fisher held regarding his
right to put away his wife and marry another, and his
intentions to carry out the same, D. S. Warner declared that he would not be thus associated or yoked
together with a man who was not straight for God,
and would never publish another issue of the Trumpet
in that way. However, he said that God had called
him to edit The Gospel Trumpet. This was when the
last issue of the Trumpet was published in June before
going to the camp-meeting at Bangor. At this time
it was not known where a man could be found who was
fitted for the place and could take the responsibilities,
and who was consecrated to take up the work without
salary or any remuneration for his work, as it had thus
far been carried on, and also there was nearly one
thousand dollars to be paid; and in the critical situation of affairs the outlook was dark for the continua-
tion of the publication of The Gospel Trumpet. Those
upon whom the burden of the responsibility of the
work lay heaviest went in fasting and prayer before
God. Near the beginning of the meeting two young
men who were students from Otterbein University of
Westerville, Ohio, attended the meeting, whom the
Lord had moved upon to help in this time of need.
One of these brethren, E. E. Byrum, entered the work
as publisher and business manager; the other one staid
a few months as a helper in the office. E. E. Byrum
had never met D. S. Warner; however, he had received

the light on the word of God a few months previous to
this time, and was in full harmony with the teachings
of The Gospel Trumpet. A few days after the beginning of the meeting D. S. Warner felt directed to
speak to him concerning taking the position. The
situation of affairs was set forth, a prayer-meeting
held, after which E. E. Byrum told them that whenever the Lord let him know he would let them know
concerning what course he would pursue. After waiting upon the Lord in earnest prayer alone with God,
he imformed them that he would accept the position,
and immediately after camp-meeting; June 21, 1887,
he took up the work as publisher and business manager.   From that time D. S. Warner spent most of his
time in evangelistic work, traveling throughout the
various parts of the United States holding revival and
camp-meetings, until the last two years prior to his
death, when he spent most of his time in writing.
About the year 1888 E. E. Byrum became office
editor, and at the death of D. S. Warner, Dec. 12,
1895, became editor. He was also editor of The Shining Light, the publication of which began in the year
1890. A German paper entitled Evangeliums Posaune
began its publication in the year 1895.

In the year 1886 the workers in the Gospel Trumpet
Publishing Company amounted to five or six in number, which steadily increased until the present time,
there being now over one hundred persons who have
consecrated their labors free as unto the Lord. These
are from many states of the Union, also from Canada.
In the year 1898 the Gospel Trumpet Publishing Company's office was moved to Moundsville, West Vir-

ginia, by a special train consisting of nine freight cars, two passenger cars, and a baggage car, which carried the machinery, outfit, and workers.

Since moving to Moundsville the Gospel Trumpet Publishing Company has been enabled to send out pure literature in larger quantities than ever before. By this means the light has been scattered into many new places in the United States and in foreign countries. About October 1, 1899 a free-literature fund was started, by means of which about $1,000.00 worth of free literature per month is being regularly distributed in missions, prisons, libraries, and through other channels, in cities and in the country, throughout the world. Let us all humble our hearts, and pray for the blessings of God to continue upon the work, and render unto him the glory due unto his excellent name.

INDEX.

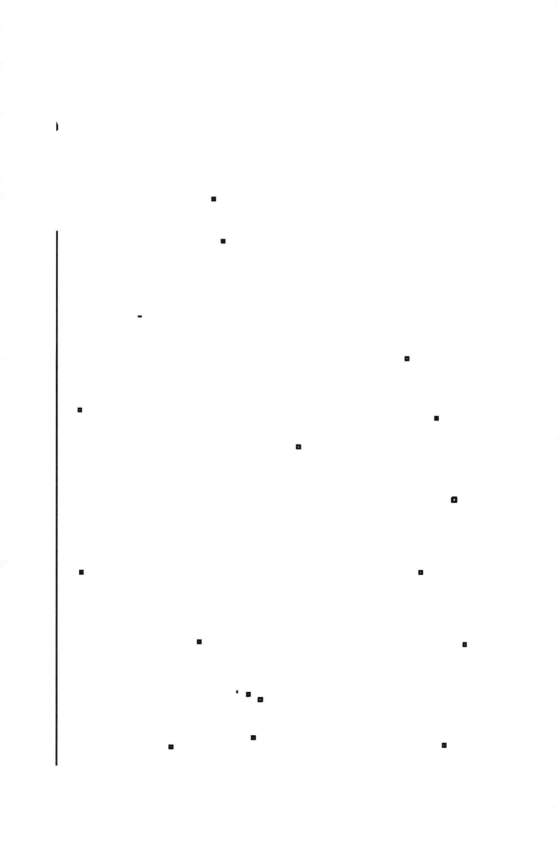

CPSIA information can be obtained
at www.ICGtesting.com
Printed in the USA
LVHW080342130520
655496LV00007B/823

9 781362 707219